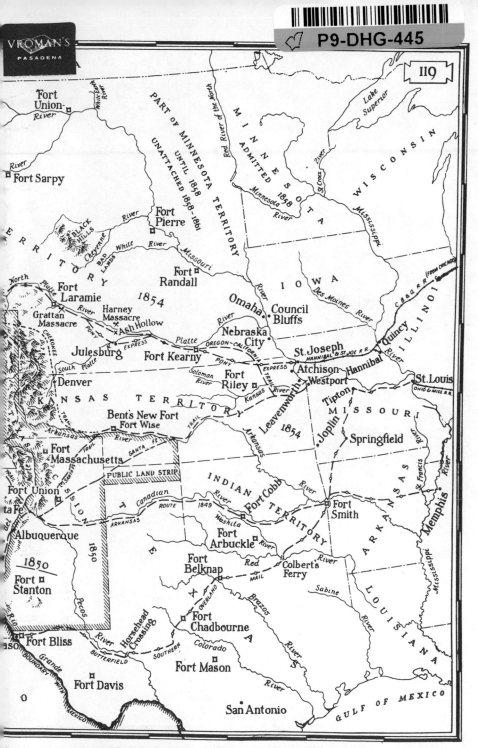

THE OVERLAND TRAIL
TO CALIFORNIA
IN 1852

Buttes, Green River, Utah

The Overland Trail to California in 1852

by **Herbert Eaton**

Capricorn Books

G. P. PUTNAM'S SONS

New York

Putnam SBN: 399-11056   Capricorn SBN: 399-50291-2
Library of Congress Catalog Card Number: 72-87612

PRINTED IN THE UNITED STATES OF AMERICA

CONTENTS

ACKNOWLEDGMENTS

———— ◄◆► ————

The journals of Jared Fox, John Lewis, Eliza Ann McAuley (Mrs. Egbert), Alpheus Richardson, Caroline Richardson, Mrs. Francis Sawyer, and John Verdenal and the reminiscences of William Taylor are quoted by permission of the Director, the Bancroft Library.

The journals of D. B. Andrews, Henry Bradley, John Clark (of Virginia), Perry Gee, William Kahler, Moses F. Laird, Thomas Lewis, R. H. P. Snodgrass, and Solomon Kingery are quoted by permission of the Yale University Library.

The journal of Dexter P. Hosley, in the manuscript collections of the Princeton University Library, and the journal of Luzerne Humphrey, in the Phillip Ashton Rollins Collection of Western Americana, Princeton University Library, are quoted by the permission of Princeton University Library.

The journal of Edward Kitchell is quoted by the permission of Mrs. Bertha K. Whyte.

The journals of Stephen T. Gage, William Hampton, Peter L. Hickman, and Alpheus Graham are quoted by permission of the California Section, California State Library. Permission to quote from the printed extracts of Alpheus Graham's journal is granted by the editors of the *Kansas Quarterly*.

The journal of Richard Keen is quoted by the permission of Bruce Adams and Richard Adams.

The diary of John Hawkins Clark and the reminiscences of James C. Carpenter and Godfry C. Ingrim are quoted by permission of the Kansas Historical Society.

The journals of Mary Stuart Bailey and Addison Moses Crane

are quoted by permission of the Huntington Library, San Marino, California.

The journal of Mrs. Lucy Rutledge Cook is quoted by permission of the California Historical Society.

The journal of Holmes D. Van Schaick is quoted courtesy of the E. E. Ayer Collection, the Newberry Library.

The journal of Jay Green is quoted by the permission of the Pioneer Museum and Haggin Galleries, Stockton, California.

The journal of Robert C. Laws is quoted by permission of the Society of California Pioneers.

Permission to quote the journal of John Dodson is granted by the Montana Historical Society.

Permission to quote from the journal of John F. Riker is granted by Professor William H. Riker.

The manuscript journals of John Brown, Esther Hanna, Lewis Stout, Mary Collins, and A. J. Wigle and the published journals of Cecelia Adams, James Akin, Jr., Enoch Conyers, Mr. Davis, John T. Kerns, John McAllister, and Cornelia Sharp are quoted by the permission of the Oregon Historical Society.

Permission to quote from the journals of Samuel Chadwick, Dr. John Dalton, Charles G. Schneider, George Short, and Thomas Turnbull is granted by the State Historical Society of Wisconsin.

Permission to quote from the journal of George Bowering and the reminiscences of John G. Dowdle is granted by the Utah Historical Society.

Permission to quote from the journal of G. A. Smith is granted by the Missouri Historical Society, St. Louis.

Permission to quote from the reminiscences of Tosten Stabaek is granted by the Norwegian-American Historical Association, St. Olaf College, Northfield, Minnesota.

Permission to quote from the journal of Agnes Gillespie is granted by the Lane County Historical Society, Eugene, Oregon.

Permission to quote from the journal of James C. David, as published in the *Annals of Wyoming*, April, 1962, is granted by the Wyoming State Archives and Historical Department.

The diary of John Hudson Wayman, edited by Dr. Edgeley W. Todd, published as *A Doctor on the California Trail*, the Old West Publishing Company, Denver, Colorado, is quoted by the permission of the Old West Publishing Company and Fred A. Rosenstock.

The journal of Mrs. Lodisia Frizzell, "Across the Plains to California in 1852," is quoted by permission of the New York Public Library, Astor, Lenox and Tilden Foundation.

My special thanks to Jacqueline F. Vlcan, who helped secure the illustrations for this volume.

INTRODUCTION

———◆◆◆◆———

WHEN James Marshall made his fateful discovery of gold at Sutter's Mill on January 24, 1848, he set in motion one of the greatest migrations in history. First gold seekers came from Mexico and Peru; then, in 1849, Americans poured across the Missouri River for the long, arduous trek to the new El Dorado. By 1851 the flood had ebbed, but then, in 1852, it swelled again. In that year the Overland Trail was crowded with a new kind of emigrant. Many men still went in search of gold, but others, with their families, were seeking a more permanent wealth: the rich lands of California and Oregon.

"Hundreds have left the Western Reserve for California," wrote the Cleveland *Plain Dealer*. "But the stampede is not confined to this district, by any means. News from Michigan inform us that the farmers complain greatly of the high rates of labor, occasioned by the depopulation of that State from the same cause. . . . The Hoosiers, too, are not a whit less panic stricken. A large emigration is now flowing thence to California from Dearborn county. A Baptist colony, a Presbyterian colony, and divers other colonies are girding themselves up in different parts of the State for an exodus to Oregon. The emigrants are mainly farmers and mechanics—the finest of stock. In Indiana, excellent farms are offered for sale all over the State, by persons intending to seek the Gold Land. What will be the end of these things? It is a grave question."

The Cincinnati *Gazette* complained, "This great exodus begins to affect business seriously. Rents are falling and labor advancing. Landlords are now looking for tenants instead of tenants for farms as heretofore. Farms . . . that last year were leased at a rent of 4,500 bushels of corn, are this year offered for 3,700 bushels, and well-stocked farms are for sale in all parts of this country at great sacrifices, by persons who are preparing for California."

By 1852 the overland journey had become a relatively routine trip, although it was by no means an easy one. The routes were clearly defined, there were guidebooks to follow, and profiting from the experiences and mistakes of those who had gone before, the emigrants of 1852 could, with reasonable care and prudence, expect to make the trip without any great difficulty.

But if the greatest hazards and obstacles of the trail had been overcome for these emigrants, it was for them still a high adventure. They were leaving their homes, their relatives and neighbors to begin a new life in a young, raw, rapidly changing country. Guidebooks might help them to grass and water, ferries and occasional rude bridges could reduce the dangers of rivers and streams, but once started on the long journey from the Missouri to the Pacific, the emigrants had to rely upon their own good sense, stamina, and courage to see them through.

While the dangers were perhaps less for those travelers of 1852, they were still plentiful. Stock could sicken and die, men were drowned in fording rivers, monotony and hardship led to murder, wagons could overturn, oxen stampede, and, most fatal of all, disease could strike down the westward traveler in a matter of hours.

Compared to the pioneering efforts of the 1840's, and the high romance of the gold seekers of 1849, the emigrants of later years may appear ordinary, but these more prosaic emigrants, many with their wives and children, their goods and

[2]

stock, had their own full share of danger, of hardship, and of tragedy.

II

Outfitting for the journey was a serious undertaking for the emigrants—wagons, stock, and provisions had to be selected with care. The wagons were ordinary farm wagons, not heavy freight or Conestogas. "The first thing father did was to go to Keokuk and order two strong wagons which were made with long wagon beds and then corded with ropes the length of a mattress . . ." Mary Medley, a young Iowa farm girl, recalled. "Tall bows were placed over the wagon bed with two covers of heavy canvas made to fasten tight in front and back to keep out rain. A large, tight box was made behind the wagon bed with a lid on hinges to let down, which could be used as a table. . . .

"The front of the wagon was tall enough to allow one to stand up straight in it. This was the family wagon. In the other wagon our provisions were stored to last through the journey."

After completing his journey from Springfield, Illinois, to Oregon, Dr. Anson G. Henry advised a friend at home about the sort of wagon he should have: "Now, were I in your place, with my present knowledge and experience, I would have made to order in Springfield, two light two-horse wagons, (wide track) close coupled, with short beds, and I would have them covered with 'cotton top sail duck,' with aprons in front and rear, that you could open or close tight, at your pleasure. . . . I would have side boards, and my bows and covers so arranged that they could be shipped and unshipped at pleasure; and I would have the beds constructed in the same way. I would have patent locks, with two light lock chains to each wagon, for the patent locks are apt to get out of order, and besides, are not as safe in bad rocky places as chains. Have a box one foot wide in the front of each bed with strong cover, that will answer for seats; you will find these very convenient for stowing furniture." Such a light wagon could be purchased for not more than $90.

Opinions varied about the stock that should be used. It was conceded that horses and mules were faster, but many thought that oxen were stronger and could better stand the trip. Also, oxen generally were somewhat cheaper than mules or horses. Messrs. Biddle and Constant, who were organizing a train for Oregon, purchased four- to five-year-old oxen in good condition at Independence for $50 per yoke, and the price at St. Joseph was reported to be from $45 to $55 per yoke. Horses sold at the same place for $40 to $60 apiece, and large mules of fifteen hands were $65 to $75, small size from $50 to $60. Cows, which could be mixed in with ox teams, cost from $10 to $15 apiece.

Although most emigrants chose oxen, Delazon Smith, after his arrival in Oregon, took the opposite view. In a letter he noted that nine-tenths of the emigrants of previous years "recommend the use of oxen. They have invariably represented them as altogether the most safe, sure and reliable, and, in the outcome, as quite as speedy. Now, whatever may have been the experience of those gentlemen, or of others who concur with them, in crossing the plains in former years, my own, and I am sure, that a very large majority of this years immigration, is, that oxen are the very last kind of a team to be preferred! They may, and doubtless have, done much better in years past than they did in the present. And it is unquestionably true that they might continue to perform the journey with certainty and satisfaction in those years when the immigration is very small. And even then either mules or horses are to be preferred. I would thus classify: 1st, mules; 2nd, horses; 3d, oxen. The present season I judge there were 50,000 persons on the road bound for Oregon and California; about 30,000 for the latter place and the remaining 20,000 for Oregon. Independent of loose stock, there were, probably, on the main route, before the separation of the Oregon and California roads,

[4]

100,000 animals in the yoke and under the harness. Of the whole number thus employed about six-sevenths, probably, were oxen and cows; the balance was composed of horses and mules, the proportion of horses to mules being, perhaps, as five to one; and yet, there were of course, a large number of mules. Indeed, if my calculations are correct, there were about 3,000 mules on the road. Out of this number, or whatever other number there was, I saw but one dead mule on the entire route! Of the whole number of horses I saw but five dead ones. Though there must have been, as already suggested, some 14,000 or 15,000 on the road. Whilst of oxen alone I saw, as I should judge, at least 5,000 lying dead by the road side! And those who work oxen usually work cows also. This I would protest against. A very interesting and flattering theory has hitherto been presented to the people of the western States in relation to their mode of getting here. . . . One item in this theory has been that they could work their cows all the way whilst they would afford them milk and butter on the journey; that they were nearly as serviceable in the yoke as oxen, and that on arriving here they would be worth from $50 to $100. All of these results are impossible. Work your cows indeed you may. But if you do two results will follow, nine cases in ten, to-wit: your cows will be worth next to nothing for milk, and what milk they do give will hardly be fit to use; and, what is worse than all, if you continue to work them, they will either die on the road, or give out before reaching their journey's end, and so compel you to leave them upon the road. I started with four and worked them. I got through with—none. If I had started with ten and worked them all I might now have one cow instead of being, as I am, cowless. Had I kept their yokes off their necks, I have no doubt but that I should now possess four cows. . . . Remember, then, I advise the driving of cows; but protest against their being yoked. I will not quarrel with the doctrines of the Woman's Rights Convention, but I must demur to the yoking up 'crying heifers' with 'cow brutes' of the sterner sort.

[5]

". . . If, therefore, the wealthy farmer or other persons are desirous of bringing oxen let them do so. His employing mules or horses for his family need not prevent his driving any number of loose cattle. Then and in that case he can employ at his option—suffer his family to proceed or accompanying the stock."

Some of the emigrants did drive extra stock; the McAuleys had, besides their teams, 20 head of dairy cows, and there were several large herds brought across the plains. A Mr. Perkins and family, from Illinois, took a drove of 560 cows with them, and Michael Smith, of Missouri, left with 270 cows.

More unusual was a train reported in the Sacramento *Union* of October 19, 1852: "We are informed by Dr. Bailey, who reached here yesterday, that a large train of immigrants have just come in across the plains, by the way of Salt Lake and the Volcano road. Among the number are three brothers, named Patterson, from Jackson county, Missouri, who have driven through fifteen hundred head of sheep, four hundred head of cattle and twenty wagons. The latter were freighted with provisions &c., for the Mormons, at Salt Lake Valley. Their freight bill amounted to the handsome sum of $11,000."

According to the *Pony Express Courier*, referring to one of the brothers: "On his arrival at the Mormon settlement he unloaded his wagons and built decks in them. These wagons (seven in number) he loaded with chickens purchased from the Mormons and delivered them in California." Also—and he must have been the busiest emigrant on the trail—a man from Illinois drove a flock of 2,000 turkeys from Independence to California.

The question of provisions occupied the emigrants through the spring. The Snodgrass-Riker company—fifteen men, two women, and one child—had six four-horse wagons, one two-horse wagon, and four extra horses. They carried 5,600 pounds of horse feed, 3,600 pounds of provisions—flour, bacon, ham, ground coffee in tin cans, tea, sugar, rice, beans, dried apples and peaches, and pickles—and 800 pounds of baggage, arms,

[6]

ammunition, and blankets—10,000 pounds for the seven wagons.

Caroline Richardson's provisions consisted of: 500 pounds of flour, 400 pounds of bacon and hams, 100 pounds of sugar, 20 pounds of coffee, 10 of rice, 7 of tea, and dried fruit, lard, and other small items.

The Captain Brandon train consisted of five wagons, one carriage or spring wagon, twenty-four men and one woman divided into eight messes. Each mess had for supplies: 350 pounds of flour, 150 pounds of sea biscuit, 1 barrel of crackers, 8 or 10 hams and the same number of sides of bacon, 11 pounds of sugar, 25 pounds of coffee, 4 pounds of tea, a small sack of rice, a box of raisins, a keg of vinegar, a keg of pickles, and a few dried apples. There was also a keg of brandy for the company.

Alpheus Graham and his two brothers traveled in a company of seventeen men, with ox teams, divided into messes. "I will here give the outfit of my mess from the Missouri river: (FOOD) 450 lbs. flour; 90 lbs. sugar; 10 lbs. cheese; 125 lbs. crackers; 1 bu. dried apples; 3 bottles lemon syrup; $2\frac{1}{2}$ lbs. tea; 1 bu. beans; 280 lbs. bacon; 6 gal. vinegar; 4 gal. molasses; 25 lbs. salt; 22 lbs. rice; 1 box wafers; 1 oz. peppermint. (MEDICINE) 5 qts. brandy; 2 lbs. tartaric acid; 1 qt. linament; 1 oz. calomel; $\frac{1}{2}$ lb. ginger; 2 oz. ammonia; $\frac{1}{2}$ oz. quinnine; 1 pt. castor oil; $\frac{1}{2}$ lb. camphor; 1 lb. sulphur; 3 lbs. soda; $\frac{1}{2}$ lb. cayene; 1 pt. sweet oil; 2 oz. opiam. (OTHER SUPPLIES) 3 lbs. rough nails; 3 cannisters for tea, coffee; 40 ft. rope; 10 lbs. powder; 1 qt. No. 6 shot; spools of thread; 2 camp kettles; 1 paper, pins, pens; 4 gal. jugs; 3 water buckets; 12 lbs. lead; 4 cinch pins; 1 gal. tar; 1 qt. turpentine; 2 water kegs; 1 bottle ink; 10 lbs. soap; 2 sugar buckets; 2,000 caps; 1 paper needle; 1 demijohn."

Newton Finley, of Saline County, Missouri, was in a party of twelve men, five women, and twenty-seven children, with eight wagons with ox teams and two carriages with mule teams. They had a total of 300 head of oxen and cows, 20 mules, and a few saddle horses. He remembered: "Each family prepared tents for themselves and also looked after their own supplies of food. These tents were of simple durable construction; the frame consisting of three poles of convenient proportions; two being the same length used as uprights; the third used as a ridge-prior and indicating the length of the tent. These three timbers being then ingeniously united, completed the framework;—then with the cloth covering and ropes for anchoring, with the necessary stakes for pinning in the earth, the sleeping quarters are complete. . . . Our supply of food was bountiful and of the best grade . . . consisting in part of: Cornmeal, flour, Buckwheat flour, Ham, Bacon, Sausages, Dried Beef, Beans, Peas, Potatoes, Rice, Coffee, Tea, Sugar, Honey, Syrup, Milk, Butter, Dried Fruits, Apples (Green) Walnuts, Hickory Nuts, Hazel Nuts, etc. . . . We had fresh milk twice daily, butter fresh daily; procured simply by placing milk at morning in the churn, put it aboard the wagon, at night we had the genuine article."

Dr. Anson Henry carried: 415 pounds of flour, 160 pounds of crackers, 100 pounds each of bacon and coffee, 60 pounds of sugar, 50 pounds of salt, 45 pounds each of apples and pickles, 43 pounds of yeast and sundries, and 30 pounds of cheese; also 70 pounds of soap, 20 pounds of powder, and 12 pounds of candles. Along with shot, clothing, and two trunks, his total load was 1,335 pounds.

Apparently Dr. Henry's supplies were inadequate. In his letter he advised that for a family of seven and three drivers: ". . . you will need for mule or horse teams the following quantities, with one-third added, if you come with cattle:— 700 lbs. of flour, and 200 lbs of good butter crackers, in tin boxes, sealed up; 400 lbs bacon, *hog round;* 50 lbs. of lard, in tin can; 50 lbs of buffalo tongues, or dried beef; 50 lbs salt; mustard and pepper in proportion, with as many pickles, sweetmeats, &c., as you can afford to buy and haul; 100 lbs white crushed sugar, and 5 gallons of syrup; if you omit the syrup,

150 lbs sugar; 60 lbs coffee; 6 lbs tea; 40 lbs soap; 10 lbs sperm candles; 40 lbs of butter, put up in 8 or 10 lbs cans, sealed up."

The doctor offered advice on clothing and general outfit he considered necessary: "I would bring nothing in the shape of clothing but what will be needed on the trip. Each girl should have two good linsey dresses and three good calicoes, with plenty of underclothes, (especially socks, which, bring by the dozen,) and one pair of light boy's boots, with three pair of shoes. Do not omit the boots for the females, for they will frequently have to wade half way to the tops through mud and water. Let them lay in plenty of coarse needles, thread, yarn and combs, and all the little fixings women are always wanting; and I would have all the clothing in light hair trunks, instead of sacks. Each boy should have one pair of coarse kip boots, made large, for when wet they always shrink one or two sizes, (if made wrong,) and at least two pairs of shoes made to order, if store shoes, three pair, and at least half a dozen pair of good woolen socks—two good stout suits of clothes, with an extra pair of pants, and four or five hickory shirts. Good stout box coats are very comfortable after leaving the Platte. . . . Do not load yourself down with sheets, table cloths, bed quilts, &c., but bring plenty of blankets and coarse towels. Each man should have an india rubber coat (do not get cloaks,) and two blankets, and an india rubber carpet for the floor of your tent. —Get your tent made in St. Louis, have a wall tent ten feet square with a fly, and have it made of the best top sail duck, with very strong chords and stakes, and when well 'pitched,' it will stand any of the storms on the Platte. . . . Get Armstrong to make you a camp table, such as he made us, and get half a dozen camp stools and have them covered with duck. . . . Have plenty of tin buckets and tin cans.

"Mrs. H. and M. suggest that a lady should have two good strong English merino or linsey dresses, with three or four dark calico wrappers; two tweed sacks in place of shawls; one good silk hood, and two sun bonnets, with three pairs of good buckskin gloves—you should have three pair for yourself for the alkali dust is hard on the skin. Each man and boy should have a good hat and cap. . . ."

The Reverend J. L. Yantis also offered general advice to a friend in the East. Writing from Oregon, he said: "I would have one wagon body made very tight to ferry in, (the simplest thing in the world) otherwise there is great imposition, . . . I would put up with my provisions several hams of bacon and several of venison to serve in case of sickness; I would get my family physician to put up my medicine, and if I had a son-in-law who was a physician, I would bring him along if I could. I would lay in a good stock of patience and perseverence. I would commit myself and family to God with prayer and fasting; set out by the 15th of April if possible not later than the 20th travel regularly consulting the capacity of my cattle; and then, resting every Sabbath, I would make the journey. . . ."

THE OVERLAND TRAIL
TO CALIFORNIA
IN 1852

PROLOGUE

———◄◆►———

"**T**HIS morning reminds me of a swarm of bees just come out, the women was busy in the hous accompanied by severl of the neighbor women the men was found out with the oxen the whips was cracking the chains rattling the men swaring the women taring and the oxen bawling and upon the hole it was one of the times that you read of when the women wold git out of humer." So wrote young John Lewis on April 15, 1852, as his family set out from Randolph County, Missouri, to join the rising flood of westward-bound emigrants.

"In the year 1852," wrote John Riker of Piqua, Ohio, "the gold excitement in California still continues, and thousands have heretofore and are still emigrating to that country." Throughout the United States upwards of 50,000 men, like Riker, sold their farms, closed their offices, gave up their jobs to join the great wave of migration to California and Oregon.

Men decided to go west for many reasons—gold, adventure, virgin lands, each drew its share of emigrants across the plains. "In consequence of a failure in business & the want of means or substantial friends to aid or brace me up again," explained John Clark of Virginia, ". . . I resolved to put forward in the world again as a new beginner. The only place, or opening I could see for a ten-strike was the mines in California, where it was said one could enrich himself with the precious mineral of the earth without the help of others."

"It is amazing to hear all the plans and several projects in view, when we all get our piles," thought James David.

[13]

The Emigrants Last Look Upon Home

"Many are the Castles built in air; piles of money, splendid farms, fine little wives and pretty children. No happiness without Gold according to our ideas. . . . Had an application from an old Lady to take her son; everybody wants to go seemingly. Oh, thou Almighty Dollar how precious thou art; but how stingy with thy favors; and with what Zeal thy Devotees worship. . . ."

Seventeen-year-old Moses Laird, working as a saddler for $8 a month, decided to try his luck in the West: "I got 2 carpet sacks and packed up my tools, some cloths, with a large oil cloth coat to protect me from the storms on the plains, and then on the 29th day of March 1852, with forty five Dollars in my pocket—that I had made by my own work—I shouldered my carpet sacks and started alone from Norwich, Ohio, to try and get through to California or Oregon if I could."

"We started for that promised land on the thirteenth of April in the year of our Lord 1852," Lewis Stout wrote as he, his parents, and his three sisters left their farm in Van Buren County, Iowa. "We sold out to an old crusty Dutchman, who kept us in hot water, as the saying is, all winter, but we tugged it out without any blood shed and with a heap of hard fixing and tearing around we rolled out today."

Leaving his wife and home, James David was tempted to give up the journey: "It was a painful matter to leave friends and acquaintances perhaps for the last time. No trial perhaps so great as starting, and probably many would have backed out had they not fixed and fear of ridicule makes many a person go to California that would not have gone."

John Hawkins Clark sold his coal business in Cincinnati and boarded a riverboat for St. Louis: " 'Twas early in the morning when we pushed out into the stream, and I for the last time walked out upon the deck to take a last fond lingering look of home, the places of my boyhood, the scenes of my earnest endeavors in later days to accomplish the dreams of my young ambition. More than all this, I was leaving all that was near and dear to me for a 'wild goose chase' overland to the shores of the great Pacific. It was not without some little regret that I parted from the shores of the Queen City and left my future fortune to fate, and this thought troubled me some: 'If a man cannot make money in this new and fertile country where can he expect to woo the fickle goddess with success?' Those and kindred thoughts troubled me some, but with as stout a heart as I could muster I choked them down and resolved upon doing the best that in me lay towards accomplishing the fulfillment of my long dream."

I

TO THE OUTFITTING TOWNS AND
ACROSS THE MISSOURI RIVER

◆◀◉▶◆

AS THE SPRING sun dried the roads and the grass began to grow, a great multitude—by wagon and team, carriage and coach, by train and flatboat, by steamboat and on foot—moved toward the towns on the east bank of the Missouri River. Emigrants traveling overland encountered bad roads, mud hub deep from spring rains, late snowstorms, mired wagons, broken wheels and axles, and unruly stock, chafing at the harness.

The riverboats of the Ohio were crowded with passengers converging on St. Louis to transship for the outfitting towns. "Every steamer that leaves St. Louis for the Missouri river is literally crowded with passengers and accoutrements, destined for the great journey across the plains to California," said the *Union*. "Men, women and children,—horses, mules, oxen, wagons, carts, and coaches, of all kinds, with all the peculiar etceteras of California outfit, throng our streets daily, and line our levee, preparatory to embarking in steamers for some one of the starting points, beginning at Independence, and going up at least as far as Council Bluffs. As one crowd succeeds another, we wonder much where they all come from, or how they are all going to reach the end of their destined journey—which with them all is the land of gold."

Lucky emigrants secured berths on the boats; the others slept on deck or wherever they could find enough space to stretch out. Richard Keen, a young man from Logan, Indiana, boarded the steamer *Alton* at St. Louis for the trip upriver to St. Joseph: "Aboard our vessel was a lot of Omaha Indians that had been on a visit to Washington City and were on their return to the wilderness. . . . our boat was very much crouded and a large number of the Passengers could not procure state rooms. I happened to be one of the unlucky number and had to take a berth on the floor the majority were California bound and were gambling day and night. I was very much disgusted could not sleep on account of the Continual noise and excitement kept up by the Gamblers. The Indians were very fond of Ardent spirits and on one occasion they managed to steal a Jug of Whiskey from some of the deck passengers brought it above and got gloriously drunk and created quite a disturbance by yelling fighting etc. One of the drunk Ones came running down the passage way of the Saloon and fell on me which aroused me very unceremoniously I then began to wish my-self in better Company. . . ." Shortly thereafter the

Alton grounded on a sandbar, and Keen was walking to Weston to find another boat.

William Taylor, of Tennessee, and his three sons "bid good buy to little Mother the ballance of my dear children and started for a long trip. . . . When we reached Saint Louis we bought our outfit for crossing the plains, waggon, provisions enough for six months, every thing complete, and went down to the landing with them,

"The captain of the Siranack who we had paid five dollars to secure our passage to Independence, told us that he would not take our freight for he was already over loaded. there was another boat the Saluda that would start in a day or two I did not like the appearance of the captain of the Saluda, and the boat an captain too, of the Sarinack had much the advantage in appearance; we had paid five dollars, I guess the captain would have given it back, for he looked like a gentleman, which he proved to be and landed us safe in Independence. The five dollars in all probability saved some, if not all our lives, for if we had not paid anything it is almost certain we would have went with our outfit!"

The *Saluda* blew up at Lexington on April 9, killing upwards of 135 persons. When Taylor heard of the disaster, he hurried to Lexington: "we found the Boat near the shore, with at least one half of the front torn to fragments! There was a large crowd of mormon emigrants on board & an awful loss of lives some blown into the river & some on the bank! the captain was blown on the bank a corpse terribly mangled!

"It appears that the river has a strong currant oposite Lexington landing, and the captain had made several attempts to stem the currant, and returned to the shore, and the last time and the last words he was herd to say that he would make the riffle this time, or blow her to Hel!

"I found nothing of our outfit but a [keg] of medical brandy, and did not get that."

The *Saluda* was an ominous warning to later emigrants. "The sight of the wrecked steamer caused some uneasiness

[18]

amongst our own passengers," wrote John Hawkins Clark on board the *Clipper No. 2*. "We are on an old worn out boat and the officers are foolhardy and desperate, caring for nothing but the gold they are making. This is the largest crowd that ever traveled up this river on one boat and any little excitement might produce a disaster of some kind."

Clark's fears were not unfounded, as Moses Laird knew from the boat's previous run upriver: "The Clipper No. 2 was a verry large boat but verry old and I had some verry dangerous times before I got to St. Joseph as they had to patch the boilers frequently and as there was a great many rappids they had to put on more steam than was safe.

"There was several instances happened on that boat that made one feel concerned. We were running after night once and the rudder rope got cut some way and the pilot could not steer her. She was in the middle of the current and the river was verry high and a great many snags. The boat and passengers was in a very perilous situation. The captain had near all his cloth[e]s off and was ready to swim if she went down. She kept floating down until they got it fixed and we went on our course. And at another time after night it was reported on board that she had struck a snag. I bounded out of my berth and as I was up in *Texas* on the top of the boat. I concluded to stay on the hi[gh]est part of the boat until it went down and then I would try to swim to shore. But it was a mistake and she did not strike that night. I was well sattisfied as it would not have been verry pleasant to swim that night as the Missouri is a hard stream to keep up in; there is so much sand mixed with the water."

An English woman of twenty-five, Lucy Rutledge Cooke, her infant daughter, and her mother-in-law shipped aboard the steamer *Pontiac* at St. Louis for Kanesville. After disembarking passengers at the village of Kansas: "Proceeded slowly till Monday morning, when about nine o'clock we saw men running and crying 'Man overboard!' But it was presently hushed up, and we saw gents laughing, which soon allayed our

[19]

fears. But in about half an hour I saw deck hands and cabin boys running into the staterooms gathering blankets and comforters. We were then informed we had run across a log on a 'sandbar' and had stove a hole in the bottom of the boat, and they were trying to stop the whole with bedding. But it failed, so in ten or fifteen minutes we were passengers on a sunken boat. But fortunately the water was shallow, so we were only submerged about three feet. Still, we seemed to be sinking lower and lower.

"The clerk (who owned the boat) came into the ladies' cabin much agitated, and told the ladies to put on their bonnets and shawls with as much haste as possible. But I cannot say any of us seemed much alarmed. Still, all was confusion, and to add to our discomfort it was a very cold, windy morning, and had just commenced to rain. We were about 150 feet from shore. Well, a colored man took baby, whilst I carried my carpet bag, and down to the front of the boat we hurried. When we arrived there the boat had so settled that water was up over the deck. So we had to walk on raised planks. But we were too late to get in the first yawl load, it being already full, and we were hurried back to the ladies' cabin, being assured we should be safe. . . . We therefore kept pretty contented for about an hour, when the boat gave signs of breaking in two. It was therefore again thought advisable to put us ashore. So to the yawl we again went, and after a big struggle in the crowd, managed to get in; but the yawl was crowded, as each passenger was anxious to set foot on terra firma. The river was very rough, and it took four men to row. However, we were soon ashore, and could then have a good view of the Pontiac in her disabled condition, and reflect on our own situation."

By dusk the Cookes' hand baggage was brought ashore, the cabin boys and cook brought enough cold meat, crackers, and coffee for supper, bonfires were lit, and the stranded passengers settled down to await rescue.

"At this juncture a boat came up the river, and as we had our baggage with us, only carpet bags (our chief things having

[20]

gone overland in our wagons with Pa), we obtained our passage on this boat, the Midas, and toward midnight we went aboard.

". . . The Midas at length left the ill-fated boat and those of the passengers who were trying to get their baggage which happened to be on deck, all that in the hold being a total loss. The boat was then nine feet under at her bows, and four and a-half feet at stern. . . . There were many horses and mules, and poor creatures they stood for hours up to their knees in water, then were cut loose, and a man in a yawl dragged one, at which the others followed to shore. But we were now on the Midas, and left our late fellow-passengers to their fate."

John Clark of Virginia, a passenger on the *Midas*, noted in his diary that with the rescued passengers there were over 600 people on board. And Thomas Lewis, also on the *Midas*, said of the sinking, "it was generally supposed it was sunk on purpose to get the insurance."

John Clark of Virginia had his first view of the town of St. Joseph from the deck of the *Midas*, the day after the rescue of the *Pontiac* passengers: "On nearing the City it shows a glowing front with high bluffs or baren banks to the rear. These, with the rich valley below are dotted with waggons, tents, horses, mules & other stock to the number of 20,000 with a great portion of other equipage. . . . I visited the heights to the rear of the city where I had a full view of the great encampment. The numerous waggons, tents & so many thousand head of stock on the ground is a sight thats seldom seen by one so old, or during a life time."

The next day, April 28, the St. Joseph *Gazette* said: "Hundreds of California and Oregon emigrants, arrive in our city daily. From present appearances, the emigration will be larger than it was in 1849 or 1850. We learn by a gentleman who came through from Hanibal by land, that the road is crowded with teams, and hundreds are daily crossing the Mississippi at various points. We notice among the emigrants several families, who go out with the intention of making permanent settle-

[21]

ments. The ferries at this city, are crossing large numbers every day, who are making arrangements to leave in a short time. In ten days hundreds will be on the plains, but how their stock is to subsist, is a mystery to us, as there is not yet a particle of grass on the plains. We find that the more experienced are willing to await the appearance of grass, before embarking upon so perilous a journey."

The day this appeared in the *Gazette*, Lodisia Frizzell, a farmer's wife from Illinois, arrived on the *Martha Jewett*, prepared to wait in camp across the river until her husband and four sons arrived overland: "We proceeded to the ferry, but could not cross for 2 hours for the crowd of teams which were in before us; while waiting there, some 200 indians of the Pawtawattimees [Potawatomis] & Winenewbagoes [Winnebagos] came down the street, affording me one of the strangest sights I ever saw. They were very dark complected, quite black, half clothed, & some few were ornamented; they had some 30 or 40 ponies which were laden as I should judge by the variety; with every thing that they possessed; for there were fastened on the top of the enormous loads which they carried, dogs, puppies, paupooses, chickens, & those who were unable to walk by reason of age or infirmity. One of the puppies thus confined kept yelping, probably from hunger, an old indian perhaps tired of hearing it, or thinking that it disturbs us, steped up & shot it in the head with a blunt arrow & killed it, and then threw it in the river. They were in a hurry to cross over and crowded down to the waters edge, the ferrymen would not take but a few of them at a time for there was not room for the waggons, one old skuaw was as mad as a wet hen, she scolded a perfect storm, one of the men who stood by understood her, & interpreted to us what she said, & it served to amuse us not a little. Our turn now come we crossed over to the wild and unhabited (except by indians) Territory of Nebraska. We soon had our tent up got some dinner, the indians came round the tent, some begging, some having a few articles to trade, and as they concluded a bargain or 'swop' as they call it, they shake hands with all around and say, good, good & then depart."

John Clark of Virginia spent several days after his arrival purchasing mules for the journey: "About one mile east of the town we were introduced into a large carroll [corral] full of stock, many of them young and unbroken. . . . We had to walk in this carol, or, pen, full of wild mules & wicked steers, risk our lives in roping them. After being kicked across the pen some half dozen times & run over as often, we at last succeeded in leading them out & hitching them to the waggons and soon made a dash, although somewhat hurt. It was laughable to all creation to see the wild devils run with all hands hanging on to the ropes to keep them in check. However, in a few hours practice we had them in the train stubborn enough. . . . Buy Canadian & Indian horses for the saddle, the latter beautiful dark animals just captured & brot in by the trappers. They were gay and swift as the antelope. Our stock was fine & well selected. We were now all ready for the start on tomorrow."

"Teams crossing the river all the while," observed Mrs. Frizzell, "but there is not half ferry boats enough here, great delay is the consequence, besides the pushing & crowding, to see who shall get across first. There is every description of teams & waggons; from a hand cart & wheelbarrow, to a fine six horse carriage & buggie; but more than two thirds are oxen & waggons similar to our own; & by the looks of their load they do not intend to starve. . . . This morning I went out walked up a hill which overlooks the town & river, never saw such a bustle, there was a large drove of cattle filling the streets for some distance, which they were crossing to the other side as fast as possible, with their little boats, where there should have been at least 2 good large steam ferry boats. . . . this I know & all others who have experienced it, that it is a great vexation to keep ones team standing for a day or two in the street, & watch your chance to get ferried over, for the press is so great that they will slip in before you if they can."

John Hawkins Clark, co-captain of a company of twenty young men, prepared to cross the Missouri on May 6: "There are several boats and among them one steamboat to ferry over the crowd that is waiting their regular turn; to wait until all who had secured regular tickets to cross over meant the loss of two or three days, and as we were all ready and not wishing to lose any more time we cast about us to see if there was no other way to cross the big muddy. As good luck would have it we discovered a small wood flat [boat] lying at the bottom of the river two feet beneath the surface of the water which the owner was willing to let if we would raise it to the surface, calk and otherwise fit her up for the surface. Many hands make light work. We soon had the boat in trim and commenced to load our animals. In this, however, our progress was very slow, for as soon as we got one mule on board and our attention directed to another the first one would jump overboard and swim ashore, to the great delight of the many who were looking on. After several turns of the kind, and finding that we gained but slowly in our endeavor to freight the boat by the single additions, we concluded to drive them all on together. In this we succeeded admirably, for on they went and we put up the railing to keep them there. A shout of victory followed the putting up of the bars; a victory was gained over the frisky mule and the order given to 'cast off,' but before the order could be obeyed the fiends in mule shape took it into their heads to look over the same side of the boat and all at the same time. Result, the dipping of the boat to the water's edge on one side, which frightened the little brutes themselves and they all, as with common consent, leaped overboard again. Three times three cheers were given by the crowd on shore. So much fun could not pass unnoticed or without applause. Of course there was no swearing done, for nobody could be found that could do justice to the occasion. Finally the mules were got on board, securely tied, the lines cast off and the riffle made. This our first trip. We had so much trouble with the mules that it was reasonable to expect a quiet time with our oxen; in this, however, we were mistaken, for they seemed to have caught contrariness from the mules and were, if possible, more stubborn than the mules themselves. Suffice it to say, we got the horned brutes on board and landed them safely on the other shore."

During early May the traffic was so heavy at St. Joseph that many emigrants started up the east bank of the Missouri. "I left St. Joseph May 3rd 1852 for Oregon, with John Drake," Moses Laird wrote. "He had a wife, 3 children, one waggon, and five yoke of cattle. I bought a cow . . . gave $15 for her, and drove her along with the loose cattle. Started from St. Joseph with 16 waggons in our train." The company crossed the river at Savannah, sixteen miles above St. Joseph. "The Missouri was verry high and we had to cross in a flat boat with oars. We had quite a time in getting our loose cattle over. I went over with a load of loose cattle and when we got to the middle of the river some of them jumped over in the river and swam back to shore and I had hard work to keep the rest on the boat. The boat came near sinking."

William Kahler's party crossed at the same place a few days later. "went up to the ferry Mr. Hathaway and one of Springers waggons went over safe then Mr. Springer family wagon and 5 yoke of cattle and all of Springer family except 2 boys went in the ferry boat and when they were about ½ way across the boat began to sink they made to drive the cattle of[f] but could not in time to save the boat from sinking I and family is still on east side and Isaac Springer with his team and we witnessed the s[c]ene and could do nothing Misses Springer and the baby and the next youngest was all under water boatman of the boat got in the river and took them out and the rest of the family got upon the wagon cover and saved them selves from drowning a Mr. A rusk jumped over board and thought he could swim to shore but was drowned he was one of Mr Springers hands by the assistance of one of the other boats the rest was saved but we thought from where we were that it was impossible that they could all be saved." Kahler blamed the

[25]

ferrymen for the accident. "the people here is as near heathen as they can be and they go for shaving the emigrants as they spent it for whisky and get drunk."

"There are many musicians belonging to the different encampments surrounding us," John Hawkins Clark wrote of his first night across the river, "and after supper all commenced to practice the sweet tunes that were to enliven us while sitting around the camp fire on the far off plains. In addition to the vocal and instrumental music the frogs in the surrounding district, as if animated by the festivities of the occasion, set up such a croaking as I think human ears had as yet never listened to. . . . Never shall I forget the hoarse bellow of the portly frog or the sharp twang of the wee ones, mingled as they were with soft strains of instrumental music. If Babel was worse confounded than I was on this memorable night I do not wonder at their leaving off building the tower, for never before had I listened to so many different sounds. This concert lasted until nearly midnight, when all was hushed except the crackling of the log fires as they were every now and then replenished by the watchful sentinel as he kept watch and ward over the sleeping multitude. Many and varied were the feelings I experienced on this the first night of my pilgrimage in the wilderness I was about to encounter. Sleep at length came to rescue me from uneasy thoughts of home, wife, children and friends."

Emigrants taking the Mormon Trail along the north bank of the Platte River gathered at the Mormon town of Kanesville, which was built three miles east of the Missouri River. "This Kanesville is a poor little mean place," Lucy Cooke wrote. "I don't think there's a brick house in it. Most of the dwellings are log cabins."

"Kanesville is not a very desirable place to live in," was the Reverend John McAllister's opinion, "being situated in a valley a hill on each side not giving room for but one street in a ravine it is $\frac{1}{4}$ or $\frac{1}{2}$ mile long extending down the hollow. Buildings a little delapidated."

"There is cursing, swearing, blackguarding and everything that tends to indecency going on," young Lewis Stout observed, and James Carpenter started downtown the day of his arrival: "just before we got to the first house a man came out of the door and nearly fell down but finally got started but went staggering down the sidewalk and I asked my Partner what was the matter and he said he was Drunk I was 19 years old and had never seen a drunken man my Parents were both Quakers and I had been brought up in a Quaker neighbor-

Crossing the Platte by Ferry

hood and therefore such a sight was new to me but my Partner had served through the Mexican war and was better posted than I was The next day when we went down town at the same place a man was thrown out on the sidewalk and the Blood was runing freely and he didn't get up he died. there I thought I was getting my experience." Kanesville, however, was far from unique in such matters. Caroline Richardson dryly commented on the village of Weston, "I should think that temperance had never been up as far as here you cannot go amiss of a good liquor sign or a good sign of liquor which may readily be discovered in almost every man you meet."

With thousands of emigrants pouring across Iowa into Kanesville, the price of provisions rose sharply, flour doubling in price in only three weeks. Lewis Stout's family had bought their flour before leaving home and shipped it by steamer up the Missouri. When they reached Kanesville, the price was $8 per hundredweight barrel: "We hunted for ours and inquired of every person that would be likely to know anything about it. Could not learn anything about it. Flour raised to $16 and none to be had. We searched every boat that came. Finally we gave up, deciding that it was on one of the two boats that were destroyed coming up the river. They were laden for this place. The eleventh [of May] four of us struck out to have flour at some price or other Hennis [his brother-in-law] and myself went down to the landing Two boats had just arrived loaded principally with flour but none to sell. It was all for emigrants but none for us. We heard of 100 barrels, we went there and it was all gone, had been sold in half a day. Went up the river some five miles from where our flour was directed and found it stored away where it had been for three weeks. You had better believe it made us grin to find it, for we were fixing to go with corn meal."

There were three ferries in the vicinity of the town: one at Council Point, eight miles below Kanesville; a middle ferry at the town itself; and an upper ferry twelve miles above. But even with three ferries, all the emigrants had delays of at least several days before they could cross.

The Cooke family put their time to profitable use: "We gave a concert last night, Ma always having an eye to business. It was a mean kind of a hall, the platform so broken I fell through when I went to sit on my chair. But we all laughed together and thought it all in keeping with the surroundings. Ma, William, and I were the performers. We knew lots of popular songs and negro melodies, which took the audience,

[28]

and they generously applauded everything. I played duets with Ma. The house was crowded, though it was but small. Our costumes were the ones we were to travel in. We borrowed a piano in town, our own team hauling it. Well, after expenses were paid we had $25, so that will pay some ferriages, and it was worth our trouble, and we always enjoyed singing together."

To raise their ferry charge, James Carpenter and his partner went to work on the boats: "While working on this boat there was a little incident happened . . . there was a man had a big nice yoke of red oxen and he drove down to the river to get his wagon and the oxen wanted to drink and started into the River to drink. I said, 'look out the water is deep there.' he said 'you tend to your business, Il tend to mine,' and the oxen only went a few steps till they were swimming and then he was in a fix. he called & called but the oxen had started back for Home. there was no small boats to follow them with and the Currant was taking them down stream. he says to me, 'what will I do,' I replied, 'you tend to your business Il tend to mine.' I know now I ought not to have made that kind of reply. I don't know how he got his oxen. the last I saw of them they were about a mile down the River on a sand bar."

Seventeen-year-old Eliza Ann McAuley was near the middle ferry on May 11. "A dreadful accident happened here today. A boat manned by green hands was taking a boat of cattle across. The cattle rushed to one end of the boat, causing it to tip and in a moment there was a mass of struggling men and animals in the water. One man was drowned. Another, who was a good swimmer, remembered that he had left his whip, and cooly turned around and swam back after it." The McAuleys, with their traveling companion, Ezra Meeker, offered to raise the boat if they could use it, which got them across the river sooner than if they had awaited their regular turn.

On May 19 there was a much needed addition to the ferry service. Enoch Conyers had arrived in Kanesville on May 9, and on the eighteenth he was still waiting to cross: "This morning a steamer was seen coming up the river, and a crowd of emigrants rushed to the landing to be in readiness to board her as soon as she touched the shore, with the intention, if possible to induce the captain to ferry them across the Missouri. W. P. Burns being one of that number and on going aboard was met by the engineer coming towards him with a 'Halloo, Burns; how are you?' He was an old friend and acquaintance from Quincy, Ill., by the name of Turner. The emigrants soon had the captain cornered, pleading with him to ferry them across the river. After some little talk he finally agreed to commence ferrying tomorrow morning at the rate of $10 per wagon and four yoke of oxen included, and $2 for every extra yoke. . . . The steamer's name is the El Paso."

The next morning the Conyers party rushed through an early breakfast and moved down to the landing: "At the sight of the steamer our joy was unbounded to know that we will now escape the danger of crossing the Missouri in one of those miserable little flatboats, for some accident happens to them nearly every trip they make, and frequently, being so heavily loaded, they sink. We waited patiently until 5 o'clock P.M. for our turn. We then drove aboard and were soon across the Missouri. They crowded the cattle on the steamer so closely that one of our oxen had his horn broken off. This was our only accident. Whilst waiting our turn to board the steamer, one of the ferry flats just below the steamer landing sunk. One man was drowned and two others barely escaped with their lives. This evening we learned of another accident which happened to this same ferry flat this afternoon a little while after we crossed. At the time of the accident there was but one wagon and several yoke of cattle on board the flat. This team and wagon were owned by a young man and his sister—name unknown—and at the time of the accident they were both in the wagon, which, as usual with all emigrant wagons had a cover on it. When the flat had reached near the center of the river the cattle became uneasy and began crowding to one side of the boat, so much so that the flat filled and the wagon and cattle all went overboard. The flat righted up, but was filled with water. The wagon went rolling and bobbing up and down as the current carried it down the stream, part of the time under the water and part of the time the top of the cover only was to be seen. The emigrants on shore were frantic with excitement, women running up and down the shore screaming and wringing their hands, children crying, men hallowing at the top of their voices for the ferryman to go and rescue those in the wagon. Finally the wagon brought up on a sandbar about fifty yards below. No one that witnessed the accident believed it possible that either of the occupants would be found alive, but to the great surprise and joy of all, the young man through great exertion succeeded in extricating himself from under the contents of the wagon and crawled out on top of the wagon cover. He immediately turned his attention to the condition of his sister and soon brought her alive to the surface. Some Indians who were standing on the shore, witnessing the accident and seeing the perilous condition of the young man and his sister, plunged into the stream, swam out to them and brought them both safely to shore."

It took the huge Mormon Council Point Emigrating Company—319 persons, 61 wagons, and 416 head of stock—four days to cross the river, from Saturday, June 12, to Tuesday, June 15. "This morning the remainder of the Company crossed the river & came up to the camping ground but why we did not cross all the wagons on saturday was inconsequence of Bro: Clark the Ferryman devoting one of the boats entirely to the removal of Californians and again about an hour before sun down the boat hands were quite Tipsey the pleasures of the Dram shop was more havenful than the salvation of we Mormons. . . ."

Eliza Ann McAuley was camped on the west side of the Missouri while her brother Tom and Ezra Meeker were ferrying wagons. "While we were getting supper, the Pawness chief and twelve of his braves came and expressed a desire to camp with us. Their appetites are very good and it takes quite an amount of provisions to entertain them hospitably, but some willow bows strewn around the camp fire suffices them for a bed. . . . At break of day the Indians awoke us, singing their morning song. The old chief started the song and the others chimed in and it was very harmonious and pleasing."

The emigrants across the river settled down to their first encampment on the plains. "A very disagreeable evening," James David wrote; "all confusion; women scolding, men swearing, children crying; dogs barking; cattle bellowing; wolves howling; fiddles in almost every camp; boys eyeing and ogling the girls cooking; some laughing; some praying; some crying; coyotes yipping; guns cracking. . . . so you have some idea of an encampment of California men from all the world; a heterogeneous mass of all for the gold regions; old grey headed men with families; old, bent, rheumatic matrons; a young couple who have just launched their frail bark on life's boisterous ocean; the minister; the gambler; the merchant; the clerk; the statesman, and the clodhopper all have forsaken home, kindred, and friends for gold."

II

FROM ST. JOSEPH TO FORT KEARNEY
AND THE PLATTE RIVER FORD

———◄◄◆►►———

ACROSS the Missouri in Indian Territory, there was a
seemingly endless train of wagons moving out from the
western shore of the river. John Clark of Virginia's company
waited half the first day until there was sufficient space on the
road to fall in behind the 196 wagons that had passed them

during the morning. "Just consider yourself one among many thousands bound for the desert, mounted on a sunburnt steed, or long eared mule with a rough Spanish saddle—something like a notch cut high enough to hang a bullock on, & still room for the lariett. . . . All hands early up anxious to see the path that leads to the Elephant. We hurry the morning grub, saddle the mules & gather in the steers & we were soon in line again winding our way to the first sumit of the great plain. On our arival I held up for a moment taking a general view of the wonderful & baren looking desert of the west. Great God, I thought, what a sight lay before us. Long ridges, dry knobs, deep gullies, few flowers, and short grass; now & then a stunted grove or lonely oak & for miles towards the mission could be seen hundreds of teams stretching forward like a great Caravan in line on the dark & winding trace leading towards the setting sun. I had little time to reflect or gaze upon the desolate looking waste as the teams were far ahead & my Indian steed had pawed a hole in the ground almost big enough to hide in. I mounted the first dash in a gallop, her mouth open, tail out, & mane in my face. I attempted to hold up, but a comon bit was of no use, for the more I strove the harder the devil went. So I could only hold to my carbine; the drivers in line giving way, and I hanging on like a Comanche for some time, when I righted up with the teams I thought so far ahead. Here I found to my utter surprise the forward wagon had met with a mishap. In going down nearly a perpendicular pitch fifty feet the hounds had given way emptying the load at the foot of the bench & the waggon on top of the steers. This was awful to see our best team, waggon, & grub all in a pile so quick. It was some two hours before we could right up & proceed to Indian Run, fifteen miles. Here is wood, water, short grass & five new graves, four dead steers. Some sickness in the crowd, so we drive up the hill & set our tent for the second time. The evening cold, some rain. No fire or sup[p]er. Make the stock all fast to the waggons, station our

[34]

guard around the Carol [corral], huddle into the waggons and tent for the night."

The first few days of travel were made difficult by unbroken and unruly stock, inexperienced drivers, improperly loaded wagons, and the unfamiliar tasks necessary to life on the plains. Moses Laird's cattle were "all wild and had quite a time before we could get them to work right. . . . Cattle was verry wild; had to put roaps around there horns and one to hold them while the other drove." Driving cattle was a new experience for a Mr. Davis, who had been a shop clerk in Illinois: ". . . this day, as usual, I have hollered and bawled and whipped our awkward cows until I am tired clear out."

The Agnes Gillespie company also had trouble with their wagons: "Cook's wagon turned over yesterday; Pa's stalled today. Have not had any trouble with our stock stampeding; except horses; they have stampeded twice, but did not go far. . . . Have had very bad luck today. Broke another wagon. . . . Osburn's hind wheel; both broke by careless driving."

G. A. Smith's party "made slow progress on the account of baulky Horses," and a few days later, "a good deal of scolding this morning as it is washing day with us we do our own washing & patching scolding & cooking it is here whare a man sees the loss of a Woman."

Wednesday, May 5, was Perry Gee's first full day on the trail from Independence: ". . . volneys mule ran away with him and threw him off Young fell down and hurt him pretty bad George Shepard got kicked by one of the oxen and John miller got kicked pitched our tents that night and put 3 men on watch at 8 oc it comenced Blowing thundering lightning and raining it blew a perfect gale and the rain fell in torrents our cattle got frightened the storm was so violent that the cattle was frightened and ran off in spite of the gard and they were obliewed to take their mules and horses and follow them through the storm in the mean time the tent that I ocupied blew down and left us exposed to the storm. . . ."

[35]

After only one day on the trail the Frizzells had to repack their wagon: "Stayed in camp to-day unloaded our waggon put every thing that it was possible in sacks leaving our trunk chest, barrels & boxes, which relieved the waggon, of at least, 300 lbs, besides it was much more conveniently packed. Water being handy, we washed up all our things & prepared to start in the morning. A boy about 12 years old came to our tent poorly clad, he said he was going back, I asked him several questions, & learned that he had run away from his folks who lived in the eastern part of Ohio, had got his passage from one Steamboat to another, until he had reached St. Jo. & then had got in with some one to go to California, but he said they would not let him go any further, & sent him back, I gave him something to eat & told him to go back to his parents, I know not where he went but from his tale this was not the first time he had ran away from home."

After a few days of shaking down, the emigrants adjusted to their new way of life, and Esther Hanna, the eighteen-year-old bride of a Presbyterian minister, began to feel almost cozy: "Our wagon is very comfortable. We have a nice, little bedroom of it at night. We shut it all up close, let down the backs of the seats, spread our mattresses, hang up our clothes on the hooks which are put in all around. I have my looking glass, towel, etc. hung up and everything in order."

"Loyd & I occupied the waggon," Mrs. Frizzell wrote, "while the boys slept in the tent, I had bought rag carpet enough to spread over the ground in the tent which proved excellent for keeping the wet, or sand, from getting in the bedding, which consisted of buffalo robes & blankets, which I considder the best for this journey, as they keep cleaner & do not get damp so easily as cotton quilts. . . . I could not sleep soundly, therefor dreamed of being attacted by bears & wolves; when the sharp bark of one, close to the waggon, would rouse me from my fitful slumbers but the rest slept so soundly, that they hardly heard them; for people sleep in gen-

[36]

eral very sound, on this trip, for being tired at night, they feel like reposing."

A day or two out of St. Joseph, the emigrants came to a bridge over Wolf Creek: "Here was not the d——l to pay," wrote John Hawkins Clark, "but instead a large Indian sat at the receipt of customs demanding $1 per wagon for the privilege of crossing over. California should be full of gold if the immigrant expects to get back all his outlay in getting there; $5 per wagon and fifty cents for horses, mules and oxen for crossing the Missouri river at St. Joe: and here again, $1 per wagon for passing over a bridge fifty feet in length, costing perhaps $150. This stream is called Wolf river, and crossing in any way except by the bridge would be a hard job. We presented a $5 gold piece but it was refused; he must have 'white money with the bird on it,' so eight silver half dollars were hunted up and passed over. The Indian was making a 'good thing,' not less than 1,500 wagons passing over to-day."

The Clark train crossed Wolf Creek on May 9 and were, it would seem, grossly overcharged by the Kickapoo Indians who maintained the toll bridge. Four days earlier D. B. Andrews had paid 50 cents per wagon, and earlier still, on April 29, Richard Keen was charged only 25 cents to cross. Some emigrants refused to pay anything. Jay Green reached Wolf Creek on May 2: "At this place there were a number of Indians of the sack and fox nation colected for the purpos of taxing the emigrants for traveling through their territory and making use of their grass and timber. This tariff I did refuse to pay as I thought it a skeen [scheme] of speculation got up by the Indian agent who resided at the mission at that time five miles west of woolf river."

Lodisia Frizzell was much impressed by the Indians at Wolf Creek: "there were several of them here, quite fine looking fellows, not near so dark as those I had seen, but of the real copper color, said they were of the Sacs & Fox tribes. One was a chief, he was dressed in real indian stile, had his hair shaved

off all except the crown lock, which was tied up and ornamented with beads & feathers, he, & one or two others, had
various trinkets upon their arms, legs, & heads, but their main
dress was their bright red blankets, There was several teams
here, which were passing over before us, when one of the teams
getting stalled on the opposite bank, which was steep and
muddy, a little pert looking indian jumped up and comenced
talking & jesticulating in great earnest; on inquiring what it
was he said? an interpreter nearby said, he was saying to the
driver, that if he could not go through there he could not go to
California, he had better go back home. We passed over when
our turn came, & went a short distance up the stream, &
encamped; having come about 20 ms, fine grass here, & some
small timber along the banks of this creek, I had a severe
headache this evening, our folks having got their supper, they
were soon seated around a blazing fire, & were soon joined by
several indians, who likewise seated themselves by the fire, &
as one of them could speak a little English, they kept up quite
a conversation. They say they no steal white mans cattle, they
good indian, but the Pawnee he bad indian, he steal, no good,
Loyd gave them a drink of brandy which when they had
tasted, said strong, strong, but smacked their lips as if it were
not stronger than they liked. I lay in the waggon looking out
upon this group, which as the glare of the fire fell on the grim
visages, & bare, brawny arms, & naked bodies; having nothing on the upper part of their bodies but their loose blanket,
& as they move their arms about when speaking, their bodies
are half naked most of the time, the contrast was striking between their wild looks & savage dress, to the familiar faces
of our own company, & their civilized dress and speech."

The Presbyterian Iowa Mission was passed by John Clark of
Virginia on May 10: "Here we find a Smith to mend our
broken waggon, also we see here a large farm under excelent
cultivation with store & schoolhouse where they teach the
young indians & learn the old ones how to raise corn. This is a
beautiful spot indeed; land rich & roling, scattering trees, &

Pawnee Family—Types and Costumes

small groves in the distance. Many fine looking indians here, with pleasing Mohalas that mounted their nags at the store facing the right, set off in a lope making the dust fly as far as I could see them. They had come in here for the purpose of buying trinkets, but hearing the cholra was in our crowd left with the speed of an antelope. Four emigrants had just been buried. Many sick & some turning back. We dread the epidemic but push forward over a delightful portion of the plain 7 miles to Buffalo Creek. This branch is quite small, a few brush thrown in to cross on, for the purpose of giving the native a chance to make a little in the way of toll, which is perfectly right for wood & grass. Two large indians nearly naked are the gate keepers. They gave me a good drink of whiskey out of their jug & told me to pass on without toll but to fill our drinking cans here as there was neither wood nor water for 30 miles. The plain is delightful to look over; game rather scarce & not a tree or bush to be seen on this wide level. In a heavy rain we had to camp without fire or supper. We had to turn in, in our wet blankets, but just before this was careful to broach the brandy jug for the first time."

The next night Clark stood guard for the first time: "The night was dark and lonely some mist. Now & then a lone skake from the evening bird, then a sharp screach of the night hawk, the prowling wolf with his hungary howl. This fearful noise with the heavy groans of the tired ox, long brays, or half-smothered wails of the pack mule, and the whining cries of the young kiote, made me rather sick & fearful of the nightly choir I thought so well adapted to the plain. I was glad when morning came when I left the haunted ground imprest with feelings I shall never forget on coming in this morning."

On May 4, a thirty-two-year-old doctor from Indiana, John Hudson Wayman, and a companion turned back from the mission to buy a yoke of oxen near St. Joseph. The next day they waited to cross the Missouri once again: "During our stay there we visited Negro Peter, of whom we baught some whiskey and grub, and became acquainted with Indian Mary, we made a bargain with Mary for some cat meat, and just as we were ready to fill our part of the contract a company of d——d Indians passed along and spoiled our fun. Mary crossed the river with us in the hope that we might come it, but we had not the time to stay."

Although the long journey was just begun, death was already on the trail. John Clark of Ohio passed the Iowa Mission the same day as his namesake of Virginia, and for the next three days, traveling from the mission to the banks of the Big Nemaha, he recorded a melancholy tale of death and bereavement. On May 11 the company camped in the rain, and Clark took the watch: "About midnight our neighbor approached our campfire and told us that his only child had just died and he had come to solicit aid to bury it. We promised that in the morning his wants should be attended to. We had an empty cracker box which we made answer for a coffin, dug a grave in the middle of the road and deposited the dead child therein. The sun had just risen and was a spectator to that mother's grief as she turned slowly but sadly away from that little grave to pursue the long journey before her. We filled the grave with stones and dirt, and when we rolled out drove over it. Perhaps we had cheated the wolf by so doing—perhaps not."

The next day: "Met some wagons returning to the states. The people with them looked tired and jaded, and had lost some of their number by smallpox. They said this was a hard road to travel and tried to induce us to return with them. Later in the day we passed an encampment where it was said there was a case of cholera. . . . Passed the grave of an emigrant, just buried, the wife and children still lingering over the new made grave, the company with which they were traveling having moved on. A more desolate looking group than that mother and her five children presented would be hard to find. An open, bleak prairie, the cold wind howling overhead, bearing with it the mournful tones of that deserted woman; a new made grave, a woman and three children sitting near by; a girl of fourteen summers walking round and round in a circle, wringing her hands and calling upon the dead parent; a boy of twelve sitting upon the wagon tongue, sobbing aloud; a strange man placing a rude headboard at the head of the grave; the oxen feeding near by, and the picture as I saw it was complete. We stopped to look upon the scene and asked the woman if we could be of any service. 'I need nothing,' she replied, 'but advice—whether I shall pursue my journey or go back to my old home in Illinois.' We could advise nothing; the journey onward was a long one and it was something of a journey back, with no home when she got back. We passed on, but not without looking back many times upon a scene hard to forget.

"Camped for dinner and while eating it the bereaved woman and her family passed by. It was a comfort to know that she was well supplied with means to accomplish her long journey."

Death visited the company of John Lewis soon after they crossed the Big Blue River. On May 30: "A. Barns wife was taken sick in the morning but we traveld on untill night as we could not find a suitable place to camp with the ill." The next morning they remained in camp. "Mrs Barns died at half past nine Amandy was taken sick this morning and died in the after noon Mahala was taken this morning and is not likely to recover." The three women were sisters. "This morning," June 1, "found us in awful circumstances Mahala died at 7 oc in the morning & was berried at 8 oc . . . her and her two sisters was beried in one grave after the girls was beried we again started there was hardly men enough that was well to start the train." The company struggled on for two days, and then: "A Barns died at 5 oc in the afternoon & was bered at 6. oc he was bered on a high gravel point on the bank of the little blew R. 5 m. west of the place whare his wife was left thare was severl of the train that was very ill in fact this is one of the most dismal times that ever I experanced it looks about like the switch end of bad luck."

After passing Buffalo Creek, William Lobenstine saw a grave, "on which lay a live dog, probably the only faithful servant to his master, howling away and paying the last tokens of sympathy to him who was resting there in a lonely grave."

On the banks of the Big Nemaha River, May 13, John Brown entered in his diary: "Here my son, about midday, took the Cholera and died about 10 or 12 that night and was buried on the right hand of the road on the east side of the creek under a white oak tree."

"The question was debated whether we should move on or remain in camp on the sabbath, and after considering all of the reasons pro. & con. it was decided that the circumstances in which we were placed justified and required us to travel," Addison Crane, an Indiana judge, wrote on May 9. "Among the reasons which impelled us to do so was the fact that sickness has already broken out in various forms, and it will never do to get in rear of so large an emigration on this account. On Thursday we passed two camps where persons had died the day before of bowel complaints, one of which the physician told me he should call cholera, superinduced however by about 5 days drunkenness. and to day about 4 miles after starting passed a camp where a woman by the name of Byles died last night of measles having taken cold, her husband and little children with their dead mother started back for Illinois. Besides the danger from sickness . . . is the further danger and difficulty of having all the grass eaten off ahead of us, by so large an emigration as we now have behind us. We are certainly am[ong] the first quarter. At the Iowa Mission we were told that 700 waggons had passed ahead of us leaving at least 2000 in our rear. Passed to day over a fine rolling prarie, and after moving about 10 miles, took a rest of $\frac{3}{4}$ of an hour and a bite for our dinner. Bill of fare Ham raw. Crackers soda, Buckwheat Cakes cold. Melted sugar, Cheese & Water. The day is cool and pleasant, and at sunrise this morning it was quite cold. . . . To day we have Joined company with two other wagons and 8 young men from Illinois and Missouri—and hope to continue with them through. They as well as ourselves are well armed. Went up to the tent of Mr Timmons who with his wife 3 sons and a daughter, are removing to California, whither he has been since 49 until two or three months ago and is now going back with his family showed them the daugerrotypes of children and wife which was much admired.

[43]

Timmons thought if I had as good looking a lot of children and as pretty a wife, I had better start to morrow morning and go back—and bring them with me. There is no spare time to any one in our camp. All have as much as we can do. What with keeping range of the cattle, cutting wood, building fires, cooking, wash dishes and clothes, keeping the tent in order, bringing water—pitching and striking tent &.c. &.c. all are kept busy while in camp and while moving I walk, Albert [his brother] drives and rides on his cart, Sam and John walk and drive, and I. sit down where I get a spare moment, and taking out my pocket inkstand jot down these ideas generally in a very inconvenient situation for the display of either penmanship or language and whenever I met with a chance intend to tear out these leaves and enclose them in an envelope for my wife. Upon the whole I am, so far quite pleased with this journey, but expect there will be trying times ahead, which I shall try and make the best of. . . . I must now retire, as all the rest have it being ¼ past 9. and we are to arise at 4."

Beyond the Iowa Mission the Big Nemaha was the first large stream to be crossed, but the ford, despite very muddy banks, was an easy one. When the Peter Hickman train reached it on May 11: ". . . two wagons from our crowd turned back, belonging to a man by the name of Richardson. His difficulty was sickness. His family first were cut down with the measles, then they took the vareloid. This morning his wife being sick, discourages him and he concludes to return. There is great sympathy for him in the company."

After waiting two hours, the Frizzells crossed the Big Nemaha on May 16 and later in the day: "We met a man who was driving several cows, the men in the other waggon recognized 4 of them, belonging to a man from their country, with whom they had intended to travel. They asked the man where was the owner of the cows? & why was he driving them back? he said first that he was the owner, & that he had bought them; but as he could not tell where the man was, nor describe him, they concluded he had no right to them; &

finaly he said them four he had found, & they took them away from him; & as one of them gave milk, we were enable[d] to live quite well; & I would advise all to take cows on this trip, if you use the milk only to make bread, for you can do very little with yeast, & the soda & cream tarter I do not like."

On a clear, starlit night, his notebook illuminated by the campfire, Addison Crane described the open prairie: "The country over which we have passed is most beautiful. No language can do justice to its description. Every acre as far as the eye could see was clothed with verdure, and the soil is as the best of Indiana. One gets but a very faint idea of what is called 'the plains' from reading what others have written. nor do I expect to be able to succeed any better than others have done. Instead of being vast levels—the country is one continuous undulation, gradually as the sumit of one hill is attained you go down another. The landscape is beautifully diversified with here a lovely valley—there a high rolling swell, and yonder a beautiful skirt of timber on some stream I saw to day one of the most beautiful landscapes the eye ever rested upon. . . . at one view the vision embraced a circle at least 50 miles in diameter all high rolling prairie—varigated with skirts of timber. That sight of itself was worth a journey from Indiana here. About 2 Oclock P.M. met a gentleman and lady on horseback returning. He had fell out with his partner some 90 miles west of here and had sold out to him, and said they were returning to St. Jo. to get another outfit, and take a fresh start. I immediately tore out the leaves of my journal & enclosed them in an envelope directed home, and shall continue to do so as often as opportunity offers and I hope these scribblings may be preserved for however unimportant to others they may be . . . they will probably hereafter be to me. But one thing is wanting to my complete happiness on this journey and that is the wife and children along. The rain and mud & labor I do not care for, as they give but an agreeable variety to the dust and sunshine and rest which are soon to suceed."

Nearing the Big Blue River, forty-six miles from the Big

Nemaha, John Lewis first experienced a common hazard of the plains: "this evening we was aroused about sunset by a nois that sounded like a grate storme and on looking about we was somewhat alarmed at the sight of our cattle approaching the camp at the top of there speed bawling & bellowing & there tails turned over there backs this was something new the women & children was in the wagons with there heads stuck out as thick as yong chickens from under there mothers wing, and the men was mounted on there horces and out to see what was the cause of all this runing when we got within 2 hundred yards of the cattle our horces was as bad as the cattle we met a swarm of bugs that was fl[y]ing and they was very thick and about the size of a bumblebee and resembled a tumble Bug these bugs is very numerous and the stock will run & snort when they light on them the horces got scart and they broke with the cattle & here we went all together round & round for about 2 hours then the Bugs appeard to settle to the ground & thare was not a bug to be sen or heard the stock becum quiet and we left them and went to bed very much astonished at the bugs as we had never heard of them untill we found them so ends the bug storey for tonight."

John Clark of Virginia was rolling toward the Big Blue River, when he camped on a small creek the night of May 14: "About 80 waggons in camp. We pitched our tents but soon found we were in a distressing crowd. Many Oregon families. One woman & two men lay dead on the grass & some more ready to die of cholra, measels & small pocks. A few men were digging graves, others tending to the sick. Women & children crying, some hunting medicine & none to be found scarcely; those that had were lothe to spare. With heartfelt sorrow we looked around for some time until I felt unwell myself. Ordered the teams got up & to move forward one mile so as to be out of hearing of cry & suffering. I almost wanted to turn back. Just as we were setting our tents there came a young hawk & lit upon the ground. Thomson, the Kentucky boy, drew his rifle & toppled the lark at a long distance. This was

[46]

A Prairie Windstorm

really gratifying; to think I would have fowl for supper. But come to look, the water cask was empty & no wood in sight. So all hands done without the supper." The next morning: "All were up. Broke the cracker barrel to make fire & roasted the hawk for myself. The rest done without."

On May 17, Richard Owen Hickman reached the junction of the Independence-St. Joseph roads: "We are just coming into the crowd of emigration. As far as the eye can reach to the east and to the west, nothing is to be seen but large trains of wagons and stock. When I beheld it first I could not help asking myself where all this mass of human beings come from, but then the thought arose in my mind that if every county in the United States should send out as strong a delegation as old Sangamon, there would be a great many more on the plains than there was. We passed a company soon after we came into the road that started from St. Joe, out of which 16 deaths have occurred within 8 days of cholera; four died one morning and was buried in one grave together."

Early in the season the weather was stormy and colder than most emigrants had expected. "We are all up this morning and dressed rather cool," Stephen Gage wrote on May 3. "Oh, Gals how the wind blew How it rained and thundered & lightened *Good Granny* how the sand blew *whew*. Left camp about 8 A.M. for Big Blue where we arrived about 2 P.M. . . . The big blue is a very nice looking stream the water is as clear as lake water and as blue."

The next morning Gage "Crossed the Big Blue . . . water not very deep down to its lowest point forded with ease," but three days later, May 7, Jay Green's party "found its waters so swolen from the heavy rains as to render it imposable to cross except in boats, and without delay wee prepared two wagon beds for the purpos of ferrying a line was made fast to eather end of the beds and they ware drawn from shore to shore by the men, and before dark wee ware all safe across wagons and baggage leaving our mules on the opiset shore as it was to late to cross them."

When D. B. Andrews arrived on May 12, the river channel

[48]

was "about 75 or 80 feet in width and between two and a half and three feet deep with a strong current," and the A. J. Wigle party "resorted to raising our wagon beds with blocks of wood, the blocks we tied to the standards to keep them in place. . . . When going into the water we had to make a short turn down stream. In making this turn one of Uncle John's wagons was upset and the load considerably dampened. Here Dennis Toome performed an exploit which is worthy of note. This Dennis was a strong 180 pound Irishman who could not learn gee from haw. He knew the larboard from the starboard side but he could not learn to turn Haw without running around his wagon and scaring his leaders around. When he drove into the river his leaders wanted to go straight across and by so doing they were about to get into deep water. He seeing the danger and not having time to run around the wagon made a dive under the chain about the middle of his team and came up on the other (or as he expressed it) the starboard side. He, by a little assistance got his team righted and got through without further trouble."

The wind was blowing strongly when Addison Crane pulled up at the riverbank, midmorning of May 13. "This is a very pretty stream about 50 Yards wide crossed both by ferry and ford, but as the water is rather high we chose to pay the $2 for ferriage." It was not just the river that was rising. On May 15, John Clark of Virginia saw more than 100 wagons waiting to ferry or ford: "Some drove through but we, like many others, paid three dollars & took the boat." When John Hawkins Clark reached the spot the next day, "if it is a wagon we want carried over the river, $4 and no grumbling."

J. H. Clark continued: ". . . the wind and rain from the northwest, and as we were going in that direction had to 'face the music' of the elements in all their disagreeableness. . . . we are on the banks of the Big Blue. Here we set fire to a pile of driftwood, cooked our dinner and smoked our pipes. On the east bank of this river is located a private postoffice, a dram-shop, hotel and a ferry, the business is all under one roof. If we mail a letter we pay $1; if we take a gram of good whiskey,

[49]

Iowa Prairie

seventy-five cents; a square meal, (?) $1.50; . . . The proprietor is doing a rushing business. During our stay of two and a half hours he crossed forty wagons, his clerks were busy handing out whiskey and the cooks getting out bacon, biscuits and coffee. . . . Rather than pay $4 per wagon for being ferried we concluded to ford the river, which we did without much trouble or danger."

A few miles beyond the Big Blue, Richard Keen's company organized for guard duty. On May 4: "Rolled out early hilly roads water scarce and no Wood. a great many of Co. are tired of traveling overland to Cal and some even say they wish that they had never started as for myself I would turn back under no consideration whatever Met 3 Men returning to the states they were walking with their provisions on their backs the Indians had stolen their horses some 30 miles ahead of us they advised us to be upon our guard as the Indians were very troublesome some of our boys laughed at the idea of the Indians stealing our horses. One of our Co Anthony Rogers had traveled this road to California in 1849. he suggested the idea of keeping a strict guard so there was a council held and after quite a discussion we decided on doubling the guard two sentinels upon duty instead of One and they to be relieved every two hours. We drew our members by lottery (ie) 24 numbers placed in a hat and each one drew a number I drew No. 7 and (U. M.) Pratt No. 8 so that placed us upon guard at the same time. I must say something of my Companion upon duty he was a small man rather slender light hair and blue eyes of an expression sufficient to command respect in any Company What ever we soon became well acquainted he gave me his history. . . . he was the youngest son of wealthy (Farmer I think) he was tolerably well educated using good language he was a silver smith had served a time received his start in the world from his father married and set up shop in Niles Michigan. but Fickle fortune frowned and business did not prosper with him he had lost all he possessed he had left an affectionate Wife and two children and was now ploding his way to the distant Gold Fields of California to retrieve his squandered

[51]

fortune he appears sanguine of success. he is a master Mason and the brightest one I ever talked with we have to walk about half the time which fatigues Pratt very much we camp to night in a small ravine good water and wood Made 28 miles."

Twelve miles beyond the Big Blue was the junction of the St. Joseph-Independence road. Dr. John Dalton had started from Independence, and after eight days' travel—progress being slowed by several accidents to the wagons, "all caused by awkard driving"—reached the banks of the Kaw or Kansas River on May 14. "Started at sunrise & had a race with and passed a train of 12 waggons bound for Origon, which had camped one mile ahead of us—took no breakfast—came to Kansas River 6 miles, about 10 o'clock—and soon commenced crossing the ferry (Papins); got all over about 4 o'clock; went on two miles and camped—Just before coming to the River a Darkey calling himself George Berryman came to us and wished to get into our waggon & cross the River—said he was the Slave of another Negro who had bought him & promised him his freedom after working two years for him in California but slaves being high, he was about to sell him to go down South. He got into the waggon, crossed the river, and next day commenced driving our team." The Independence road continued on across Big Vermillion Creek, the Big Blue, and on May 22, the Dalton party came into the St. Joseph road.

John Clark of Virginia passed the junction on May 17 and met a band of fur traders returning from the headwaters of the Platte. They reported grass was good, but there were 3,000 wagons ahead. One of Clark's company, George Ball, was dangerously ill, so the party stopped and a doctor was summoned from a passing train: "He could do nothing for our friend as mortification had began. So we drove on to Cottonwood, 3 miles. Here we take our lunch & tell Ball he must die. The tears was full in his eyes when he said, I am sorry to leave you & die on the plain; O my God is it so. Imagine our feelings when the teams were got up & ready to go. He requested I should go forward & select the place. I did so going over a beautiful level 10 miles to . . . a high, level & gentle rise. By the wayside I reined up, waiting for the teams until sundown. When they came the young man was still alive & spoke. Water we had none, but two of the boys put down toward the ravine near two miles and found a little. They brot in a cup & gave it. Soon after he said Sister & Mother then expired. We then wound him in his blanket, the green grass his cooling bord until morning.

"May 18th. We procured a spade, selected the spot, dug narrow & deep & laid him down. His hat covered the face, the coat over the breast & body. Then we turned in the sand & clay until it was full; a bone at the feet, while at the head was a bord inscribed in pencil mark: George Ball. Died May 18/52, Measels. Age 20. Clark & Companys train, Portsmouth, Ohio. It was now about sunrise & the teams had gone forward while we were filling up the grave. After we were done, stood in silence for some time imprest with feelings of the deepest sorrow for him we leave."

The trail crossed the Little Sandy, the Big Sandy, and fourteen miles beyond reached the Little Blue River: "This is quite a fine stream with a channel about three rods wide with a very strong current," D. B. Andrews wrote on May 15. "The water in this stream is very turbid and to me not very palatable; skirted on its banks with cotton wood and some ash; a great scarcity of feed. From the Big Blue . . . to this stream, a distance of sixty-five miles, there is no good water, none other than slue or muddy creek water and in many placcs no wood can be obtained without going off the road a great distance. The first part of the road from the Big Blue passes over a tract of high rolling prairie and of a rich soil. The last half of the distance passed over the prairie becomes more barren in appearance and is much cut and broken by runs or small drains with quite abrupt banks and quite broken. The soil is light sand and gravel presenting rather a barren appearance. Roads for the last few days good."

John Hawkins Clark approached the Little Blue five days after Andrews: "From an elevation we first caught sight of the river and a beautiful sight it was, the river winding through groves of thick timber and a small undergrowth, the branches dipping into the clear, silvery flood below, presenting a picture of quiet repose altogether in accordance with our wishes. Happy were we to rest beneath such grateful shade as was here presented for our comfort. Here, too, was wood, water and grass in abundance. Another bear was seen to-day, but made his escape. One of our men, an old bear hunter from the wilds of West Virginia, is badly disappointed in not being able to catch a bear and has promised to kill the next bear he sees or break his rifle over a wagon wheel. After supper drove our stock over the river to good grass. It was a satisfaction to see our cattle on good feed once more."

The next morning: "We were surprised . . . with the bluster of wind and the discomfort of rain; the wind blew a gale and the rain fell in torrents. We are elected to remain in camp all day. . . . This was a day of discomfort, and could our friends at home seen us as we sat huddled around the camp fire, smoked, burned out, (and I was going to say rained out) they would have been greatly amused; but, as it happens, man is neither sugar nor salt, and it would take a good deal of rain to wash him out entirely."

Dexter Hosley was on the Little Blue on June 5: "I went fishing to day, but was not successful enough to get any, I pulled some three or four up most to shore but they were too large for my hook, they bent my hooks out straight and got away, they would have weighed five or six pounds I should think, they were the large Pike, the game here is very shy there has been so many passed, they have left the main road and gone to safer quarters."

The trail did not cross the Little Blue, but followed up its north bank forty miles before striking off toward the Platte. "At 6 AM we struck our tents and renewed our march," Holmes Van Shaick began on May 27. ". . . At 11 we reached the little blue and traveled along its banks about 1 mile, and halted to take in wood and water & let our animals graze. About 11 our Captain was attacked with the Cholera, but not considering himself his condition very dangerous, he ordered the train not to stop. We accordingly at the usual hour ($1\frac{1}{2}$ Oclock) harnessed our jacks and rolled on. Having gone a distance of 3 miles, and while passing a difficult spot in the road the right fore wheel of one of our waggons broke. Being thus disabled we were thus obliged to stop and repair. A traveler hapening along at that time told us that he had passed a wheel about 4 miles back, which he thought would answer our purpose. Three of our boys then went in pursuit of the wheel, others in pursuit of a suitable place to encamp while others stayed with the broken waggon. While standing there two ladies dressed in the Bloomer Costume came along cach in possession of a riding beast. They were so uncommonly talkative that they soon drew the attention [of] all who were standing near. One of them bounded astride of her prancing steed, placed her feet in the sturrups, and with an air of Supremacy drew the reigns rode a few rods, and waited for her associate to follow her example. Her associate, feeling the effects of Nature modesty, concluded she would wait till she reached the other side of the hill. Well thought I these are the women for the over land route to California—Such are the women for me. Having found a suitable place on the banks of the little blue to Camp $\frac{1}{2}$ mile distant, we went there with the unbroken waggons, and pitched our tents (having left a guard with the broken one) The boys in pursuit of the above wheel returned with it about dusk. Our afflicted Captain still grew worse till about Midnight, the cause seemed to be measurably removed. Thus passed a beautiful, though partially unfortunate day with us."

The company lay in camp the next day, and several of the party, including Van Schaick, were taken ill. On May 31, he wrote: "Our Captain has so far recovered that he is again able to lead the train. This morning I found myself a little better. In view of our being in a very sickly place, and surrounded by the sick and dying, it was considered expedient to roll out of

Camp. A bed was accordingly fixed in the waggon for me, on which I placed myself, and as soon as the teams were harnessed we rolled on. We rolled on over the plains till 5 PM when my condition made it necessary to encamp the remainder of the day. Our encampment was on the table lands of the little blue 50 rods from the stream and most of the night I endured the most excruciating pain in my bowels and stomach, that I ever had experienced."

R. H. P. Snodgrass was traveling along the Little Blue on May 17: "Found the body of a man today that had most likely been murdered by his companions. Assisted in burying him decently." Lodisia Frizzell, on the twenty-third, provided some details: "We passed a spot where there was a board put up, & this information upon it, that a man was found here on the 17th, horribly murdered, with wounds of a knife, & buckshot, his shirt was lying there, with the blood & wounds upon it, . . . I never learned any more, but I hope the murderer may meet his reward, sooner or later." John Hawkins Clark passed the grave the same day: "How strange that man will commit murder at all, and still stranger when he does it in a desolate country where there is so much need of aid and comfort from one to another."

Later in the day Clark encountered what was, for the emigrants, an unusual sight: "At noon camped near a train of Rocky mountain traders coming into the states loaded with furs. They were the first we had seen and excited some little curiosity from their rusty looking appearance. Men, animals and wagons looked as though they had spent their existence in the bad lands of the great northwest." To Lodisia Frizzell the wagons piled high with buffalo robes looked "like so many huge elephants, & the men, except 2, were half breeds & indians, & a rougher looking set, I never saw," while Esther Hanna thought they "were savage looking creatures, part of them Spainards, one or two Indians, and the rest what once were white men, but a season's exposure to all kinds of weather had so tanned them that I scarcely recognized them as such!"

John Clark of Virginia identified the mountain men as belonging to one of the famous Robidoux brothers' trains: "The drivers were greedy & filthy looking with six or eight span of poor mules or oxen to each waggon that was filled with robes & furs at least eight & ten feet above the beds. The wild odor or smell from the train gave vigor to our stock that would not face them but left the road in spite of drivers until the black & greasy crowd was far past."

Robidoux Trading Post, Scotts Bluffs

And where the other John Clark was camped: "In our immediate vicinity lay the ruins of an immigrant train—broken wagons and scattered goods, men running here and there, women wringing their hands and children crying. I asked one of the unfortunates, 'What happened?' 'The devil and Tom Walker; can't you see for yourself?' he answered. 'I can see Tom Walker, but the devil I can't see,' I replied. 'Well, look over there,' he replied, pointing to the train of peltries, 'if you can't see him you can smell him.' That explained the matter; the Rocky mountain train had quite a number of green hides, poorly cured, and a dreadful smell was the consequence; this the immigrant oxen objected to and concluded to run away, and making a strong run of it upset wagons, ran over some of their drivers, spilled women and children, bags of flour and other articles upon the highway. It looked like going west under difficulties; some of the wagons had lost their wheels, some had broken tongues, others had covers smashed, and nearly all had some injury to repair."

The plight of the stampeded train caused John Hawkins Clark to give some thought to the general lack of helpfulness among the emigrants: "A word here to all who expect to cross these plains; never get into trouble with the expectation of getting help; carry nothing but what is absolutely necessary, and mind your own business. There is but little sympathy for anyone on this road, no matter what may be his condition. Everyone thinks he has trouble enough and conducts himself accordingly. However, if one is stuck in the mud and there is no way of getting around, over or under, he may get a lift at the wheel, but then he is cursed for having a weak team or for overloading or maybe for bad driving."

Dr. Anson Henry took a barely more charitable view: "The saying that men become selfish *on the plains,* and often mean and dishonest, is not true. They were always so, and when away from the restraints of organized society, they show out their real characters. A really good man in Springfield, will be a good man on the plains. It is true every body becomes more [or] less irritable and ill-natured; so it is very necessary to keep a strict guard over ourself, and observe the good old maxim of 'thinking twice before speaking once.' If a good man has any dog in him, it is sure to break out on the plains sooner or later, in spite of all his care in concealing him."

Passing up the Little Blue two weeks later, John Lewis had camped for noon near the head of his train: "I was first in-teruped by one of the girls that was in my wagon at the time she hit me a tap & spoke very short What—is—that John, I was laying down taking a nap just as ushel but seing her eyes

flash like fire and then to see the oxen prick up thare ears &
me about half asleep it was sum if not more but I had got
somewhat aquainted with the Plains by this time and did not
git excited I jumped from my wagon locking it as I got out
with a paten lock then ran to the lead ox took him by the
Wont you ho buck, G.D. you ho. ho. ho wont you never ho but
as they was very good to mind they did ho. I held them by the
horn till severl wagons ran past but at last one of them come
up and ran on the off side and unlucky locked wheels with me
as he past whitch broke my off hind wheel and his near hind
wheel all in to bits and turned my wagon over with a yong
Woman and two little children in it this was nearly h.l. but I
dun some of the tall snatchen untill I got the yong out from
under the wagon box and its contents they was lik the most of
the Co. more scart than hurt after I got them out I started
after the oxen and the rest of the wagon here was fun the teems
was runing in every direction the loose stock was runing bawling kicking up thear heels all over the botom and the Women
& children Men & boys was all in a h.l. of a sweat and to top
out the spree it comenced raining just for fun and we had
plenty of green cotton wood & willow for fuel hurraw for hurraw who cares if corn is 4 dollars per bushel upon the whole
we had one of them old times we struck camp and made our
selves at home as for my part I took a (yank) of old (ned) and
some bread for my supper and went to bed just as sadespide as
if I was at home thare was no one hurt in the scrape but some
of them was scared half way back to Pike. Co. Mo."

The question of observing the Sabbath caused dissension in
many trains. Being a minister's wife, Esther Hanna had particularly strong feelings on the subject. "There is some dissatis-
faction in our company today," she wrote on May 23. "Some
want to travel, others want to spend the Sabbath here as we
have good grass, wood and water. Mr. Hanna took a decided
stand—told them that whoever wished to go might, but that
he would remain and spend the day in suitable manner! They

have agreed to stay but might as well be travelling! Some are washing, others fishing and shooting, some sawing and hammering, fixing up their wagons, etc.

"I had hoped that we would all be a Sabbath-keeping company but such is not the case. They claim that what they do is the work of necessity!"

On the same day, George Short gave thanks to God for his blessings, then continued: "whilst i writing the most of the company are breaking the holy Sabbath one is shoeing horses one a hunting 4 others are doing there washing it is not necessary to do so May God have mercy on their souls."

The Dexter Hosley party—twenty-six men—were on the Little Blue on June 7: "This morning started at 5. O'Clock and came better than any day as yet. The United States Mail, went by us this forenoon bound for Fort Laramie, 600 miles from St. Joseph, they had four Mules to draw it with, a driver and four men mounted on four other Mules as guards, they were on a smart trot and looked very fine, about 3. O'Clock this afternoon we were surprised by about thirty Indians dressed in their war fixings with their Guns, Spears and Shields. they come upon us from a hollow so very sudden that we had not time to think, they rushed into our teams, and came very near turning us all over, but we ran on both sides of them and succeeded in getting straight again, they commenced begging for tobacco but we did not give them any, they were very bold, they caught hold of one of our mens Watch Chain, but did not get it. they were perfect robbers, and no mistake we happened at the time to be in a bad fix to meet them, as we had just been cleaning our Revolvers, there were but few loaded, but as they turned back and followed us a little time, our Captain Mr Baldwin thought it best to turn from the road a little and take our teams from the Wagons, for it was evident that they were trying to stampede our teams and turn us over so that they might plunder from us, some of the men that had their arms in readiness took care of the Cattle, as they were in the yokes, and the rest were not long in preparing their Guns for defence, as soon as they saw that we were well armed they rode away a few rods and left their pack Horses and took their Flag of truce and the Chief with two others rode up with it, this was to show that they were friends to us we gave them two pieces of tobacco, and they rode away. but not satisfied they left their pack Horses, with one to watch and then rode up the hill, as though they were going away, but we thought there might be some cunning about that so we put a man on to our smartest Horse, and sent him back to the next train, about half a mile, he told them about it and they got their Muskets in order for them and come on, there were thirteen Wagons in the [train], and when we were all together we numbered about fifty men. We hitched up and drove on with them, when we had got one mile we met the same Indians coming scattering along, we supposed they intended to attack us but seeing our numbers enlarged they dare not undertake it. they wanted to shake hands with us but we told them to be off and they did not trouble us any more, we drove thirteen miles and encamped."

Leaving the Little Blue, the emigrants traveled over thirty miles in a northwesterly direction to the Platte River. There was little water, no fuel, and poor feed between the two streams, so it was an occasion of great relief when the Platte finally came into view. "when we come on the last hill which overlooks the great Platte Country the foremost of the Boys raised a shout in which all joined," Richard Keen wrote on May 9. "We could see the mighty Platte for miles and miles either way with her broad expansive bottoms extending back for miles to the sand bluffs on either side. Away to our left could be seen Fort Kearney and Close by could be seen Grand Island with its heavy timber."

When John Hawkins Clark reached the Platte on May 25, there were "Many immigrants . . . camped on the shores of this river, many busied themselves fishing, hunting, running and jumping, playing cards and dancing. Boys will amuse themselves one way or another; many wrote letters at this camp, intending to mail them at Fort Kearney. Caught some fish and took a rest for the balance of the day."

The next day: "Out early this morning, and our pathway now lies in the valley of the magnificent Platte river. What a beautiful and pleasant looking stream; for several hundred miles we are to follow its meanderings, camping opposite its banks, fishing and bathing in its cooling waters, we promise ourselves much comfort while we keep it company, for it is indeed a lovely looking picture, studded with beautiful little islands of every shape and size, some single and at times clusters of them, always covered with grass and sometimes timber. While looking and viewing this broad sheet of water as it comes rolling down from the great west one almost feels that it has come from fairy land. Picture to yourself a broad river winding through green meadows covered with grass which grows to the water's edge, beautiful little islands setting like gems upon its bosom, on some bright morning when the sun first spreads his golden rays over the same, and tell me if you do not see 'enchanted land.' "

The same day Lodisia Frizzell camped on the Platte five miles below the fort: "Several indians of the Sioux tribe came to our tent, the best looking indians I ever saw, they were tall, strongly made, firm features, light copper color, cleanly in appearance, quite well dressed in red blankets, and highly ornamented, with bows and arrows in their hands. We gave them some crackers & coffee, with which they seemed very much pleased. They signified that they wished to trade, & pointing off to the right, we saw, many more indians seated on the ground not far distant, with some 20 ponies feeding around them, as we started out there, we saw a train of waggons which were passing, halt, & appear to be perplexed, we soon saw the cause, a huge indian, naked to the waist, with a drawn sword, brandishing it in the road, & seeming to say 'stand & deliver.' But when we came up, he signified that he wished to trade, but they wishing to proceed, & not wanting to be detained, they gave him some crackers &c, each waggon as they passed, throwing him something on a blanket, which he had spread on the ground beside the road; but I saw the indians chuckle to one another, upon the success of the old chiefs maneuver. This old chief accompanied us to the rest of the indians, & he gave the doctor a buffalo robe for his vest, which he immediately put on, buttoned it up, and appeared much pleased with his bargain; but not better than the doctor with his."

Mariett Foster Cummings had crossed the Missouri at Old Fort Kearney, and this same day—May 26—was on the south side of the Platte, five days out on the trail:

"Before we started this morning we were visited by quantities of Indians that followed us all the forenoon and camped for their dinner near us. They cut willows and stuck them into the ground and spread their buffalo robes over them so as to form quite a primitive tent.

"Their fires were kindled in a trice and a single crotch stuck into the ground obliquely supported their kettles over it. We broke up our noon camp before them to avoid them if possible, but we had not gone out of sight of their encampment before we met five of their number returning driving a mule, and screaming in the most terrific manner and screaming to us to 'Hold on.'

"We caught sight of their pursuers who followed them almost into camp, rode around awhile and then slowly retreated to the hills. There were but 11.

"The returned Pawnees created a great sensation in the camp. There was stripping and mounting in hot haste, and as they got ready they came singly and in groups, screaming in the most devilish, unearthly style imagineable. We were between the contending parties.

"As the Pawnees came running their horses by us each one would point at the Sioux and at us, and motion us to stop and join them and whip their enemies. They were very angry that we did not, and we were apprehensive of an attack, but they were too cowardly.

"A portion of the foremost scouted the hills for their enemies, while the rest as they came screaming and yelling, singing their war songs, running their old ponies, gathered in a group on a slight eminence on the east side. Directly they discovered the Sioux and squaws, 13, in the north, and they commenced a running fight.

"We heard three guns and arrows in abundance. The Pawness had not the courage to join the fight, many of them, but the Sioux killed one of them, and then the Pawnees fled. 150 of them, before 13 Sioux and left their dead man on the field of battle. They came back stiller but full as fast as they went out.

"In the meantime we had stopped and driven into a huddle, and the men had got their guns and ammunition ready for instant use. When the old chiefs returned they were perfectly beside themselves with rage and fear. One in his impetuous gesticulations struck at one of our company with his bow. He showed him his gun and the chief left suddenly. There were two guns among the Pawnees and my brother gave one of them some ammunition but he had not courage to use it.

"The Sioux and squaws got two scalps, one on the battlefield and one in the hills. We thought there were none of them injured but the emigrant train that overtook us said they met the Pawnees in full retreat driving before them on foot a Sioux that had been shot through the body and otherwise badly wounded. He was bound and weak with loss of blood but they drove him on with whips. A brave nation truly! One hundred and fifty of them vanquished by 13."

Mrs. Francis Sawyer was following close behind Mrs. Cummings: "A large party of Pawnee Indians passed us this morning going on to their hunting grounds after buffalo, and this afternoon we met them returning. They had met a party of Sioux, and the result was a battle took place. The Sioux had whipped them, killing and scalping two of the party and wounding several others. The Pawnees were very angry and badly frightened. Some were armed with bows and some with guns. I met some ladies that saw the fight, and they said that they were scared almost to death themselves. The Pawnees

Pawnees Looking Out for Enemies

had made a poor fight. There were only thirteen Sioux and they whipped sixty or seventy Pawnees. When we came to where the battle had been fought, Mr. Sawyer and I drove off the road a short distance to see one of the Indians who had been killed. It was the most horrible sight I ever saw. Four or five arrows were sticking in his body and his scalp was gone, leaving his head bare, bloody and ghastly. I am sorry I went out to look at him. I have had the blues ever since. We are in camp with a large company of emigrants to-night, and have out a strong guard. So we women are safe and secure from danger, and may rest in peace and comfort, if we don't dream of dead Indians."

D. B. Andrews arrived at Fort Kearney on May 20: "This fort consists of a few frame buildings of not very fine appearance and a number of stores & out buildings built of prairie sod or turf. About sixty soldiers are stationed here. The buildings are situated on the Platte bottom about three-quarters of a mile from the river on a level piece of ground. The whole establishment taken together has anything but a neat & tidy appearance." But Mrs. Sawyer observed: "The Fort is a neat little place, kept in the best of order, and the best of order is kept in it."

John Hawkins Clark was at the fort on May 26: "It was quite a lively place when we passed; an hour or two and we were satisfied. . . . In looking about among our neighbors this evening some of the boys found a wagon where whiskey was for sale, and made a purchase of the article, brought it into camp and as the auctioneer would say, 'gone.' However, the liquor did but little damage as there happened to be more water than whiskey in the purchase, and but a limited quantity of both; no ill effects from its use was perceptible, but no more whiskey in camp was allowed after this. Fiddling and dancing was a recreation that most all of the immigration indulged in; we had plenty of it to-night."

The Clark party camped several miles beyond Kearney, but Richard Owen Hickman's company was unaware that all the grass within one mile of the fort was reserved for the army horses. "we came to the Fort just at 12 o'clock, stopped and got some of the best water I have drank since I left home. Came out half a mile and stopped for noon. After remaining there some time the captain sent us a message to leave within 30 minutes or be canonaded. We chose the former."

The captain's name was Horton, and upon his arrival on May 22, Addison Crane paid him a visit. The captain was "very much of a gentleman. He was from Philadelphia, and with his family has resided here 2 years. There are four two story wood houses in which the officers and their families reside, and several adobe buildings for the soldiers. They are very kind to emigrants as an instance of which I may mention that a blacksmith shop has been opened for their accommodation, where they may mend their numerous breaks free of charge. Procured here a good meal of bread, fresh butter and milk, and eat so much that it gave me a violent headache and made me quite sick all night."

Beyond Fort Kearney the wagons stretched in a seemingly endless line. One emigrant, Seth Doty, described the scene in a letter: "We have now been eighteen days on the plains, amid the greatest show in the world. The train is estimated to be 700 miles long, composed of all kinds of people from all parts of the United States, and some of the rest of mankind, with lots of horses, mules, oxen, cows, steers, and some of the feathered creation, moving along about 15 or 20 miles per day; all sorts of vehicles from a coach down to a wheel-barrow; ladies on horseback, dressed out in full-blown Bloomers; gents on mules, with their Kossuth hats and plumes, galloping over the prairies, making quite an equestrian troupe and a show ahead of anything Barnum ever got up."

A typical evening on the Platte was recalled by Mary Medley (Ackley): ". . . when we stopped for the night all the wagons were drawn up in a line and the tents were pitched behind them, forming a street. Then preparations began for supper. We had a little sheet iron stove at the begining of the trip, but

[67]

it proved to be a nuisance and was discarded. The cook, one of the men of our party, used to dig a trench about a foot deep and three feet long, build a fire in it and then hang the crane over the trench with the coffee pot and camp kettle. As soon as he had coals in the trench he baked bread in a Dutch oven, fried the meat, made coffee and tea, and when supper was ready a coarse cloth was spread on the ground to protect us from dust and the prickly pears. Then the tin dishes were taken from the box behind the wagon and placed around our table on the ground for eleven people. The milk can was brought out with a lump of butter on top, churned by the motion of the wagon.

"After supper was over preparations were made for bed. Our tent was pitched behind the family wagon and a ditch dug around it to keep it from being flooded, for we had some terrible rainstorms on the Platte River. A heavy canvas was spread on the ground in the tent and two feather beds were placed on it, where part of our family slept, the rest sleeping very comfortably in the corded wagon bed which took the place of a spring mattress."

When the emigrants reached the Platte, they could see the teams and wagons on the Mormon Trail across the river. Sixteen or seventeen miles west of Fort Kearney was a ford, and some, hoping to escape the sickness, or because the grass looked greener on the north side, decided to cross the Platte and join the emigration from Kanesville. Addison Crane was three miles beyond Fort Kearney on Sunday, May 23:

"Left camp at 7, and proceeded on our road laying most of the way immediately along the bank of the Platte. This River is from 1 mile to 1½ miles wide—and the soil of the bottom appears to improve as we go up. The bottom lands on this side are from 3 to 6 miles wide, skirted on the south by high and rolling prairie bluffs. There is no timber of any kind except occasionally a few green willows near the River bank. There would be grass, but it has all been eat off by the immense herds which have preceeded by. . . . It looks green and fresh

On the Way to a New Home in the West

across the Platte, and I have no doubt there is plenty of grass there, and I wish we were on the north side instead of here. . . . After moving about 14 miles, from camp, came to a point where emigrants sometimes ford the platte. This was at 2½ P.M. . . . By crossing here we should . . . save some 60 miles in distance, and what is of great importance get grass for our cattle and wood to cook with. But then the task of fording such a looking stream was by no means inviting. . . . Let my friends at home imagine a dark turbid stream, . . . with a sand bottom which slides away and sinks the moment the foot touches it, water from one to four feet deep, and they may form some faint idea of what lay before us in attempting to work our teams through—However we resolved to try it, and elevated our loading on the top planks of our wagons & cart so that it should not get wet, and drove in, with some of our company ahead on mules to pilot the way, Albert wading one side of the cart team & I the other, & Lovejoy & Sarre the same with the wagon, and with hard pulling, our teams often getting stalled in the sand bottom, and then pulling out again, frequently stopping to rest on the harder bars in shallow water, we at last, all wet and tired, after two hours the hardest work man or beast ever did, landed all safe on the north side. Here we found grass up to our cattles eyes and they did full justice to it. . . ."

Four days later Lodisia Frizzell's company also crossed the Platte: "We had proceeded some 4 or 5 ms. up the river; when we saw several waggons standing on the bank, & the men watching something in the water; we soon saw there was a waggon & team fording the river, we could hardly descerne the team which was nearly under the water, and the waggon looked like a little boat, it was preceeded by two men on horse-back, who rode side by side, surveying out the ford & marking it by sticking up little sticks in the sand; we watched them till they were safely across, & the pilots had returned, but there was a board stuck up here which informed us, the ford was

safe, & that a large train had passed the day before. I felt a little nervous when we were about to cross, for the river here is
all of one mile & a half wide, & a more foaming madening
river I never saw, & its banks being very low, & the water the
color of soapsuds you cannot see the bottom where it is not
more than six inches deep, consequently looks as deep as the
Missouri when it is bank full, & the many islands & bars
which obstruct this swift current makes an awful noise, you
cannot make a person hear you, when you are in the river, at 5
yds. distant; and I call this one of the greatest adventures on
the whole route, for from the quicksands giving away under
the wagon wheels, there is danger of upsetting, which would
be a very great disaster indeed. Blocking up our waggon bed,
we started in, for our cattle do not mind mud, or water, the
men with their coats, hats, & boots off, with a kerchief around
their heads, with whip in hand, into the Platte river we go; but
we are only one team in 20 that is now in the river, making a
line from bank to bank; we were about 2 hours in crossing, & I
do not think our team pulled so hard & for so long a time on
the road, at any place; for our waggon was heavily loaded
with about 15 hundred lbs, & the wheels sunk in the sand
about six inches most of the way, but we did not stop but once,
for fear the waggon would get fast in the yielding sands, for
there were 2 or 3 teams stuck, when we crossed, 2 were mule
teams, their feet being so small they sank in the sands & could
not pull out; but when we got across, one of the men who traveled with us, went back & pulled out one team; but there was
no one anxious to go in a second time."

When Alpheus Graham forded: "The quicksand giving way
under the wheels make a wagon shake and rattle as bad as any
frozen ground I ever saw." And Mariett Cummings:
". . . never dreamed of anything like this river. It is impossible to see an eighth of an inch into it and the bottom is quicksand so that an animal can gain no sure footing and a wagon
runs as though it were the roughest stones, one constant jar;

[71]

. . . I drove the wheel mules and was very much frightened for fear of their drowning. I surely never was so glad to gain 'Terra firma' before."

John Clark of Virginia crossed to the north bank the same day as Lodisia Frizzell—May 27: "I mounted the new steed & put forward to sound the ford. Some half mile from there accidently fell into a hole or swirl that was near drownding us both. In the scuffle lost my revolver but hung to the animal until she swam out & made the opposite shore. We were all day making the crossing, having to make two trips. Of course the boys were all wet having to wade & drive the teams. We broached the brandy keg & took too much of the criter which ended in a broil with Gibs Gilman & others. Two bunged eyes and a bloody snout ended the farce & day's ferrying."

III

FROM KANESVILLE TO
PLATTE RIVER FORD

———— ◆◄◆►◆ ————

AFTER crossing the Missouri river at Kanesville, the emigrants had a drive of twenty-seven miles to the Elkhorn
River ferry, which Edward Kitchell reached on May 15:
"Camped on the banks of the Elk Horn river; ferried this
river—it is deep & rapid. 30 or 40 rods wide—but little timber
in places heavy cotton wood—Tolerable grass we made about

18 miles to day. grass on the prairie is getting good—camp is in bottom—passed a good camping ground 8 or 9 miles this side of last night's camp—saw some Pawnee Indians there. . . . These Indians were half starved—they begged of us money & something to eat. I gave them some bread—he was well pleased. At noon we gave four more there dinner—They were not satisfied with that, but wanted to steal a sack—

"The road to day has been crooked very much so, but smooth. The prairie is rolling and beautiful. land poor—Day has been cool—morning rain—afternoon clear & pleasant. I stood guard last night for the first time, from $\frac{1}{2}$ past 12 until daylight. I saw no sign of Indians. All was calm & peaceable—no sound was heard, but the howling of wolves. it was a clear & cold night. . . . Am sick tonight—got a very bad headache."

The Cooke family arrived at the Elkhorn ferry the afternoon of May 11, in a company of thirty wagons, but were unable to cross until the following day: "We were detained until nearly noon by the ferry. The oxen had to be driven into the river and made to swim across, a man on horseback leading the way. It was a long time before they would attempt to cross. The men shouted, and whipped and kicked the poor frightened creatures before they seem to understand what they were to do. Some floated downstream a distance; others would go straight across. It was an exciting scene to us all. . . . A little episode occurred here. It appeared three or four wagons, not of our company, had gone ahead and were being annoyed by the Indians, so a man was dispatched on horseback to warn and obtain help. He had not gone far when, looking back, he saw someone in pursuit, and fearing it to be an Indian, jumped off his horse and took to his heels and hid in the tall grass, leaving his horse for Mr. Indian. The pursuer proved to be one of his own men, so he got well laughed at for his fright, and would have lost his horse had not an Indian caught it and brought it to camp. This caused much merriment to us all."

Elkhorn River Ferry on the Mormon Trail

But the next day, while in company with two other trains, fifty or sixty wagons in all: "We traveled on till noon, and when we halted the Indians came around begging for corn and money. A man came riding in haste, telling us that one of the wagons in a company ahead of us had been stopped by Indians, and trouble was feared. Our company at once came to a halt, but no one seemed to know the real cause. But the men took up their wagons and got ready for a fight—somewhere. Fortunately a chief of the Pawnees was on a pony near the head of our company. Mr. Perrin [captain of the train] communicated to him through a squaw who spoke some English, and the chief galloped off to ascertain the trouble ahead.

"Then the cry was given, 'Corral,' which means turn back and form a circle for protection. So we feared a fight. But no one knew, and thus we were in suspense. But in time the Chief returned with a man who said the Indian had been caught who stopped the wagon, and a few sharp cuts were administered with the whip the chief carried. We paid a small tribute in provisions, tranquility was restored, and on we proceeded to Platte river, where we halted to water our cattle. The chief accompanied us to the river, and each wagon donated something to him, so we gained his good-will."

"The Indians gave us no trouble last night—besides our company (of 26 ox teams & four horse teams) there came up thirty or forty horse teams & camped near us," Edward Kitchell wrote on May 16. "The Indians appeared friendly—shook hands with us, but they were after something to eat. They were half starved. . . . I saw at last night's camp several pappooses, they were pretty & greasy little fellows. They were not tied to a board (as I supposed they would be) but the mothers held them to their backs by means of there buffalo cloaks just leaving the legs of the pappoose exposed. No signs of Indians tonight—Cool, clear & windy—In fair spirits & feel well."

Encamped for the Night

The Mormon Council Point Emigrating Company was at the Elkhorn on June 20, and even though it was a Sunday: "This morning the First, Second and Third tens got safe over the river and the greater part swam their cattle and the others had theirs took over by the boat. . . . then we moved a short distance and formed in correll. In the afternoon the Company was called together for meeting. It was opened by the Brass band we have in our midst playing . . . then an hymn was sung and played, Prayer by Captain John M. King after which the Captain of the Guard Elder James D. Ross was called upon to address the assembly, he gave a most able and impressive discourse upon the principles of gathering showing that we are know in the act of rushing to fulfill prophecy that was spoken of by the prophets of old &c &c He was followed by Captain Tidwell who made some remarks on the same subject and also said that we have had some hinderences by the misfortunes and other things that transpired in our midst and in conclusion said we have made some new arrangements respecting the order of things and the following things are to be done. A trumpet will be blown first in the morning to arise from bed and unloose the cattle for herding at the same time the herdsmen to be ready to go with them. The second time it is blown for prayers, the third time it is blown is for the herdsmen to bring up the cattle and all hand is to yoke up and prepare moving. And the fourth time it is blown is for the camp to start their journey. John Holdredge then arose and said that he promised that we raise our Captain a horse either by subscription or some other means Eleazer King Jun said he might ride his horse if he had a mind it was young, and had never been rode with a saddle yet but it was at his service. It was moved and carried that we accept this offer. Then the Captain of the Guard read over some by laws which Captain Tidwell had requested him to draw out for the regulating of the guard and herdsmen. . . . Immediately after the meeting five individuals went down to the water and was Baptized under the hands of Captain John Tidwell in the Elk Horn their names are as follows, Martha Dinna Howland Aged 28, George Goddard Aged 11, Eliza Goddard Aged 10, Joseph Goddard Aged 9 and Emma Broom head Aged 13."

Twelve miles beyond the Elkhorn River the Mormon Trail struck the north bank of the Platte, where the Kitchell party camped on May 17: "About a mile back, two Indian Chiefs came up to us with a request that we pay them for the grass our cattle eat—we did not at that time give them anything.

[77]

but they followed us to camp. Each waggon then gave something—The Chiefs (Pawnees) spread their buffalo cloaks for the provisions—The remaining Indians, stayed outside the encampment. . . . After the Chiefs had collected together all they could get they took it out of camp & distributed it among the Indians—each one was called by name & came forward to receive his share of the corn meat & bread &c. There was no grumbling, but as soon as each one received his quota, off he put for our fires, to parch corn & beg something more to eat. John wrestled with one of them this evening, but got thrown every time. We apprehend no danger, only from their thieving disposition—They are half starved—and like a pack of hounds. I gave them half a dollar & a duck & a snipe that I killed today. We gave also some corn & swapped corn for moccasins."

Enoch Conyers noted some of the outfits on the road: "One wagon just passing, their team consisting of four yoke of two-year-old calves, with the motto, 'Root, little hog or die,' scrawled on both sides of the wagon cover," and also, "a splendid four-horse coach in which is seated four richly dressed young ladies and two young girls, aged about 10 and 12 years, and a young man who was handling the lines. . . . One of the young ladies was making music on an accordean, another was playing on a guitar; all were singing as they trotted past, gay as larks."

There had been some trouble between the emigrants and Indians at Shell Creek, which the Conyers party reached on May 26: "We see quite a number of Indians along the road, all dressed up in war paint and having bows and arrows; their hair cut very short, except one small bunch on the crown of their head, which is allowed to grow its full length. In with this little bunch of hair they had stuck a lot of quills. Their quivers were full of arrows all ready for use. The Indians were all on the beg, pointing over towards their village, saying, 'Help Pawnee, all hungry.' They wanted to exact one steer from each team for the privilege of passing through their country, which, of course, was refused. The Indians became more

[78]

plenty and threatening the farther we go, therefore our captain has ordered the company to keep our teams as close together as possible. It is our turn to drive in the lead of our train today and tomorrow we will fall back to the rear and let the next wagon take the lead. As we now have sixty-five fighting men in our company, we could put up a pretty good fight, and all we are now waiting for is for them red devils to endeavor to put their threats into execution. We certainly would very soon make a small starting for a good-sized Indian graveyard. We came six miles further to the creek where we expected to meet resistance from the Pawnee Indians. This creek runs through a low, flat prairie country. The bed of the creek was cut down into the soil by the freshets to the depth of about eight feet and about twelve feet wide, with abrupt banks and bordered with a narrow strip of willows. These willows the emigrants cut and piled into the creek level with the surface, thus forming a temporary bridge for their teams to cross. The company that done this work on the willow bridge, after crossing laid by and collected toll at the rate of 50 cents per wagon until they had received what they considered sufficient pay for the labor performed, then left the bridge and went on their way. After they left, the Pawnee Indians took possession of the bridge and demanded one steer from each team that crossed the bridge. This demand was refused. We offered to give them some flour, rice and sugar, but these articles they indignantly spurned, saying, 'Help Pawnee; much hungry,' and pointing to a steer in the team to give us to understand that was what they wanted. So many of the emigrants had already crossed this bridge the dirt and willows were pressed down so close that it had made the bridge almost waterproof, therefore by the time our turn came to cross the water was packed up almost on a level with the banks, and it seemed about ready to go out and dangerous to cross. Nevertheless cross we must, and cross we did. Our captain gave the order to proceed, and I started our team on the bridge, whilst the Indians on the opposite side were taking off their blankets, intending to shake them in front of our cattle to run us off the bridge into the water. Noticing this maneuver,

[79]

our company made a demonstration with small arms. The Indians, seeing our determination, resisted, saying, 'Pawnee heep good.' Then the old chief pointed to the sun and following its course to the west laid his head on his hands, thus giving us to understand that we would all be dead men by the setting of the sun. But we took no stock in these gyrations. After crossing we came about one mile and stopped for lunch and to let our cattle graze. . . . We have no more trouble with the Pawnee Indians."

When the emigrants reached the Loup Fork of the Platte River, they had the choice of ferrying at $3 per wagon or moving up the east bank twenty-seven miles to the middle ford or nineteen miles farther to the upper ford. "Loup Fork is a hard stream," wrote John Kerns. "It is 50 rods wide, with low banks and sandy bottom and full of sandbars besides; the water is as muddy as a hog wallow."

Just as Henry and Jane Bradley arrived at the Loup Fork ferry the afternoon of May 15, one of the two boats struck a snag near shore and sank: "We lay over here to day. last night & P.M. it rained & hailed very hard. Not rained but poured. in the Night the wind Changed into the North, & Blew a Gale almost & it was very cold also. We had to hold the hoops of Waggon Covers to Keep them from Breaking. It hailed Yesterday P.M. so much that it was a good deal of difficulty that we could keep Our Horses from Breaking from us & Running off Several tents were blew down. . . . & Some were flooded out. this day is Sunday, & it is a very cold day. Great many trains comeing in all the time some waiting to Ferry others going up 25 Miles to ford."

The Cookes came to the ferry the same day as the Bradleys: "We had to wait at Loup Fork from Saturday to Tuesday before a chance to cross, and then had to swim all the oxen. That was a tiresome job, as the river is wide at this point and full of quicksands. William earned a dollar by swimming a horse over for a man. I took the dollar for safe-keeping, but unfortunately I had a hole in my pocket, and so lost it."

Jared Fox arrived the day the Cookes crossed and was told

Loup Fork Ferry

he would have a four-day wait. So his company decided to go to the middle ford: "After dinner I had to settle and divide with Vail and Phelps. When we took up our teams Old Jack could not be found. It was on a level prairie and not a stick for 3 or 4 miles and after looking 3 or 4 hours with 4 horses on a jump, we gave up. Thought he had gone back. The company started on slowly to a feeding place and I took a horse and went back till I was satisfied by meeting hundreds that he was not on the road back but was stolen but how I could not tell. I turned to overtake my company and after riding awhile I found I had lost my dog. The wind having blown a perfect gale all day and cold and I began to get over my sweat and was cold, tired, had a hard headache and when I began to count up the day's work—2 men gone and took one horse and what was of the waggon I did not know, my old Jack stolen, my dog lost, my stuff all torn up and divided and I did not know where it was or how it was and I left behind in the dark, cold and sick and not knowing where they were, I concluded I was elected for a trip to California alone, but I found the company and the dog had got there first."

The next day: "Joined in with my brother Levi. He had 3 horses. He throwed away stuff too numerous to mention. Levi left his waggon and hitched on to the one Vail left. I hired a horse for the day to put beside mine and sent Charles on ahead with the other to overtake some teams that passed yesterday to see if they had not stolen my horse. Levi put 3 horses to his waggon and we started on. Weather good. Passed an old Pawnee Indian town burnt down in 1846 by other Indians. Passed an old missionary station gone to ruins. At noon Charles met me and had found my horse and if it had not been for our Capt. the men would have been whipped to all intents and purposes. The afternoon fine. Passed some of the prettiest land I ever saw. Made 20 miles to ford and camped and unloaded and cut blocks and put under our boxes on the bolsters to raise them and our loads from 6 to 10 inches to fetch them above the water and keep dry as all depends on grub now.

"Thursday May 20th—Weather good but cold and frosty. Commenced early to ford what is called the Loopfork of the Platte. The two first teams came near drowning and 3 or 4 men would have drowned but for the timely aid afforded. I should have been among those who have passed away but for help afforded principally by Charles. The water is swift, deep and cold, and quicksand bottom, but notwithstanding all the obstacles in the way—by being in the cold water till noon and suffering almost to perishing—we were, by the Lord's Blessing, all across and alive. Some had been all under water and some teams and waggons all under but by ropes fastened to them beforehand they were drawn ashore and our provisions were not as badly injured as we feared and we had rendered timely aid to Cummins and Pierce's Companies who had come up and got into serious difficulty in trying to cross just below us. In the afternoon we made ten miles wet and cold in the wind and before night it began to rain. We camped on the open prairie with very little wood or water. This night it came our turn to watch in the cold and rain and it was not the most pleasant night of my life to tramp in the grass and rain after the day's work we had endured but it must be done. The Indians must shoot us or not get our horses. In the night something scared our horses and some broke loose and ran but we finally secured all of ours but another company lost 14 horses."

The Mormon Council Point Emigrating Company elected to use the ferry at Loup Fork, and because of the size of the company, the ferryman agreed to charge them only $1 per wagon, they to swim their own cattle. There had already been three deaths in the company: "June 26. Saturday. This morning very rainy but in a few hours it cleared off. Between five and six A.M. Ann the wife of Franklin J. Daves departed this life by the grasp of that foul and dreaded disease Cholera after laying only a few hours. . . . And was buried about eighty rods East of the Loup Fork Ferry. To day our company crossed the Ferry. The ferryman were rather saucy and wanted to put over the river at the same time he was ferrying us over some Californians but our Captain would not suffer it this he wanted to do because he could get more pay. About six o'clock P.M. after the company had got in correll we had a slight thunderstorm and heavy rain for a few minutes. The Seventh Company of Mormons has just arrived at the Ferry."

Edward Kitchell's company went to the upper ford, arriving on May 21 in a heavy rainstorm, and crossing on the twenty-second: "We are in devilish fine spirits to night—no wonder we have forded the Loupe Fork, safe & sound. We crawled out of our steaming bed (our clothes still wet) eat a good breakfast & started for the ford—the morning was damp—cloudy & chilly—and we cared not for the wet—The river at this point is (straight across) about $\frac{1}{4}$ mile wide—but to cross you go down the stream quartering a distance of $\frac{3}{4}$. The water is not deep but the infernal quicksand is: you can't stand still a moment if you do, you are 'still' going down. The water is clear & rapid. One german company, of 3 ox teams & 80 head of cows, were in company with us. We doubled teams and took two waggons across without much difficulty save the swamping of a yoke of oxen & the waggon running over a Dutchman—But when we came to our heavy waggon we seen sights—9 yoke of oxen poke the chains at every pull while the

[83]

hind axeltree was buried in the sand—we had to unload a part
& haul across in another waggon—we blocked up our waggon
beds & kept dry our bedding. two women in company so bad
'scared' they cried. We were all wet from head to foot—sometimes up to the waist flounder in the quicksand & then
crawling on your knees for a foot-hold—We found most
difficulty with our horses. All of ours got thorough 'duckings.'
My black horse Tom carried me over safely twice, the first &
last time: but the second trial he went over his back in water
& sand. & I the same way—he floundered on his side some
time before he got up. But at last we all got across safe & felt
very much obliged &c for our good fortune. We are camped
on the banks of the Loupe, at the ford, in a good spot for
everything but grass. It cleared up about the time we got
across (2 o'clock) the sun came out warm & we dried our
clothes & aired our provisions—we made a good cup of coffee
washed our faces—changed our clothes & now feel inclined to
go a little further 'on the morrow.' "

The next day, Sunday, May 23, the company rejoined the
Platte River road: "Made 17 miles. . . . Country handsome
low & highland—grass poor—antelope & prairie dogs—killed
none—prairie hens, ducks, snipe plenty—killed 12 snipes—
Camp on the verge of a pond—water bad—grass short. no
wood 5 miles to prairie creek. no timber in sight. As far as the
eye can reach one vast expanse of beautiful,—green prairie.
Emigrants camped near by the hundreds—150 teams within
half a mile of us. Day has been clear & beautiful—warm.
Ferry road & fork roads of the Loupe intersect about 7 miles
back. ford road is not out of the way. passengers from the horse
teams 'hunger & thirst' after milk—plenty of applicants—Tomorrow morning my turn for Cook, for one week, commences.
I don't like to cook: night is beautiful. & before we thought of
Sunday we were dancing a cotillion. a german in our company
can 'fiddle' very well: every day is alike with [us]. This trip
doth makes heathens of us all, 'cept a 'few.' " Perhaps Kitchell
did not like to cook because, the next day, "I bake us bread
but that of unsifted meal & the boys have their own fun about

its quality," followed by the next day's terse entry: "Had mush & milk porridge for supper. the boys got sick of my corn bread."

Emily Adams traveled from the Loup Fork ford back to the Platte on June 14: "Very hard west wind. Took an early start this morning, calculating to stop and rest our teams as soon as we come to good grass, which our guide book says will be two or three days' travel. Here we find toads with horns and long tails. They are about three inches long and very slender, and tails as long as the body; they are spotted, white, yellow and brown; can run as fast as a man, and very wild. Mosquitoes annoy us very much, and sometimes the air seems to be filled with large bugs. Dust is very troublesome, roads good, water scarce, grass poor, no timber. This afternoon we passed seven new-made graves. One had four bodies in it, and to all appearances they were laid on the top of the ground and the dirt thrown over them. Most of them were aged people. It was written on some of the headboards that they died with the cholera. We find good bedclothes and clothing of all kinds, but do not pretend to touch one of them. Encamped for the night on the wide Prairie creek. Find good grass and water, but no wood, but we brought wood with us, as our guide directed us to do. Made twenty-three miles."

The Mormon Trail followed the Platte River for nearly ninety miles to Elm Creek, opposite Fort Kearney—for Edward Kitchell an easy and pleasant journey. "Morning drizzling—cleared up before noon—warm & still," he wrote on May 25, "made about 17 miles today. road within a mile or two of Platte all the while—or rather Grand Island. This Island is formed by a very small body of running water (6 inches deep—5 or ten feet wide) separating from the main body of Platte, several miles up & running below last night's camp for some distance. . . . A skirt of cotton wood, & Elm surrounds it—prairie in center very handsome. The country between here and wood creek is one vast level plain, of rich prairie as beautiful as the eye can behold. high & dry, raising gradually from the river. . . . I stood (or rather laid) guard part of last night—the musquitoes were very bad—heavy dew. I lay down in my blanket, slept tolerable we are having a real pleasure trip. delightful country and delightful weather. The roads are as good as one could wish. perfectly level & dry. no hills—no deep ravines. but one or two wet spots of a few feet. We have nothing to do but hollow 'get up' & we go along. . . . I get about as much sleep as I want during the day—find a good grazing spot tie my horse to the strap of my boot, lay down & in a minute am fast asleep. My horse can walk more than twice as fast as the oxen."

Jared Fox was a day ahead of Kitchell and took a gloomier view: "This day," May 24, "began to witness the destruction of property and life. Plenty of old bones and several old graves and waggon irons. Today passed 4 new graves, one a mile from our camp, buried an hour ago and left a wife and several children just gone on a mile ahead. . . . Plenty of teams—miles of them—on the other side in sight from this side and many crossing and some drowning in the attempt. Passed some gun barrels and a part of a new waggon, the remainder burnt up for wood. When we pass 4 new graves in a day it reminds us (me at least) that death has been along the track."

"Dock Ballard and I went horse-back riding this morning down to the river where we saw a train that had just crossed from the south side of the Platte," Eliza McAuley wrote, June 1. "They report a great deal of sickness and a scarcity of grass on that side, so we feel that we did well to stay on the north side." John Kerns camped on Elm Creek the following night: "The emigrants are crossing over from the south side on account of cholera. We have heard of twelve cases this evening and all very dangerous ones. I begin to feel like I would rather it was somebody else than me. I believe I could count 5,000 wagons this evening in sight. I do not know where all these people intend going to make fortunes, but I am going to Oregon myself, so I am, go it while yer young, when old you can't."

IV

THE CALIFORNIA TRAIL FROM FORT KEARNEY TO MORMON FERRY

———————◄◄●►►———————

"O**N UP THE** Platte," R. H. P. Snodgrass wrote on May 20. "Heretofore we have had plenty of fuel but it is very scarce now. We use a light willow mostly. There is some wood on the Islands in the river but none on the mainland, and the river bottom is so treacherous that we are seldom able to get any wood. The river is from $\frac{1}{2}$ to 2 miles wide and full of Islands. The water is color of milk or more yellow and needs to stand and settle before it is fit to use. The river bottom is from 2 to 6 miles wide and tolerable good land, then you strike into sandy hills perfectly barren. We have determined to pass a large portion of the large emigration ahead of us so we make long drives for that purpose. We passed over a hundred teams today & camped 4 miles west of Plumb Creek on the Platte."

Before long even the willow on the islands gave out, and there was virtually no timber on the Platte for several hundred miles. There was, however, a practical substitute, without which travel across the plains would have been impossible. "rose early and left our place of encampment," wrote Caroline Richardson on May 28, "we traveled along the river saw a great many fording . . . we encamped about a mile from the road to night for the first time we cooked our supper by buffalow chips and I think it is an exelant substitute for wood it makes a clear hot fire and burns very much like turf."

The John Hawkins Clark company first used the buffalo chips on May 29: "We gathered them by the basketful, by the armful and by the handful, and as they were plentiful I guess we gathered a wagon load, set the heap on fire and cooked our supper. The 'chips' worked like a charm and are really a godsend for the traveler in this part of the country—a staple which would be hard to dispense with. It is now no longer wood, water and grass. The inquiry when camp is announced is whether or no there is 'plenty of chips.' If there is we can stay, but if not we must move a little farther on. Sometimes a man goes ahead to hunt a camping ground and if nothing is lacking when he finds one he turns his horse loose and commences piling up chips. When the train comes up it stops before the largest pile and the teams are unhitched. Men, women and children are sometimes seen gathering chips—the men in their arms, the women in their aprons, and the little boys and girls will sometimes be seen carrying them on their heads. The horses, oxen and mules get so used to camping where there is plenty of them that it is hard work getting them

[88]

past a spot where they are thickly strewn; and if a heap has
been left unburned at any place near the road our oxen will
make for it and there is no stopping them until they are alongside."

Any delicacy the emigrant may have felt over using dung
for fuel was soon dispelled. "We had quite a laugh when we
saw Anthony Rogers gathering his Arms full and Carrying
them in to camp," was Richard Keen's first reaction, "and
when we learned that we would have to follow suit there was
some funny excuses Made however we broke in and took them

Hunting Prairie Hens

up very delicately. a kind of self reproach however this soon
vanished and it was hurrah Boys Who could get the best
Ones." John Lewis was amused by the women in his company:
"but here comes the fun just notice the Women how well
pleased they are with those large chips that we have to use for
fuel but to see some of the boys broiling their meete on the
coles is the fun of it and to see how poticlar the Women take
holt of one of those chips a fine spree we had over the first fire
we made of the Buffalo chips the Women did not like to tetch
it with thare hans for fear of giting thare hans spoiled but this
will ware off in a short time."

[89]

A. J. Wigle was well satisfied with the fuel: It made a hot fire with little smoke or odor. "We would dig a narrow trench long enough for our use, make our fires in the trenches and put our teakettle and frying pan on the fire and we would soon have a supper that any of us could eat."

While the food consisted mostly of the monotonous bacon, bread, flapjacks, and hardtack, it was possible along the Platte River to vary the diet occasionally. Antelope was fairly plentiful, and most emigrants managed to get at least one meal of fresh meat. R. H. P. Snodgrass killed snipe and ducks along the river, and John Lewis partook of prairie dog, which, he reported, was "very sweete and . . . very good." John Verdenal, a day west of Fort Kearney, found mushrooms in large quantities: "Elsworth said they were poisonous, there were some botanists in the train that knew better, we cooked and found them to taste exceedingly nice. . . ."

It came as a surprise to most of the emigrants that there was a scarcity of buffalo along the trail. Many travelers had confidently expected to eat fresh buffalo meat all the way across the plains, but the great herds stayed well clear of the thousands of wagons lumbering along both sides of the Platte. There were, however, enough small herds and stragglers to provide one or two kills for many of the companies. Jay Green was nearing the South Fork of the Platte on May 20: "my attention was drawn to some men riding at the top of their animals speed upon stoping my team I saw four buffalows one was runing in the direction of my wagon one was coming across the river and the other two had taken shelter in some willows on the bank of the stream I amediately drew my rifle from the wagon and was determined to have a shot I set out on foot to head the afrited animal when a man gave me his mule to ride I rode quickly over a ridge and stationed myself the hidious looking animal soon made his appearance and with a well directed shot I pearsed his heart he bounded up with grate speed for a short distance then settled into a lazy trot for about one or two hundred yards—he then stoped turned and looked back and seeing his perseuers near he turned again to run he made a few leaps as if mad and fell—by this time I was overtaken by some of my train wee took a goodly portion of the beef . . . leaving the carcase for the wolves which inhabit this country in grate numbers."

Dr. John Dalton was, on June 2, some forty-five miles west of Fort Kearney and had "laid by over three hours at noon and traveled very *slow* on account of its being *extremely warm*. It being near sundown, and no chance to get wood for cooking, we soon fixed up and dispatched our suppers, pitched our tents and prepared for rest. But soon after we had striped off all but shirts and pants, and laid down, there came up one of the most tremendous thunder storms I ever witnessed—the wind blew a perfect gale the rain poured down in torrents, the thunder rolled & the lightening flashed, *almost incessantly:* which rendered the scene, if not sublime, at least somewhat terrific. At nearly the first the wind came whistling & knocked our tent into a *cocked hat.* tearing up the pins and letting the cloth right down upon us, when the rain came through as though there was nothing over us and it required all our exertions to keep the whole concern from blowing away. In a few moments where we lay the water was over shoe mouth deep; & there we *poor monomaniacal gold hunters* had to lay, sit, or stand and take it for three long hours. As soon as the wind slacked a little I drew on my overcoat which having laid inside up was dripping wet, went out and repin[n]ed down the tent while others, inside held the cloth in its place; it still raining quite hard—I then went to hunt a light and on returning with one, found the boys had all left the tent and crawled into the wagon *with the darkey.* Found everything in the tent as wet as a soaked sponge. Threw the bed clothes aside, hunted the higher spot of ground without a dry thread of clothes on me laid down and tried to go to sleep. Got up at daylight still wet and shivering put on some dry clothing, it having turned very cold—roused up the boys, cooked a little breakfast, the best way we could boiling our coffee with a few little sticks we had brought along with us, struck our tents, packed our wet clothing into the waggon

[91]

while the oxen were being yoked, and soon found ourselves again on our wending way—plodding along in fine spirits, with lighter hearts and *strong hopes,* determined, like true hearted Yankees, not to be skeared at trials but to brave all difficulties, and yet *see the Elephant* on the other side of the Sierra Nevada."

On May 19, two days beyond Fort Kearney, Thomas Lewis: "Saw a beautiful mirage of clear or transparent water as it where a Large Lake before and behind us with trees with Borders I showed it to some of the men they thought it was a Large Lake the wagon trains behind us seemed as if they were traveling or wading through it, it seemed to us as if the only dry spot of ground was where we was an that we should have to wade through it. . . ."

On June 1, John Hawkins Clark climbed a bluff to survey the Platte Valley: "As far as the eye can reach the broad river can be seen stretching far away to the east and west, the wide bottom lands covered with a carpet of green which gives to the scene a color rich and beautiful to look upon. And then there is another picture. Look at the long lines of immigrants, stretching as it were from the rising to the setting sun; and when one does see it, as we do at this moment, he cannot but wonder where such a mighty multitude of men, women, children and animals are marching to. Echo answers 'where'; but ask of the throng and they will tell you 'California and Oregon.' Yes, California and Oregon have lured that crowd from many a happy home, and here they are, this beautiful morning, marching to those beautiful shores whose golden sands have set the world on fire."

Dr. Dalton was moving up the Platte on June 4, when: "A messenger came to me to go in haste to see Capt. White of Mo. 6 miles ahead. Found him nearly gone with Cholera & 12 others in the same train sick most of them with the same complaint; some very bad; did all I could for Capt. W. but after reviving a little, he sunk very fast, and died in about two hours—Capt. W. was said to be a very *fine* & *most excellent* man.

[92]

He had a very intelligent wife & family of six children, who took his death very hard, though they behaved with much propriety. Indeed, the whole train had looked up to him as a father & consequently were grieved exceedingly. He had been to California, was largely engaged in Quartz mining, had done well & was now moving his family there—I prescribed for the others sick and about 10 oclock started to hunt our train which had past, found it about 3 miles ahead 1 mile from the road camped—having traveled about 18 miles—"

On June 16, one of John Verdenal's company had an experience common to emigrants who would leave their train to hunt: "started at six during the day one of the Cohen brothers was missing he had been out early hunting not arriving at night we kindled large board-fires, and fired guns, in the hope he would arrive, and he did arrive at two oclock in the morning, quite weakened, and fatigued. He said that during the day he lost his way and fatigued his poney much in endeavoring to go different paths, and night approaching he descended from his horse, siezed the lariat and let the poney go on ahead. the poney followed in his former footsteps and he soon was again on the road. he walked 10 miles to find our camp which was the cause of his late arrival. He saw our fires and heard our guns which enabled him to find our camp came 23 miles."

"Still on the Platte," noted Esther Hanna a day's travel east of the South Fork on May 29. "Have a most delightful road, not having any rain for some time. The roads are smooth and level. The river lies on one side with the high bluffs on the other. The cliffs look beautiful in the distance. This day is calm and beautiful. It reminds me of an Indian summer in the States. There is a smoky, hazy atmosphere. I do not know the cause of it unless it is that there have been several fires burning on the praira. Some of last year's grass is still sunburnt, and the fires left by the emigrants often set it on fire. It must be a grand yet terrible sight to see whole miles of praira on fire, sweeping along with the rapidity of lightening.

"We arrived at our camping ground at 12 O'clock. We pur-

[93]

pose staying over the Sabbath. Have stopped early to wash
and bake. We have not washed any since we left! We are on a
small branch of the Platte, and have an excellant spring of
clear, cold water, which is quite a luxury. The water of the
Platte is very muddy in taste and color. . . . We have no wood
here. Have had to haul for two days.

"Evening. Feel tired. Have baked pies and bread and
washed. Mr. Hanna assisted me. Have to wash without either
tub or board but get along very well with a large bucket and
pan set on an ox yoke. Still it requires me to stoop considerably. All our work here requires stooping. Not having tables,
chairs or anything. it is very hard on the back.

"Sabbath, 30th: This morning very bright and lovely. Yet
we were not permitted to enjoy its calm repose. As usual part
of our company wished to travel! The other part took a decided stand against it. So 11 wagons started with our captain,
seven of us only remaining. After they started, we had a lec-
ture and spent the remainder of the day very pleasantly and
quietly. Four of the wagon that went were very unwilling but
were obliged to as they had an interest in some of the other
teams. I think they will wait for us tomorrow; as for the rest, I
feel glad that they have left us. I hope that we shall enjoy the
Sabbath hereafter.

"This afternoon a party of Indian warriors passed our camp.
They were Sioux and have been at war with the Pawnees. Five
of them with their chief, stopped with us. We could not
understand each other only by signs. They had three scalps
with them which they had taken in battle. We gave them
something to eat and a few articles of clothing. They seem to
prize any article from a white man very much. I gave them
some finger rings with which they seemed highly pleased.
They wear a profusion of ornaments but are almost entirely
naked with exception of their blankets and moccasins. This
tribe is friendly to the whites."

Francis White, one of the Hanna party, added: "A party of
Cheyenne Indians came to us today. They were all warriors

Cheyenne Village

and had been on an expedition against the Pawnees. They
were very friendly and took great pleasure in showing the
scalps they had taken. These they had made fast to the ends of
long reeds which they carried elevated. After eating with us
and receiving a few presents they inquired for our 'cap-e-tan'
whom they shook by the hand and left us."

The Holmes Van Schaick party also rested each Sabbath:
"This being the Lord's day we did not roll out of camp but
spent the most of the day in reading conversation &c. The
messes united and cooked a general supper, which was spread

on the ground, and all hands with the Captain at the head, seated themselves around this rude table, and enjoyed what we called a union feast. Our meal consisted of a pot pie made of Antelope, biscuit fried cakes, tea, coffee, cheese &c. At 5 PM we held a religious meeting, in which our Captain addressed us in a very appropriate and profitable manner. I felt much benefitted by his remarks, and felt to thank God that our leader was a man who lived and walked in the fear of the Lord."

Another viewpoint was expressed by William Lobenstine: "It is Sunday to-day and the great bright luminary of the day is peeping over the horizon in its full spleandor. . . . The remark so frequently referred to by Christians that the sublime beauty displayed by the sun proved the existence of a God, was made to me last night by a Universalist. True, the beauty is grand and sublime, but it is so without divinity connected with it. It is not something beyond nature but a planetary phenomenon following the great arrangements, the great and external laws of Mother Nature. No reasonable man will doubt the existence of a great incomprehensible principle which pervades throughout all nature, but this principle is nothing separated from the universe but is the great whole itself which can exist only all and not other ways which always was, always is and always will be, although things may be subjected to great changes.

"We stopped in our camp a considerable part of the day, Orthodox Christians objecting to our movement. Calling, however, a meeting, and taking every single vote, the majority carried the motion for moving onwards."

Beyond Fort Kearney, Dr. Wayman expressed his views of observing the Sabbath: "We have no preaching, though we have a Minister in our company. If we do not serve our Maker directly with flattering songs of adulation and humble petitions for kind rememberances and favors, we do so quite as acceptably to Him & agreeably to my self, resting ourselves & animals and providing for the further prossection of our Journey." And four weeks later he noted: "I am devoting my servises to necessary business while some are card playing—others lounging, some Cooking, and some looking on, while I am very sorry to say our Minister seems disposed to spend the day trimming heads, some bad heads too yes very bad ones. I might say with propriety rascally ones. If he would first convert the reprobates, then he would be excuseable, but as it is I know not where he expects pardon for Heaven denies him."

One hundred and twenty miles west of Fort Kearney the trail crossed the South Fork of the Platte River. There were three fords, and D. B. Andrews came to the lower one on May 26: "Morning fair and warm, roads very dusty. Shortly after sunrise we saw the first buffalo—it passed down the bottom between our camp & the river, under a full run with a pack of large grey wolves in close pursuit. About noon we forded the south fork of the Platte. The ford at this place is at this time good, the water not averaging over ten inches, water not being over twenty inches deep in the deepest place; a good running current and sand bottom. This ford is a short distance above the junction of the North & South Platte and distant from Ft. Kearney one hundred & twenty-three miles agreeable to *Platt & Slater's* Guide to California. The land to the left has been considerably rolling. A small stream of clear water makes down through the bottom parallel with the river for some distance. This creek is crossed soon after leaving the road, running along the bluffs bordering the south side of the south fork to the upper ford some forty-five miles above the lower one. Crossing the lower ford we hove across the bottom land, the road running near the hills on account of rather low ground near the river. The river at the lower crossing is between a quarter and a half of a mile in width. The hills on the opposite side of the river present a very barren appearance. Abundance of game abounds along the Platte such as elk, antelope, deer, grey & prairie wolves, panthers, buffalo, prairie dogs, cranes, wild geese, ducks, &c. Camped on the bottom; no timber in sight. Alkali quite abundant."

Caroline Richardson arrived at the lower ford on June 1:

"there are three fords some distance apart we first thought of going to the middle ford but in order to do so we would be obliged to cross some high hills and as there were some crossing here we concluded to ford the water was very shallow not touching the hubbs very nice gravely bottom the river where we crossed was I should think about half mile wide though intersected with small islands and high sand bars." Ten days later, Mrs. Cornelia Sharp at the upper ford "found the waters so deep that we were obliged to raise the provisions from the bottom of the wagon."

"The river at that place," A. J. Wigle wrote of the lower ford, "was about one half mile and had a strong current. We doubled our teams and drove in and across without any halt until we were out of the water. The deepest place just ran over the hubs of our front wheels. The water was muddy so that we could not see anything in it. The boys thought that they would have a swim . . . they selected a nice eddy where the bank was suitable for a good dive. The water looked as if it were fifteen or twenty feet deep. Our impetuous Irishman got ready first, took a running start and plunged in head foremost. His head struck the bottom which was only sand and not very solid or it would doubtless have killed him. As it was, he complained of his neck for several days. The others put their clothes on and did not swim any that day. I waded across the river 3 times, the bottom felt smooth and solid. We had always heard that in crossing this stream that it would not do to stop but must keep moving or we would sink in the sand. The bottom felt so smooth and hard that I doubted the truth of what we had heard which led me to experiment on a small scale. I stood several times while wading across. At first the bottom would feel to my bare feet, as hard as a floor but in a very short time I felt the sand begin to slowly crawl from under my feet. I did not stand still long enough to find out how far I would go down but a few inches convinced me that it would not be good policy to remain very long in one place while crossing South Platte."

John Hawkins Clark reached the lower ford at nine o'clock the morning of June 2: "There is, perhaps, more fun, more excitement, more whipping, more swearing and more whiskey drank at this place than at any point on the Platte river. Many loose cattle were being driven over when we crossed, and the dumb brutes seemed to have an inclination to go any way but the right one. Loose cattle, teams, horses, mules, oxen, men and boys, all in a muss; the men swearing and whipping, the cattle bellowing, the horses neighing and the boys shouting, made music for the million. It was an interesting scene. It reminded one of something he had never seen nor heard of before, and if he is an actor in the play he is so much excited that a looker on could hardly tell whether he was on his way to California or going back to God's country. One would think by his actions that he had lost his individuality and had become half horse and half alligator; sometimes pushing at the wagons, at others whipping the stubborn oxen, then splurging through the water to head some curious old cow who had taken it into her own sweet will to go contrary to the right direction.

"Having but few cattle, our troubles were comparatively light; we gave the team all the water they would drink before starting and then whipped them through. When safely landed on the other shore the captain passed around the 'big jug.' It must be remembered that we took brandy along for the sick folks. If ever brandy does good it is perhaps when one gets into the water and stays there long enough to get chilled; the most of us had waded the river and came out chilly."

Dexter Hosley came to the lower ford on June 17 but did not cross there. "Last night I had a first rate meal of Antelope," he wrote on June 20, "and it was fine eating no mistake, I think it is the best meat I ever put into my mouth, we had some this morning. We started this morning and before we had gone two miles, we found ourselves in the midst of a Prairie Dog town, I should think that there were 1000 holes or burrows, and at some of them there would be one, at

[99]

Prairie Dog City

others five, looking at each other and then at us, as if they were preparing to defend themselves, they are about as large as a half grown Woodchuck, and will bark like a Dog. The Deer and Antelope, are thick here.

"About twelve miles brought us to the upper ford of the South fork of the Platte River. we gave our Cattle a little grass and water, and at 2 O'Clock commenced unloading our Wagons, this done we roped the top of our Wagon bodies, by drawing them tight over and under, and then placed our provisions on top of the ropes, we did all of this work on four Wagons in one hour. at 3. O'Clock we were in the water, we put our best Cattle on two Wagons, and sent two Horses, on ahead with men to pick out the best place to cross, the bed of the River is so changeable that it is almost impossible to cross the same place twice, the River . . . will average two and a half feet deep, in some places up to a mans arm pitts, at others half way to your knees.

"I was in the water four hours with nothing on but my hat and a woolen shirt, and a cotton one on. We have got our train across without any injury to the provisions or our Cattle, and no accident happened to us whatever. We are now encamped on the California side, all feeling first rate."

After crossing the South Fork of the Platte, the trail led to Ash Hollow, where John Hawkins Clark was on June 4: "nothing we have yet seen can exceed the beauty of Ash Hollow. It was a lovely morning as we entered it; birds were singing joyously amid the branches of beautiful trees; flowers were everywhere blooming, making fragrant the air we breathed; women and children were gathering wild roses and singing some sweet song which put us in mind of other times and other localities. There were many camps in this valley; the shade of the green trees was truly inviting, and a stream of clear, cold water and plenty of wood made it a desirable place for a few day's rest. From the head of the valley to where it opens out on the Platte bottoms is perhaps two miles, one side of which is an abrupt bluff 100 to 200 feet high. Thousands of birds have their nests high up in these perpendicular cliffs and clouds of them are hovering about filling the air with their chattering noise. On the opposite side the land rises with a gentle grade and is covered with a variety of timber, ash being most prominent. . . ." Six days later Holmes Van Schaick saw there "three kinds of wild roses, wild onions, Choke cherries, black cherries, 1 wild currants, Grapes, Ash and Cotton wood trees."

Idyllic as Ash Hollow appeared to John Hawkins Clark, there was, at the head of the valley, a very steep, difficult hill to descend. John Dalton described it as "a very rough rugged & picturesque looking place & a very bad hill, a mile & a half long to go down. Just as we started O. Claygert broke the fore axel of his waggon—No. 12—Took out the load, divided it around; fastened the waggon, with a pole underneath to our waggon & drove on—stayed here all day and mended up the broken waggon—" Richard Keen's company was at Ash Hollow on May 19: "where we descended in to the Hollow we had to let our Wagons down with ropes (i e) we took off all but the wheel horses with 10 or 15 men holding to the ropes tied behind the Wagon with both Wheels locked."

Esther Hanna and Francis White passed through Ash Hollow on June 5. "Ate breakfast with candlelight," Mrs. Hanna wrote. "Started about 4 O'clock. Came to Ash Hollow. . . . There is a great profusion of wild roses in full bloom. The sides of the bluff are literally covered with them and the air is heavy with their fragrance. I was enchanted and could scarcely tear myself away!

"Caught up with the wagons that left us on the Sabbath. Met another train of fur traders. Have seen seven fresh graves this afternoon. The number of deaths on the plains is truly alarming but so far the Lord has dealt very mercifully with us all. We have had neither sickness nor death among us. We have passed over a very bad road this afternoon. Nothing but deep sand all the way. It was nearly up to the hub of our wagons in many places and we were almost blinded by the dust from it. This dust is very bad on the eyes causing soreness and inflammation.

"Have travelled since 5 O'clock this morning till nearly dark this evening. We were unable to find a good camping place. We are on the banks of the Platte again, without fuel except what was hauled with us. Do not expect to get any more wood for 60 miles. Have seen some very rare and beautiful flowers, the corea and orchid among the numbers." (Mrs. Hanna was, inexplicably, the only overland emigrant who never mentioned using buffalo chips for fuel.)

There were many deaths between Ash Hollow and Fort Laramie. On June 6 John Hawkins Clark met three dispirited men returning east: "These three are all that are left out of a company of seventeen men who left Ash Hollow a few days ago, bound for California. Sickness commenced soon after leaving the Hollow, and by the time Fort Laramie was reached fourteen of their number were dead."

On June 21, near the hollow, John Verdenal recorded: "Mr. Davis in the morning 1 of the passengers purjd himself, in doing so he caught cold. . . . not finding grass, and being in a thick cold fog, we did not wait here. perhaps it would have been much better had we did. poor Mr. Davis begged for the sake of God to stop. But Ellsworth would not. we camped at 8 oclock in a place where there was plenty of water and grass; Mr Davis at 11 oclock in the night expired he [had] a wife in the train but no children . . . the first thing in the morning we did was the solemn spectacle of interring Mr Davis, two men proceeded to dig a grave, which they quickly finished, it was six feet deep, two and a half wide, and six feet long. he was lowered envelloped in his blanket, and in a few minutes was in that bourne from which no traveller returns, at the head of his grave we placed a board which bore the following inscription,

('John Davis'
of Saint Louis, Mº.

[103]

died June 21st 1852.
aged 52 of Choleral.)

and so the solemn and impressive spectacle ended, and again we travelled on for that land we seemed never to reach 'California.' "

Forcing the sick to travel was blamed for many deaths by Dr. Anson Henry. He said in a letter that most of the illness on the trail was diarrhea, which could have been cured by diet and rest: "People, however, though sick, would rush on, and the result was death, which was charged to the account of cholera." In writing to a friend, Dr. Henry advised: "In cases of cholera morbus, *lay by* until the disease is arrested. If this policy had been rigidly observed on the plains this season, many valuable lives would have been saved, and there would have been a saving of time in the end. It was a very common thing for men to drag along for a day or two, and then be compelled to stop for three or six days, and often die at last, when one day's delay at the start, would have saved all."

Moses Laird's train was stricken on June 11. "Went about 5 miles and laid over the rest of the day as Mrs. Drake had a attack of the cholera and another of our company, a young man. He was riding along by me and helping drive loose cattle and he was [taken] and fell off his horse. We rubbed him and tried to bring him to and I have set up at night with him and put hot irons to his feet, but our efforts was of no avail. He lost his reason and the man he was with hauled him to Fort Laramie and left him. Mrs. Drake was not [taken] as bad and got over it in a few days. The principal caus of cholera along Platt River is the water. The water of Platt River is mixed with alkily and there are a great many ponds of alkily water that we had to keep our cattle from as it kill cattle to drink the water."

Moving up the south bank of the North Platte, the emigrants soon passed two of the most impressive sights on the trail, Courthouse and Chimney rocks. Of Courthouse Rock, most emigrants copied into their diaries the description from their guidebook: "This is a singular structure very much resembling a court house or some large public edifice. It is situated some 8 or 10 miles south of the road, though it appears to the emigrants generally to be not more than one or two miles from it.

"It is here more than anywhere else previously, that inexperienced travelers on this route begin to be deceived in relation to distances and the size of objects."

Some emigrants, like those with the John Hawkins Clark company, ignored the warning: ". . . after traveling an hour or two concluded it would not pay. The object of their visit appeared no nearer after a five mile tramp than it did at starting."

Richard Keen, the morning of May 22, started with two companions to walk to Chimney Rock: "We were afoot and started at a fast pace not thinking it worth while to take our Canteen with us as we would soon walk it. Well we traveled until about 11 O clock at the rate of about 4 miles pr hour the day was exceptively hot and we began to suffer for water Chimney rock was far a head of us yet. We had left the Road to our right and was wending our way along the foot of the sand hills. We looked back to see how near our train had approaced. When to our sorrow we saw that the road was gradually leaving us and turning to the right. some of the boys wanted to turn back and overtake the train for Water as we were very thirsty, but after some little time spent in Consultation it was agreed that we go ahead to the rock. it was a sever undertaking but I started ahead and told my companions that I was bound to visit the Rock they followed me we went ahead at a faster rate than ever we were getting intolerably dry and some of the Boys said they were getting thick tongued and could not talk plain. I was as dry as any of them I thought but laughed at them. I was in advance when I descried a pool of water directly before us. I called to my companions and we all started on a run. it proved to be a very large spring of clear cool water the prettiest I ever saw the water boiled up three or 4 inches through the White pebles. we sat down and quenched our thirst by degrees washed our faces and wet our heads. we then bid farewell to this glorious spring and again pushed onward arrived at the rock about 12 oclock."

"Chimney rock is about, from its base to its apex, four hundred feet high, consisting of a low and second platform. Upon the latter is the chimney or shaft of the rock nearly one hundred feet high," wrote William Lobenstine. "This rock is principally composed of marl and clay, intermixed with several strata of white cement. Joining the chimney rock, right above it, I beheld a most beautiful sight, being a section of rock of singular construction resembling in its appearance very much some of the scenery along the Rhine. The whole consisted of five rocks, one approaching the form of another smaller chimney and giving with the rest a most grand view, just like an ancient fort of the feudal barons on an average steep ascending hill, with cupola on the top assuming the forms of ruins. Had I the talent of a Byron or the skilled hand of a Raphael I might give an adequate idea of the landscape, but as I am, even common language is wanting to give an appropriate description. I thought it, however, romantic, and truly felt more than my tongue may express. O what a pity it is to be deficient of *Brain!*"

"We ascended about 150 feet and carved Our Names," Richard Keen continued, "there are thousands of Names out here which will attract the attention of a man that loves to reflect and study human nature. You will see names cut a high as any man could ascend you would think he leave his Name and date above all others when probably there comes another More Ambitious than he and ascends by cutting a little higher and leaves his Name above all others. after a While another Comes he to is possessed of Ambition and cut a few more notches to stand in and leaves his name yet above all others. this is the case of Chimney Rock. I ascended as far as I though[t] safe not daring to look downward but my Ambition was not sufficient to carry me any higher there is Many Names above Mine."

Leaving Chimney Rock, the traveler could see the high cliffs of Scotts Bluff some twenty miles in the distance. "For forty miles we had caught frequent glimpses of these celebrated rocks," John Hawkins Clark wrote on June 9, "and their appearance when first seen impressed one with the idea that he might be approaching a great and magnificent city. Court House Rock stood a temple upon the plain, Chimney Rock had the appearance of a watch tower from whose lofty

Chimney Rock

height a watchman could command a view of the surrounding country; and last, though not least, in the extensive view, stood Scott's Bluffs, like fortified ramparts to guard the safety of millions. Here are castellated walls and ramparts, towers and domes, built in that grand and massive style which only nature knows so well how to plan. The natural ruins of this neighborhood are on an extensive and grand scale, wonderful to behold, and what makes them of more interest is the strong resemblance to decaying monuments erected by the hand of man, making one believe, almost in spite of himself, that yonder ruin is the handiwork of man. It is only on a near approach that the delusion wears off, yet there still lingers a curiosity to examine, to see if, after all, there are not some chisel marks, square joints or plumb corners that man can claim; but there are none. It is all the work of nature's master builder. . . ." At Scotts Bluff, Richard Keen achieved the ambition thwarted at Chimney Rock. "No man was ever higher on these bluffs and My name is above all others."

In the vicinity of Scotts Bluff, John Hawkins Clark wrote: "About 9 o'clock we met an old black cow returning to the states; she appeared to have had enough of this wonderland and was returning to pastures green and more plentiful than she has had for the last hundred miles or so, traveling day by day in search of a bare subsistence. Some of the boys thought the journey too long and too lonesome for a single traveler, and after much coaxing induced the old thing to turn back. But no sooner had we camped than her alleged owner made his appearance, and recognizing her old and familiar form claimed his child's pet; a sad blow to some of the boys who hungered for milk in their coffee."

Holmes Van Schaick was approaching the bluff on June 14: "We had traveled about 2 miles, when we came to a blacksmith shop, made by sticking up 4 poles and by laying some of the same on tops and plastering them over with clay. The house was made by sticking poles in the ground in the form of a hay stack, and covered with dried skins. This constituted the settlement."

The army and trading post of Fort Laramie was visited by John Hawkins Clark on June 12: "Fort Laramie is located at or near the junction of the Platte and Laramie rivers, near the banks of the latter and about one mile from the former. We crossed Laramie river over a bridge just above the junction of the two streams for which we paid three dollars per wagon— teams and passengers free. Camped on the Platte river as usual; here we again wrote letters for home. Fort Laramie is a great place in the immigration season; a good many wagons are left at this point, many coming to the conclusion of getting along without them. Many pack their goods from this point; a hard way to travel, I should think. A hotel, store and post office are located here. I saw about 150 officers and men belonging to the Fort; all appeared to be well behaved, and I think ready and willing to help the unfortunate. The hospital, I am told, contains many sick immigrants."

William Newell, an emigrant from New York, had a decidedly different opinion of at least one officer at Fort Laramie. When he reached Salt Lake City, he wrote to the *Deseret News*. After paying high tribute to the officers at Fort Kearney, he continued: "I regret that I cannot say the same of all the officers at Fort Laramie, there is a young man stationed at that post who, I believe, has the honor of being assistant Surgeon, to whom the Emigrants (such of them as were so unfortunate as to become invalids) frequently had occasion to apply for advice, and in some instances for medicine, being entirely destitute, but they met with poor consolation, the reply they received was, that they could not be accommodated, and were assured that the post was not established for their benefit nor he (the assistant Surgeon) placed there to be annoyed by them, he was also often heard to remark that it was a matter of no consequence to him whether they died or not, he should give himself no trouble on their account.

"He claims also to have a great dislike to the American people and particularly such as traverse the plains, and has (he says) sent into the heads of the department his resignation, which will undoubtedly be accepted, and I trust his place supplied with one who has at least, the common feelings of humanity.

"The commander of the Post Capt. Ketchum, as near as I could learn has been very obliging, and ever ready to do all he felt himself authorized to do to administer to the wants of the traveler."

An emigrant signing himself "G. W. H." wrote from Fort Laramie on June 9, to the St. Louis *Intelligencer*: "I find the

Fort Laramie

buildings in good repair and well adapted for their present use; the dwellings are of frame, two stories high with double porches and railings, painted white; the small outbuildings, stables, &c., are of *adobes*. There is a good blacksmith and wagon maker's shop here, very accommodating to those who pay them handsomely; there are also three bakeries, where the poor emigrant can obtain an apology for a loaf of bread for 40 cents, and a small dried apple pie for 50 cents. Capt. Ketchum is in command here with 64 privates, all now in good health. Mr. Tutt superintends the store, where a full supply of 'chicken fixins' can be obtained at remunerating prices. The Government have a ferry across the Platte within two miles of the fort, in charge of two mountain men, very accommodating also, at the most exorbitant prices—eight dollars for ferrying four horse team, 25 cents for foot passengers. . . . We leave here to-morrow for Salt Lake, where I shall again write you. . . . [we] are all here well, in good health and spirits. We are all getting fat, and wear terrible mustaches and beards."

The toll charge over the Laramie River seemed to change almost from day to day. Mary Stuart Bailey on June 23, and Mrs. Cornelia Sharp on June 20, each paid $2.50; Richard Keen, on May 26, and Stephen Gage on the twenty-ninth were charged $1, and Caroline Richardson on June 11 paid $2, as did the Verdenal party on July 1, and they were additionally charged 10 cents per head of stock.

John Verdenal did not think much of the fort which he considered poorly built: "the front is a three story frame house and a large yard enclosed with adobe walls there are also many small adobe houses in its vicinity being populated mostly by Indians and mountaineers." But Caroline Richardson thought the fort "quite a bustling place containing between twenty and thirty houses there is one house that looks quite like home."

At the fort Robert Laws bought a meal consisting of a pint of buttermilk with ice in it, a loaf of bread, and a piece of roasted buffalo meat, for which he paid 25 cents; "this was," he wrote, "the best meal I ever eat." G. A. Smith, on May 15, "got a bowl of sweet and bitter milk wheat bread and butter this was the best meal I ever eate in my life."

Dr. Dalton's company, on June 18, purchased additional supplies: "Stayed Camped all day. Overhauled the Provisions; appointed a Committee of One from each mess to ascertain what was wanting and the Captain went back five miles below the Fort and bought them of Mr. Campbell—a freighter who had traveled along with us, with six waggons having 6000 lb. in each waggon. Stayed about Fort Laramie all day—took dinner on Buffalo meat, Bread & Butter, Coffee &c.—at 50 cents—All things kept for sale here are *extremely high*—Coffe & Shugar, 75 pr. pound. Tea 2.00—Rhubarb, aloes &c. 1.00 per ounce—A Big Indian (*Louis the brave*) came to the Fort to see the Capt. with two wooden pins stuck in each arm; having killed his Brother in a Spree."

The Smith party had come through from St. Joseph in only twenty-eight days, with disastrous results: "Our boys not being accostumed to driving Horses we drove to fast and animals got verry poor and we concluded to pack which we done and disposed of all the clothing and bagge we could spare and sold our waggons not having but one Horse a piece to carry our baggage we all had to go on foot which was rather hard at first." Six days and eighty-four miles later: "this was a solem morning among the Boys our Animals became worn out and we concluded to Shirk for our selfs divided what little property we had left with good feelings." Smith and a companion went to a nearby train and paid $60 to be carried through to California.

Leaving Fort Laramie, the trail entered the Laramie range, then called the Black Hills because of the dark covering of pine and cedar. "The scenery, after passing the Fort and proceeding a few miles up the river, assumes quite a different aspect from that which we have passed before the Fort," William Lobenstine observed. "The monotony of the prairie land disappears, and a varied highland scenery is offered to the traveler. The road leads generally over the bluffs at an average height of about seventy to one hundred feet above the bed of the Platte and in advancing approaches sometimes toward the Southwestern mountain chain with the Laramie Peak, whose summit is six thousand feet above the sea and covered with snow throughout the greater part of the year. This mountain can be seen at a distance of one hundred miles. . . . The Platte River above the Fort Laramie takes a different appearance from its lower course. The low fertile land through which it runs for nearly seven hundred to eight hundred miles to its mouth, is changed into a highland scene. Its course is rapid and cut through the solid granite rocks. . . . The beauty of the mountain chain is greatly increased by the scattered trees of cedar and pine and by the interruption of numerous streams which are bordered with a most beautiful growth of cottonwood and other trees."

There were two roads entering the Black Hills, one over the hills, which Lobenstine took, the other along the river, taken by John Hawkins Clark: "The river cannot be followed only on its general course; it is now quite a narrow stream, rapid and very crooked. For days we see nothing of it, then again we are upon its banks where it goes rushing, foaming and thundering over great rocks or between high and nearly perpendicular walls of stone, almost a terror to contemplate. This region is very interesting; we pass many curious shaped mounds and ruin-like looking places that would in the states attract a great deal of attention. . . .

". . . This afternoon our road lay across an elbow of the river and over a grassy plain, at the end of which we saw a little white tent, and at a near approach found that it contained within its canvas walls a sick man in the last stages of cholera. We called at the tent door and asked if we could be of any service. He replied, 'No; my time is nearly out and I feel beyond any power of help, but am willing and ready.' . . . I had almost forgotten to say that the sick man had two attendants who had, as they told us, 'attended to his every want,' and at the same time dug his grave alongside his dying couch, 'to have it handy,' they said."

[113]

Scene in the Black Hills, Bitter Creek Valley

There was a rich meadow along Deer Creek where many emigrants laid over for two or three days. "here is first rate camping," William Kahler found on July 1, "there is thousands of cattle resting on this crick the most of the emigration stop here to recruit their stock this is a lovely place . . . we are taking out our things to air and dry this day I spent hunting went up the black mountains saw some elks and antilopes and some buffalows but killed nothing came back allmost tuckered out seen curiosities that paid me for my jaunt these is some hills you had bettcr think some of them are at least a ½ mile high and allmost strate up I could find places to scramble up on some of them but they were mostly stone some pine and Seder on them and as pretty flours heads as you ever seen rite on the tops of them all kinds and sorts of strange flowers."

The wild flowers served a sad use for eleven-year-old Harriet Scott whose mother died in the Black Hills: "The rolling hills were ablaze with beautiful wild roses—it was the 20th of June, and we heaped and covered mother's grave with the lovely roses, so the cruel stones were hid from view."

A day past Fort Laramie there was a large Indian village where John Hawkins Clark laid by on June 14: "At dinner we were visited by a party of native Americans, and as they were on a mission of peace added greatly to the pleasures of camp life. It was a change in our dull routine, and but for the slight difference in our looks one would have sworn we were brothers of the same mould. We immigrants had been so long on the plains and lived so much like Indians that now, while sitting round the camp fire, passing the pipe from mouth to mouth, from white man to Indian, a stranger would have sworn we were all the same tribe as we smoked together. So we dined and a good time was had. But I must say that a little envious feeling was manifested towards that happy brother who had the extreme pleasure of sitting by and now and then helping to dainty bits (pork and fried bread) a 'dusky daughter' of the far west who happened to be one of our visitors. It was rather hard to let one man monopolize so much pleasure, but we were getting used to 'hard things.' The lucky fellow was left alone in his attentions to the fair one, who seemed very grateful for the devotions of the gallant immigrant. Whether the fellow will remember this as the happiest hour of his life I cannot say, but from the efforts he made to please and his polite farewell I am half inclined to believe she made a lasting impression.

"When dinner was over and the pipe again went round we exhibited the pictures of our sweethearts and wives; these appeared to be greatly admired by the 'stalwarts,' but the lady Indian passed them by with supreme indifference."

Caroline Richardson lay by at the same place the day before John Hawkins Clark: "this afternoon we were again visited by more indians we gave them something to eat after which they left us carrying with them such victuals as they could not eat they took a sharp stick and placed some boiled ham and cheese on it they did not seem to relish this cheese very well they scrutinized it very closely before they ventured to taste it and when they did they made up a terrible wry face."

Mrs. Richardson put the day of rest to good use: "we made use of our soft water and done our washing we also baked up

[115]

pies and cakes to last a week some of the company took a turn
over the hills in search of game and returned with a young antelope which furnished us all with the first dish of fresh meat
since we have been on the plains it had the flavor of veal."

The Clark party, unlike Mrs. Richardson, had baking prob-
lems: "We have been eating fried bread ever since leaving the
Missouri river and some of the boys are very tired of it. How to
bake bread is a question that has often been discussed. Some
say on a board before the fire; others tell us a hole in the
ground and a fire over it is the way to do it, and still others tell
us the way to bake 'white man's bread and to be decent about
it is to bake it in a cast iron Dutch oven, and then you have it.'
This afternoon one of the boys came into camp with one
turned bottom side upward over his head. All hands shouted
'Hurrah for the bake oven! Hurrah for the man who found
and brought the bake oven into camp; we will now have good
bread.' The poor fellow who found the oven said, as he threw
it from his head, that he had 'toted it five miles and would not
do it again if he had to eat slapjacks and hard bread all the
way to California.' 'Why d——n the thing, there is a hole in
the bottom,' said one who had turned it over. 'Yes, I'll swear
there is two of them.' Sure enough, there were two bullet holes
as near the center of the unfortunate oven as a marskman's
skill enabled him to place, and through those two bullet holes
vanished all our present hopes of good bread. It is but fair to
say that the holes had been plastered over with mud, and the
finder, not scrutinizing it closely, had been deceived as to its
soundness." Luckier was Jay Green, camped in the Black Hills
on May 30: "As wee encamped erly in the afternoon and having plenty of dryed fruit spices and brandy, and a good supply
of antelope meat—the too Cooks—Mr Dye and Mr Ellis
thought it advisable to make a few mins pyes."

"yesterday morning," July 6, Dexter Holsey and a companion "started out hunting we took it into our heads to go a good
way off took some lunch with us and started for the mountains
we went about 3 mls and come to one of the coldest streams in

[116]

the world we followed it up about 5 miles through the wildest and most romantic spot I was ever in but did not see any game the rocks were at some places 200 ft high above us we then left the ravine and went up on a higher land for about 4 miles when we come to a steep Bluff and decended on to a large meadow where there was plenty of game it was six OClock when we got there we saw 12 Buffalo comming down out of the mountain about 1½ miles from us we went after them and in about 2 hours we caught up with them they were walking away from us but 3 of them turned and looked round to see what was going on it was so duskish he could not see very plain and we got very near him about 20 rods we put two Balls into him and they made him hop up and down well but he finaly gathered up and went on with the rest it was so late we did not feel like running after him so we went to the mountain and built a fire to keep away the wild animals we found plenty of water and we sat down by the side of it with our guns on our laps and ate a little supper that we had brought with us we slept first rate by the fire and the next morning we started out at 3½ O'clock after game we crept and crawled about trying to get close to the antelope and sometimes Blazing away at them 80 rods off until 5 Oclock when it commenced raining and we started for home and left the game to take care of themselves we got home at 12 Oclock and found that our Boys had killed a fine elk and it was good eating and no mistake. . . ."

On June 17 the Clark party crossed Labonte Creek, more than seventy miles west of Fort Laramie, and saw evidence of the rough justice that prevailed on the trail: "One mile from the ford we passed the grave of a man just hung; it appeared that the culprit committed an unprovoked murder yesterday, was caught in the act, confined until this morning when he was tried, found guilty of murder in the first degree, and 'hung on the spot.' The fellow kicked against the proceedings with much argument and wanted to be taken back to a civilized country before being tried; but as he had committed murder on the plains, he should be tried on the plains, and if found guilty should be hung upon the plains. The murder was proven fair and square, the jury prompt in its verdict, sentence pronounced immediately and the hangman's rope finished the job."

Godfry Ingrim, a member of the Clark party, provided more details of the murder in his reminiscences: "There was a large train two days ahead of ours that was owned by a man named Brown. Brown's wife was with this train but Brown himself was behind with a drove of cattle. There was a young man by the name of Miller in charge, and two young men, brothers, by the name of Tate, who each drove a team in the train. The Tates did not like Miller. Mrs. Brown told Miller, the boss, that he had better lay over until her husband came up with the cattle. Miller told the drivers to stop and unhitch. One of the Tates told Miller that he was putting on style, but Miller told Tate that it was Mrs. Brown's wish that he would stop the train until Mr. Brown came up. One word led to another and Tate called Miller a low mean name. Miller grabbed up one of the whips and said that he would not take that from any man and at once struck Tate. Tate's brother Lafe ran up behind Miller and stuck a knife into his back and as he fell nearly cut his head off. As soon as he did this he went to Miller's wagon and took Miller's pistol and knife and started ahead on the road to California. As fast as the trains came up they were stopped until there was a crowd to pick from to send after Tate. In a short time fifteen men had volunteered their services and started in pursuit of the murderer. The party overtook Tate at a creek called Labont. Here they arrested him, but he told the party there was no law on the plains. As fast as teams came up they were stopped until there was a big crowd. As soon as Brown's train came up with the witnesses there was a judge and jury picked out of the crowd and a man on each side as lawyers. The prisoner was given a fair trial. The evidence against him was overwhelming. He was found guilty and hung on a tree at the hour of midnight and buried close to the road. A large headboard described the horrible crime and hanging. His brother said that it would be the death of every man composing the jury. This was more than the jury could stand and he was tied to a tree and whipped. As our train came up the next day, I learned these facts from one of the men at the trial. . . . So much for a man to let his passions get away with him."

Caroline Richardson came along just after the murder, which occurred on June 15. Her party camped near the trains gathered for the trial, and several of her company attended, although Mrs. Richardson herself did not: "It was near midnight when our men came back to the camp the jury gave in a verdict of guilty the prisoner was but nineteen years of age named Lafayette Tate of Jackson Co Mo the judge told him he had but thirty moments to live and asked him if he would like to have a prayer he answered it is too late to pray and he cared nothing about the bible he went into his tent and threw himself on his face and appeared perfectly indifferent to his fate his brother asked him what he should tell his parents he stubbornly replied you may tell them what you please he was leagly tried. and hung about eleven oclock at night. . . ." When John Verdenal passed the spot on July 6, "we noticed his grave from which one of his bones protruded forth and his hair was strewed around the grave. It was a shocking sight."

The day after John Hawkins Clark gave his account of the Miller-Tate murder, he wrote: "The sublime, the pathetic, the outrageous and the ridiculous follow each other in quick succession on this road. This morning while in advance of our train caught up with an old lady trudging along after her two wagons. 'Well, how are you getting along?' I asked. 'O, terrible bad,' she replied; 'one of my grandchildren fell out of the wagon yesterday and both wheels ran plum over his head; oh dear! I shall never forget yesterday!' Thinking the accident a painful one for the old lady I changed the subject; in the meanwhile several little fellows that were in the wagon making a fuss, climbed up the side boards, swinging to the roof of the cover, and otherwise disporting themselves. The old lady ever on watch called out to 'Johnny' to behave himself. 'Do you want to fall out again and be killed, Johnny?' 'Is that the boy who got run over yesterday? I thought surely he must have been killed.' 'No, it did not quite kill him, but it made the little rascal holler awfully.' I thought that boy's head must have been a very hard one; or, possibly there might have been a very soft spot on the road somewhere. I asked the old lady if the children fell out of the wagon often. 'They fall out behind sometimes when the wagons are going up steep places, but that don't matter much you know, for then there are no wheels to run over them,' she replied."

Others were not as fortunate as Johnny. On June 27, near Labonte Creek, William Hampton noted: "Hyde's little girl fell out of the waggon and it ran over her, hurt pretty bad." And Mary Medley recalled that four days after her mother's death "my two brothers were playing in the wagon on the bed, the curtains were rolled up and the front wheels went down in a rut which jarred the wagon, throwing brother John out. A hind wheel ran over him, breaking one of his legs. Had it not been for deep sand in the road he would have been killed. His leg was set at once by Dr. Mason and he got along well, but was confined to the wagon for the rest of the journey."

Clark continued the story of Johnny's grandmother: "As this old lady is something of a character I am inclined to give something of her history; as a washerwoman I became acquainted with her at St. Joe, Missouri. She told me that herself and husband joined the Mormon church in England, moved to America and Salt Lake, where her husband died, and she, becoming disgusted with Mormonism stole away and returned to St. Joe where she had resided ever since, making a living to the wash tub. When the California fever broke out she determined to go to the Pacific coast, and saved money sufficient to equip two wagons with teams and provisions. She crossed the Missouri river the same day that we did and here she was, safe and sound, without a broken head in the 'outfit,' which consisted of three women besides herself and five boys, big and little, including a son-in-law and a grandson."

A week west of Fort Laramie, Perry Gee, on July 3, was nearing the Mormon Ferry: ". . . found a Drowned man floting Down the Platt by the name of R. Talbet. Case got him out and Buried him had in his pocket a peace of gold just as it was Dug from the mine the value of it we judged $5.00 one note of thirty Dollars knife silver pennsil money purse and money in the exact amount I never could find out by them but as near as I could find out thare was about $60.00 Dollars worth in all those that toke him out and buried him . . . Divided the spoils between them and would not tell how mutch they Did get."

Nearly 140 miles beyond Fort Laramie the California Trail crossed the Platte River at the Mormon Ferry, and the emigration joined with those who were on the Mormon Trail from Iowa. The Platte was more than 300 yards wide at the ferry and swift; this made it dangerous to ford the stock. Esther Hanna reached the ferry on June 21: "We came over with our wagons, carriage mules and horses, intending to swim our cattle as that is generally the way they are gotten across. The men drove them in 3 or 4 times but they were unwilling to stem the current, it being very rapid and deep. We were then obliged to have them ferried over at a cost of 50 cents a head; wagons, five dollars; horses, mules, and persons, 50 cents each! There have been 15 men drowned this spring in attempting to swim across. The water is very cold, producing cramps immediately. We were detained until late this afternoon getting over."

"Three boats are constantly running at this point," D. B. Andrews noted on June 12. "Current very rapid. About $\frac{1}{2}$ a mile below the ferry, swam our cattle. This is attended with some danger, besides much fatigue to the animals. A number of lives have been lost here by those who were engaged in driving over stock by their venturing too far out into the current which is very strong at this place. The boats carry over

Red Buttes, Laramie Plains, Utah

about 24 wagons per hour at $5.00 per wagon, men 50 cts per head, cattle $1.00, man & horse $1.00. About 1000 wagons have already passed this season up to this date."

John Hawkins Clark set out for the ferry the morning of June 22 and was soon in trouble: ". . . in crossing a deep and muddy ditch our ox team went contrary to good conduct and broke the wagon tongue, leaving the wagon half upset in the worst mud hole on the Platte river. We were now in a fix, and if the wagon was not a 'fixture' it appeared to be, for with all our ingenuity we could not move it. The most of our men and all the other teams were ahead and out of call. As we had done once before, so we had to do now—unload all our freight before we could extract the wagon. After an hour's labor in mud and water we had made things all right except the broken tongue, which we expect to get mended at the ferry. All set for the ferry, which we soon made and bargained for the transit of the whole outfit by paying the sum of $32; these plainsmen do not forget to charge. All have to ferry their wagons, but most of the immigrants swim their stock. Many cattle have been lost at this point and the ferryman has a record of fifteen men drowned within the last month. The boatman had, I think, located this ferry on a difficult place in the river in order to force custom over it.

"There is a big crowd of people here and a great deal of stock is being driven into the river. They are driven in promiscuously and allowed to find their way over as best they can. I saw many of them drown in the swift, whirling and turbulent stream. Some men in their anxiety to get their stock over wade in after them, and as the records show, many are drowned. I saw one man go down and another would soon have followed had he not been rescued by a negro who, as he heard the cry of 'another man drowning,' jumped upon a big mule, and then, mule and man, over a steep bank four feet high into the foaming current. Then came the struggle for life—now on top and then beneath the surface. The drowning man was making desperate efforts to save himself, the whirling and shifting current

[123]

often preventing the negro from making a sure grip at the unfortunate man's head. Now he has him, now he has 'lost his grip,' and now he is again reaching for a sure hold, and fortunately, he has it. The mule and his rider and the half drowned man land on a sand bar half a mile below, and the excitement of the hour is over.

"The negro, when the alarm was given, was busily strapping his pack upon his mule. Now again he is busy getting off on his journey, and as he is about to start he is detained by an old gentleman who tells him that this crowd of people cannot afford to let him proceed on his journey without showing their appreciation of his heroic conduct. Then calling the crowd together he dwelt upon the heroic deeds recorded in ancient and modern history and declared none of them more heroic or more deserving of praise than the one they had just witnessed, and ended with the proposition of giving the dusky hero 'three cheers and a tiger.' It is needless to say that three cheers and the loudest 'tiger' that ever was heard upon the banks of the upper Platte river were given, and with a low bow of his wooly head the negro turned and resumed his journey toward the setting sun. 'Honor and fame from no condition rise.' He had acted well his part and is now as 'happy as a clam at high tide.' God bless him."

A Michigan emigrant, Gilbert Cole, crossed the Platte on June 14: "We had to wait nearly a whole day before it came our turn to take our wagons over. In the meantime we were detailed as follows: Ten men were selected to get the wagons aboard the boat, cross over with them and guard them until all were carried over; three or four men were sent across and up the river to catch and care for the stock as it came out of the river near a clump of cottonwoods. One of the company, named Owen Powers, a strong, courageous young man and a good swimmer, volunteered to ride the lead horse in and across to induce the other animals to follow, the balance of the company herding them, as they were all loose near the edge of the river. When everything was ready, Powers stripped off, and mounting the horse he had selected, rode out into the stream. The other animals, forty-seven of them followed, and when a few feet from the shore had to swim. Everything was going all right until Powers reached the middle of the river, when an undercurrent struck his horse, laying him over partly on his side. Powers leaned forward to encourage his horse, when the animal suddenly threw up his head, striking him a terrible blow squarely in the face. He was stunned and fell off alongside the horse. It now seemed as though both he and his horse would be drowned, as all the other stock began to press close up to them. He soon recovered, however, and as he partially pulled himself on to his horse, we could plainly see that his face and breast were covered with blood. We shouted at him words of encouragement, cheering him from both sides of the river. While his struggling form was hanging to the horse's mane, the other animals all floundered about him, pulling for the shore for dear life. The men on the other side were ready to catch him as he landed, nearly exhausted by his struggles and the blow he had received. They carried him up a bank and leaned him against a tree, one man taking him while the others caught the animals, or rather corralled them, until the rest of us got across and went to their assistance. We brought the young man's clothes with us and fixed him up, washing him and staunching his bleeding nose and mouth. He had an awful looking face; his eyes were blackened, nose flattened and mouth cut. However, he soon revived and was helped by a couple of the men down to the wagons. We then gathered the stock, went down to the train, hitched up, and drove into camp."

V

THE MORMON TRAIL FROM
PLATTE RIVER FORD
TO MORMON FERRY

AS EMIGRANTS in increasing numbers crossed from the south to the north bank of the Platte River, they brought "the sickness" with them, and fear, almost amounting to panic, spread among the trains from Kanesville. Jared Fox, who was in the forefront of the emigration, had encountered no sickness until he reached the Platte River ford, and his entries over the next few days reflected the emigrants' alarm: "(May 25) Cholera raging on the south side of the Platte at a dreadful rate and all were hustling over to try to escape it if possible, but they are falling now on this side. We gathered up our traps and started as soon as possible. Passed before night all the teams that passed us and some others. . . . (May 26) Everyone seems to be in a hurry. Ox teams are on the move. Drove fast. . . . Plenty of teams hustling through the river wherever they dare as it is so sickly on the other side. . . . (May 28) We made 28 miles—too far for the going and the weather. Our stint is to pass 50 teams per day but today we have passed near 150, some droves of loose cattle, making in all near 3000 head of cattle, horses and mules. . . . (May 30) Our Capt. seemed to be anxious to bring his company through but feared for grass, there were so many teams. He said we ought to keep ahead of the 3000 that we passed Friday and we started out early and travelled till $\frac{1}{2}$ past 9 and passed 3000 more, the most of them on the move. We then stopped till 3 o'clock. I suppose 1500 or 2000 passed us while we were there. This day has been very warm. Here we lighted up again by throwing away. We have now got rid of our tools mostly, some of our ropes, some of our harness and 3 feet off the hind end of our waggons, $\frac{2}{3}$ of our bags, all of our horse blankets, some of our clothes and some of our dishes, etc."

Moving up the Platte, Edward Kitchell, undismayed by the death around him, was thoroughly enjoying himself: "Made about 10 miles today," May 30. "Day excessively warm. morning threatened a hard shower, but blew over & cleared up— road good save a couple of miles over the sandy bluffs—that very heavy—These Bluffs come down to the river at this point (6 or 7 miles back) & the only place since we struck the Platte. They are about 280 miles from Council Bluffs. they are not very high, but from their top you have a splendid view of Platte, with its large islands & small green Islands, covered with willow & cotton-wood. Bluffs on other side near river & handsome bottom with large cotton-wood. The large islands

[127]

are mostly prairie & are very beautiful. Camp is on Skunk creek, an ugly, low, flat swampy stream of clear running water—No wood, ('chips') dug a well and have excellent cool water—grass good—most day it has been poor. Went hunting today with Milton—he lost my saddle blanket where he killed deer—we couldn't find it & so went hunting deer. Started four—got no shot. I had two fine chases after wolves. I saw four gray ones. My black horse runs upon them & while we are going full tilt I shoot. I killed two in that way & today never missed a shot—one was a very large one. Saw ducks & wild geese

"This is a beautiful moonlight night & the frogs are singing merrily—we are a mile & half from the river, near bluffs—passed some fine rich prairie today—perfectly smooth & level. 'prickly pear' abounds in the prairies ever since we crossed the Loupe Fork.

"Last night (fore part) I stood guard—it was a delightful moonlight guard so still & pleasant—one could dream of *happy* days gone by—could wonder if the moon awakened such thoughts as ours in friends & relatives—could bring up home before my imagination could see a father, mother, brother & sister—I dreamt of old times in Madison in Hillsboro, in Olney. reviewed my whole life. Could let my mind go whither it willed but my body, staid with the oxen, wrapped up in a blanket—well this is going to California 'pleasuring' it so far—we live like Lords, venison, biscuits hot coffee & tea occasionaly. Musquitoes are confounded bad tonight—gosh what pretty songs they do sing in my ears. When I cross the 'plains' again I take with me an umbrella for the hot sun & a musquito bar. Nearly two o'clock—good-by to you musquitoes 'vamos.' " Addison Crane also complained of the mosquitoes: "I do not wish to be impious—but really it does seem to me that musquitoes, gnats, and sand flies never ought to have been created." He was particularly annoyed that "they work both day & night, without cessation—a most ungracious and ungentlemanly proceeding. . . ."

But the mosquitoes were a minor irritation, and Crane's journal was typical of the emigrants traveling the Platte Valley the last week of May: "Travelled yesterday about 18 miles. Encamped at 6 Oclock—night cool enough to sleep well which I improved to good advantage. Saw deposits of Alkili (called saleratus) in spots all about. It looks like a hoary white frost, and to the taste has the flavor of common salt and potash combined. It does not dissolve in the rain or dews. . . . Dug two holes for water—and found it in both—in one like lye and unfit to drink, in the other barely palatable—but we were encamped 2 miles from the River and had to get along the best way we could. Happened to have 2 or 3 gallons of good water in our cans which made tea & coffe for supper & breakfast and choppcd up a span ox yoke for wood. Found tolerable grass. Started out 7 this morning and in about two miles found an encampment where they were digging a grave. On enquiry found that a Mr Ware of Mo. had died of Pneumonia leaving a wife and 5 small children who were on their way with him across the plains This train 5 wagons were to start back to day and by one of the men (Mr Calloway) sent back my journal for the last 4 days. It is two months this day since I left my home, and all that is most dear to me, and which sccms more like home, and the objects of my affection there more dear, the longer I am absent from it. I have wished sometimes that they were all along, but the more I see of life, of hardships, deprivation, sickness and death—the better I am satisfied that they should be where thcy arc. The country we have passed over to day is much the same as yesterday. These bottom lands of the Platte are a sandy and naturally dry soil, and except in spots produces poor grass—next to no grass at all Have as yet seen no Buffalo, although we are in Buffalo country. Should be glad of some fresh meat—but must wait the fortune of time. (Eve.) We are encamped to night near the banks of the platte. plenty wood water and grass. Water very indifferent but not poisonous—Evening beautiful—slight shower this P.M. just enough to lay the dust and cool the air. Gentle breeze all day from the

[129]

north, but for which it would have been excessively warm. Sun is setting clear—prospects of a good night for sleeping. Met, and travelled along a mile or two with a man from Marietta O. who like me has left a wife and 6 children—said if he were back where he was before he arranged his business to go, he would let California go, and I presume there are many such. It is one thing to be a fireside warrior—entirely another to go into actual battle. But a good soldier will not shrink when the contest thickens. Two of our company go out this moonlight night on a buffalo hunt and say they will not return without fresh meat if they dont overtake us in two days. There are quite a number camped about us within half a mile—several families. Observed to day a great many specimens of the cactus. gathered a mess of mushrooms but could not cook them so that they were palatable and consequently threw them away. The moon shines brightly—frogs sing sweetly—night clear and calm—and I am wearied and will retire. Distance to day 20 miles.

"Thursday May 27 (23d day). The night was beautiful for sleeping—morning quite cool, but as soon as the sun raised himself in sight his influence began to be felt. The morning is calm—bright beautiful, and spread in every direction to the extent of the vision is bright green endless prarie. The beautiful warble of a meadow lark is heard from a neighboring bush. The gold seekers who are camped about us are driving up their oxen to commence their days journey. We give ours a little more time to eat this morning—having driven them on to an Island in the River where the grass is very good. Our boys who left about 1 Oclock last night on their Buffalo hunt have not as yet returned—when they do we hope it may be with some fresh meat. Unless they are back soon we shall move on and leave them to overtake us as they can. Sarre met with an accident last night in unyoking, the cattle jumped and struck him in the side and knocked him down—bruised him some, and he thinks injured him inwardly—but he is able to be about this morning and we hope is not seriously injured. The

Crossing the Platte by Emigrant Train

water is most miserable—but we must endure it—it is part of the game we are playing at. (Noon) Moved about 8 miles this morning, and at about 11 Oclock came to most excellent grass, and water (fit for stock) & concluded to lay by a couple of hours and let the cattle feed. Teams require great care on a journey like this, and especially for the first month out. Ours so far have kept in most excellent order, although we have not at all times grass enough for them. . . . The day so far has been most beautiful—breeze enough to moderate the heat of the sun and render travelling comfortable. I cannot say that time hangs heavy or that the journey on the whole has been an unpleasant one. There is a constant succession of new Scenery, and new views arising to the vision. This morning the bluffs across the river began to assume a bare mountainous appearance, and the width of the bottom lands there cannot be over a mile or two while on this side the whole character of the country has suddenly changed from one of comparative desolation to good heavy green grass. I have sometimes thought that if I could pass into a deep sleep and awake only at the end of my journey, it would be desirable, but then again I cannot afford it—I cannot afford to loose the splendid scenery yet to come, with all the adventures of three months campaign still before me. To one kept constantly busy as I am there can be no ennui, and even homesickness cannot get a fair hold. The roads are yet good and level, and so far we have had none of the cold bleak storms so generally spoken of as prevailing upon the platte. . . . (Evening) The sun shown very hot this P.M. and I do not remember of ever feeling more intense heat from the sun. . . . We are encamped in a very narrow bottom near the banks of the Platte. Supper is over—the cooks are stewing beans &c. for to morrows dinner—our three boys who left this morning at 1 Oclock to hunt Buffalo have not as yet returned and some concern is felt on their account—but I reckon they will turn up after a while. We are encamped entirely alone to night, only 9 men, and might be easily cut off by the Indians—but I have no concern on that account. Passed this P.M. a new grave which the wooden head board informs us was that of a Mr. Beach of Va. aged 23. who died yesterday. Our progress to day has been slow on account of the heat—distance estimated at 16 miles.

"Friday May 28th (24th day) Our hunters came in 10 Oclock last night with the quarter of a Buffalo. The animal was shot with my gun at 75 yards, of course we are revelling in fresh meat this morning. . . . Several others came in and camped about us after dark last night. The buffalo meat was that of a *venerable male*, and consequently neither so tender nor well flavored as would have been a young cow—but then it tasted good and relished well. . . .

"Sunday May 30th (26th day) I have been walking a great deal since I commenced this journey, and last night in addition to being tired my feet were quite sore, and I resolved to have a horse, and purchased a fine bay mare for $90, *on a credit of three months* of an emigrant with whom I have become acquainted with on the road. . . . I have been thinking how strange an operation my buying that horse was last evening. It happened on this wise—the owner who had been out hunting buffalo (but had killed none) rode into our camp about sunset —his own train being still ahead. I had not seen him for perhaps two weeks and did not even know his name. Some two weeks ago we had travelled and encamped together some two or three days. As he came in I shook him heartily by the hand, made some few enquiries, and asked him what he would take for his horse saddle & bridle. He at first said $100. but after some bantering fixed his lowest price at $90. I told him I would be glad to buy her—and pay in Cal. or Oregon, but had not the money to spare. He replied, 'It makes no difference . . . you can pay as you say—I don't want the money now.' and thus the bargain was closed and the horse delivered to me. The seller took supper with us and then went off on foot to find his own encampment, and we may never meet again. I have his wifes name and address and shall send the money to her in case we do not meet. The transaction was certainly a

[133]

strange one. I have rode Kate ahead this morning and am now sitting in the grass writing this while she is feeding about me. She is 5 years old—bright bay, medium size, kind & gentle—but rather poor in flesh having had hard usage. I intend to get her fleshed up and if I can get her thro. shall no doubt do well in the purchase. . . .

"Tuesday June 1. (28th day) A most beautiful clear morning—up at 4. Breakfast before sunrise—all the work done & off at 5¾—passed a great many teams just ahead of us which had not yet 'rolled out.' . . . All our cooking and washing yesterday was done by the *bois de vache*, which can be collected in large quantities, and, dry, burns very well. I wish I could convey on paper an idea of this region as it now strikes me[.] at the distance of from 3 to 5 miles apart run nearly paralel two bluff ridges like small mountains, broken and uneven on their summits and from 60 to 150 ft. high. Between the bases of these bluffs lays a beautiful extended plain varying in width as the bluffs approach to or recede from each other, and midway through this plain flows the broad, noisless, swift current of the Platte interspersed with numerous little Islands of from ⅛ of an acre to 10 acres in size. All these bluffs and plains and islands are entirely destitute of timber, even to a shrub, covered with their bright green grass carpet—except an occasional barren scared point which shows it self on the bluffs. All this scenery spread out under the bright sunshine of a fine morning, and viewed from the bluff where I am now (alone) seated strikes me as one of those enchanted scenes of nature which to be fully realized must be seen. From the reports of other emigrants I had heretofore only thought of the valley of the Platte, as a cold, rainy muddy, barren and desolate region, one of those dark spots in the journey which the sooner passed the better—but to me it has seemed far otherwise—too much sunshine if anything. And yet I cannot doubt there are multitudes who will after having passed here, have about as intelligent notion of the valley of the Platte as their oxen. All they will remember will be hot sunshine, dust, sand, bacon, bread coffe whiskey and swearing. Such are the masses. . . .

"The great mass of those moving upon the road are from the unrefined portion of the community, among whom the most horrid profanity and degrading vulgarity and obscenity of language is nearly universal. Their blasphemy is generally vented upon their oxen, and is of a character too horid to defile my paper with. Card playing is also a general custom the game being at all times well seasoned and interspersed with oaths and imprecations. There are however several companies of very respectable people, with whom I have met, who entirely eschew all these vices. Sometimes one meets here a gentleman or lady of refinement and education but not often."

Richard Owen Hickman had crossed from the south to the north bank of the Platte on May 25, and three days later eight of his company set off on a buffalo hunt: "After going some six or seven miles off to the right of the road they saw a herd of 300 or 400 down on a valley still further off by a couple of miles; so they laid their plans how to make the attack so as to kill as many as possible. The plan was about in this way,— four of the company were to go to the right and the others to go to the left, so that when the four to the right made the attack the ones to the left could have an opportunity of cutting off their retreat and in this manner surround and take them down in numbers; but they were sadly disappointed. After running down there a distance of two or three miles, they expected to immortalize their names, but they had just come in about 100 yards when they looked down in a deep ravine and saw five old ruffians making at them. Some were delighted at seeing them so tame, whilst others thought they were too tame. Those of the former began to look for some place to secrete themselves and the latter took to flight. One of those delighted was a little Vermont Yankee with long red hair and whiskers. He fixed himself in a sort of ditch and was waiting for the word 'fire.' When he looked around for the rest of the company, the first he heard was 'Come Yankee they'll have us.' Two of the company was then forty yards off and running for life. Boo-oo went the foreman of the band of bulls. Now for the first time poor Yankee saw his danger and his red hair rose so that it pipped his bearer. Grabbing it in his left hand he began to make tracks in a hurry. How were they to escape? Only by flight. The band of bulls were bearing down on them strong, coming up in Indian file; and as they run Yankee took occasion to look back, Boo-oo went the old fellow again who had now come within 40 paces of him; and Yankee said, 'Now legs if you expect to do me any good now is the time.' About this time one of the foremost boys fired his gun, which caused them to slacken their speed, and poor Yankee thus saved his bacon. After fairly outstripping these five they stopped to rest, and one of the three foremost broke silence by saying, 'Boys I'll not run another step; I'll die first,' but before he got fairly through he looked up and saw them coming on their trail and he spoke more emphatic and said 'I will not run;' then turning around again and looked he saw they were still coming and he began to walk pretty fast, but they gained on him so fast that he saw that to run was the only chance for saving himself; but he looked around and in the place of five saw ten, five on his track and the other five coming in from the right forming a tie, so he took to his heels and so far outrun the others that he made them ashamed of themselves. When they got back to the river they found they were about the same place where they left it in the morning, but the teams were at least ten miles further off so they dropped in with us one at a time till dark, when little Yankee come marching in and said 'Boys, I've seen the elephant, darn old roper if I ain't.' "

On May 29, having crossed the Platte, John Clark of Virginia wrote of a different sort of hunting: "This afternoon our boys must have killed some thirty or forty brown or black looking Snakes from two to four feet long. Saw several others much larger but feared to attact them with the ox goad. I fired on some with revolver but they run like hell for the high grass. We fired the plain so as to turn them out but we had to pass on and let them flicker. We camp near the river & gather buffalo chips for the first time. The odor from the new kind of fuel gave our Slap Jacks & broiled meat a strange flavour. Just after dark a light breese sprang up starting the fire afresh that we had kindled in the grass miles back. This gave a brilliant light for the evening as the flames spread far & wide. We could now & then see bctween us & the lighted blase animals runing like fury too & fro. We supposed the snakes had gone."

John Dowdle, a member of the Eighteenth Mormon Company from Kanesville, shot a large buffalo bull seven miles from his camp: "I then haistly made my way to camp, to have someone go back with me to fetch some beef to camp but all seemed beef foundered, for no one appeared to care to return with me that night. . . . Old sister Clark sent for her old horse, which she called Pete. She mounted old pete and bid me get on behind, and she said now we will have some beef for breckfast. . . . and away we went for the seen of the old bull, ariveing at the sean at about dark off we got from old pete, the old lady with tobaco mouth and knif in hand she fell to work not feeling to care much for the order neat butcher bull. but soon had the hide striped from one of his hind leges and soon a large chunk from the round and firmly fastened to old pete back and that was followed with another and another, until we had on board all that we thought sufficient to do for breckfast.

"So all abord, and old pete was switched onto the main track again with plenty of steam and any amount of tobaco juse to fill the air."

Of all the hunters—and hunting hopefuls—who tried their skill on the trail this year, easily the most astonishing was a young lady, Mary Collins, who casually remarked in her reminiscences that one day in the Black Hills she and her sister "went up in the hills and killed birds with our oxwhips and cooked them for supper."

If emigrants in good health could take pleasure in traveling up the broad Platte Valley, others were aware of the darker side of the journey, as death kept pace with the slowly moving trains. Edward Kitchell, opposite Ash Hollow on June 4, observed: "There is a great deal of sickness now. Almost every train has a sick person—and the sickness (diarrhoea) is very fata[l] several deaths today & it is far worse behind. Two men died today from the effects of bad water they drank at a fine clear spring, about a mile the other side of Wednesday [June 2] camp. They had been hunting & drank a good deal—Our boys tried it; it smelt bad & tasted bad. We have such good milk & drink so much of it coffee that we do not fear the sickness characteristic of this trip. . . . We are in a perfect swarm of Emigrants and and one continual train on the south side—more sickness below, than here—most sickness on this side is amongst those that forded the Platte above Ft Kearney."

James Akin's aunt died, and young Akin wrote the sad news home in a letter from Fort Laramie: "Aunt Louisa Richey was taken with the diarrhoea about the 10th and they gave her medicine and she got a good deal better. And on the 14th she was taken with cholera morbus a little after dark, and got worse all the time, till about noon the next day, when she appeared to get almost easy, and stayed so till about 1 o'clock the next morning, when she took worse and died about five minutes past 2 o'clock. We buried her about 9 o'clock the same morning. She was buried in as decent order as circumstances would admit of. Being so far from timber, we could not make a coffin. The grave was dug very deep, with a vault. We took the sideboards of a wagon and covered the vault with them, and then covered it up. We sent about two miles for tombstones. Her name, age and date of death were cut upon one of them. She died about 75 miles east of Ft. Laramie. She did not express any fears of death, but she was unwilling to die and be left on the plains. Uncle Stuart took it very hard."

Richard Hickman was opposite Court House Rock on June 6: "On the 3rd, 4th and 5th we done some good traveling, for we were in the midst of sickness, pain and death, and thought if we could manage to out travel the bulk of immigration we

[138]

would not be so much exposed to the cholera, measles and smallpox, which is scattered along throughout the whole road thus far. James has been gradually growing worse since the second, and last night I thought he would surely die. Our medicine did not seem to have any effect on him as we could give him nothing but what he would immediately vomit it up. This morning I looked for and enquired after a physician for some time, but without success. I was then persuaded by one of the company to give him some morphine. Then the question arose; who knows how to administer it? The prescription said, from $\frac{1}{4}$ to $\frac{1}{2}$ grain per dose, so I had to guess at it and began by giving a small portion and thought I would increase it. I believe it is having the right effect as he appears to be a good deal easier. During the last night he was calling for water constantly and if he did but swallow one tablespoonful I could see his nerves or flesh begin to draw and he said he was cramping. After I saw the effect it had on him I did not let him swallow any when I could help it. We burned some brandy this morning for him to make use of instead of water and have been giving small portions of the cholera medicine we brought from St. Louis." A week later: "James has been on the mend slowly ever since Monday last, but complained a good deal today, as the road was rough."

Death and bereavement were the worst but not the only trials of the Platte Valley, and crossing the plains was a hard and wearisome journey. An anonymous correspondent to the St. Louis *Republican* forcefully expressed his opinion of traveling to California: "To enjoy such a trip along with such a crowd of emigration, a man must be able to endure heat like a Salamander, mud and water like a muskrat, dust like a toad, and labor like a jackass. He must learn to eat with his unwashed fingers, drink out of the same vessel with his mules, sleep on the ground when it rains, and share his blanket with vermin, and have patience with musketoes, who don't know any difference between the face of a man and the face of a mule, but dash without ceremony from one into the other. He must cease to think, except as to where he may find grass and water and a good camping place. It is a hardship without glory, to be sick without a home, to die and be buried like a dog."

Under such conditions patiences wore thin, tempers were short, quarrels frequent, and in the neighborhood of Fort Laramie many trains began breaking up. "At night there were some of us dissatisfied with the balance of the company," Jared Fox wrote on June 7, "and had been for some time and we hauled off and would like to have taken our capt. with us but he was so linked in the teams of the others that we could not. The haul-off party numbered 14 men, 3 women, 7 waggons and 23 horses, leaving 15 men, 1 woman, 6 waggons and 21 horses. We that hauled off joined Cummins Co."

The Bradley party divided on May 29: "just before Starting Myself and F. T. Mason had quite a sharp time for about a minute when it all cooled off again, & we are going to divide our loads to morrow. . . . lay over to day. We are going to divide Provisions with the Boys. They take $\frac{2}{3}$ & we $\frac{1}{3}$ of all the Provision & Corn. they allow us $10 for their part of the Butter Pickles & other Stuff of Ours (except Medicines) that we Brought from home. We made a new tent at Kanesville which they take at $4.00."

The James David company was three days east of Fort Laramie when they, too, began to quarrel: "This morning Sylvester's team left us. They got mad because we told them they did not do their part in watching, driving up cattle, etc. There is more or less quarreling in every train which is much to be regretted. The fault is in persons not doing their share of work. The best way is for every one to lend a helping hand until all is done. Camping is another source of dissension; and driving, taking care of teams. Men are more irritable here than any place in the world. I was sorry the boys should leave but could not help it. We had loaned them a yoke as they had broken theirs. We had to take it from them." But the quarrel ended well two days later. "Sylvester joined us today again; much all right; everything goes off smoothly. Cattle no doubt will be well taken care of now. The reconciliation of old friends is always gratifying."

The huge Mormon Council Point Emigrating Company proved too unwieldy for travel. After camping on July 31, "there came rolling into camp Ezra T. Benson and company on their way to Salt Lake Valley. They were received into our midst with rejoicing and all faces seemed [to] sparkle with gladness, in a short time the company formed into correll. At dark in the evening the company was called together for meeting it was opened by the brass band playing several tunes. . . . Ezra T. Benson Arose and addressed the congregation on the necessity of dividing the company into two parts called the first and second Wing. In a few minutes it was moved and carried that we separate into two wings for the benefit of feed for the cattle and in the whole to accelerate the speed of travelings Then Elder Benson nominated Captain Andrew Whitlock to be the Captain of the second Wing and to be subject and under the control of Captain Tidwell and to take the weak teams and to go an head of the first Wing Carried Uanimous And tomorrow the company can make all necessary arrangements."

Approaching Fort Laramie on June 11, John Clark of Virginia went out hunting alone and then rode eight miles to catch up with his train: "Here I come up with Williams, Thornton, Price, Thompson & others that had found 3 dead indians tied on a cottonwood limb. Williams made out to get up the tree 20 feet then went out on the large limb that held the three dead Sioux. They were shrouded in Buffalo robes & lashed to the branch with strips of rawhide that was hard to cut even with the hatchet; but down it came with a crash when Giles Thornton more reckless than the rest stove his ax into the breast part. Out flew a number of white and blue beads. A little further, & a long roll of flowing black hair showed it was a young female & for all we know the flower of the forest. I for one felt mortified at the degraded act of my fel-

[141]

low being. A beast in the shape of man, the warior of the Red man is generally buried with his pipe bow & quiver, also the mohala in her best, decorated with beeds, jewels & other little trinkets of their fashion. We left the spot in a hurry for Poney Run, 3 miles & no grass. To the trees on the river bank where we dine oposite to a number of indian wigwams on the other side of the Platte. Just as we were leaving this point a terable gust or squall of wind struck us splitting one of our waggon covers, threw down several people, carrying away before it. Everything that was loose in the shape of saddles, blankets, tents, old hats and umbrelas flew with the sand & dust so far as we could see. Some passengers lost nearly all, while one fellow complaind that the filling of his shirt was gone with a part of the pants. Two waggons were blown over & one or two persons more or less hurt. After the floury we hitched up & drove on pasing several indian lodges & French trading huts. We saw many young & old Squaws engaged in making moccasins, belts, bags, baskits & some dressing skins. We bot some for the purpose of a look at the mohalas. Some of the younger had pretty faces but their legs were awful crooked, so we drove up near the ferry and camped below the Garison, 11 miles. This day, 25 miles. Seven graves, 5 steers, 1 horse & 2 waggons. Lots of Sioux Indians this afternoon."

For the benefit of emigrants on the north side of the Platte, there was a ferry at Fort Laramie. It carried passengers only and was not prepared to cross wagons. Addison Crane went over to the fort on June 10: "Have been over and visited Ft. Laramie, formerly a trading post of the American Fur Co. of whom it was purchased by our government three years since. The old Fort is used as soldiers quarters and quite a number of new adobe buildings have been added outside the old fortification for the same purpose, and 2 two story wooden house for the commissioned officers. There is here one company only of about 40 men under command of Cap. Ketchum. I called on the Capt. and found quite a clever sociable fellow. There is here a store quite well supplied with a

Sioux Camp—Skin Lodges

great variety of goods, most of which are sold at reasonable prices. I purchased of a canadian frenchman a pair of moccasins for one dollar, and sold the same man 6 pounds of coffe (of which I had an over supply) for $1.50. The Fort is situate in the delta formed by the confluence of Laramie River . . . with the Platte, and is surrounded on every side within two miles by high bluffs, so that it is really in a vale—Capt. Ketchum told me that it was perfectly healthy and that he had rather reside there than in any city—but would prefer more society—that there were but two Ladies there—his own wife and that of a private soldier. . . . The Indians which I saw at the Ft. (not more than 50 in all) impressed me very favorably. They are a well formed race—tidy and neat in their dress, and of pleasing expression of countenance. I noticed one party who appeared to be moving and who crossed the ferry. Their goods were neatly packed in buckskin packs clean & nice, and the women were dressed (Indian fashion) very neatly, with abundance of bracelets and ornaments. I noticed also an Indian girl (say 18) and who doubtless thought herself a beauty, riding out in her gala costume her face duly painted with ochre, a branch of a tree in one hand as a parsol and seated *other*wise on her pony in a grand gallop. A large oversupply of provisions had been sent forward by the government to Ft Laramie in anticipation of keeping a larger military force there, than it has finally been deemed necessary to keep—and provisions (Capt Ketchum informed me) the government had ordered him to sell to the emigrants for cost and transportation—and so he is selling them, to the great accommodation of many who found they were getting short. Flour could be had for $10½ per cwt. hams & bacon 15¢—dried fruit 12½¢ per lb—&.c. We did not find it necessary to replenish, having, as we hope quite sufficient."

"I saw a number of Sioux Indians," Edward Kitchell observed on June 11. "They have fine trappings & good horses, are better looking than the Pawnees. They have buggies as well as 'whites.' They take four long poles and lash them to the sides of the horse two on each side & the small ends dragging away behind the horse & about $2\frac{1}{2}$ feet from the tail they tack on a seat & there they ride *a la grande*. I saw several of these buggies.

"Saw several squaws (wives of traders) dressed in calico The fit of their dresses took my eye. They didn't get whale bone out here."

William Cooke went to the fort the same day as did Addison Crane. His wife had been suffering for some weeks from a sore throat and an ulcerous tongue which made it difficult for her to eat: "My dear husband has just been over to the store there to see if he could get anything to benefit me, and bless him, he returned loaded with good things, for which he had to pay exorbitantly. He bought two bottles of lemon syrup at $1.25 each, a can of preserved quinces, chocolate, a box of seidlitz powders, a big packet of nice candy sticks, just the thing for me to keep in my mouth, and several other goodies. Oh, it all seemed a Godsend to me, and I was so careful of everything that I hated myself for my seeming selfishness in not dividing the candy with the children every time they looked anxiously at it. The preserved quinces seemed so grateful to my poor throat, and I took such tiny swallows of them each time, and then hung the can up overhead to the wagon bows. William bought a small bottle of ink also. It was only a ten-cent bottle, but he paid thirty cents for it. He says it's a splendid store over at the Fort, and it was crowded with people, and clerks were as busy as at any large city store."

When the James David company arrived at Fort Laramie on June 12, they began lightening their loads: "All as busy as bees this morning; a general resurrection of California goods. Lightening up everything for the Black Hills. Threw away everything useless. Got everything in order and started on. There is a Ferry opposite the fort above the mouth of Laramie River. . . . This ferry is a very poor concern; some had difficulty in getting over; appears to be badly conducted. . . . The river is deep and narrow and runs very swift.

". . . In the evening in crossing the river the boat came near to sinking, it being rather heavily loaded. There was great stripping of linen and drawing of boots and some pale faces; but finally got over without going down which if we had done, would have been several lives lost."

The next day, June 13, Mrs. Francis Sawyer celebrated her twenty-first birthday, but remained with the wagons and did not visit the fort . . . "I have been in bed most all day, taking a good rest and trying to sleep."

John Udell laid over at Fort Laramie on June 22: "This is my fifty-seventh birth day. I feel that age is creeping on, and I shall soon be in the sere and yellow leaf. Yes, I have lived many days, and have seen good in them all, and though the days of trouble have been many, yet the hand of a merciful Father has conducted me safely through them all. Many, very many, of my fellow mortals die daily on these plains, while my life is spared. Oh may I be duly thankful to him by whose care we live, for his goodness to me, and may I always be endowed with wisdom from his holy word, to guide me in the path of duty."

For seventeen-year-old John Dodson, the most memorable thing about Fort Laramie was: "we went and fixed a swing on a tree and had quite a time of it for the girls were full of life and gaiety."

On June 9, Jared Fox was in the Black Hills: "Camped close on the bank of the Platte. This is the first time I have seen any fog on this river. The other side seems to be lined with teams. Feed not as good tonight. Most of the country between here and the Fort is good for nothing, as I can see plenty of stone in some places but no timber to speak of and the land is not good." But Mrs. Sawyer thought: "The scenery is very beautiful. Pines and cedars are scattered over the hills and beautiful flowers are abundant. I gather tulips and larkspurs and many other lovely kinds that I cannot name."

John Clark of Virginia was one day into the Black Hills on June 13: "To the Lime Kiln Spring, 15 miles. We dine here, then cross over the Sumit of the Black Range that appears full of wild goats or mountain Sheep. They are very wild & dark looking, with enormous horns from the top of the head & branches off in two & falls away back & turns down. From the top of the ridge go down an awful steep through Grannies Gut, a devil of a place with four broken waggons at the foot. We had the wheels all tied & cattle off but one yoke, then the men with ropes to hold back, and a small tree for a draging ancor. Our damage was scattered all the way down. However, we gathered it up with little swearing & drove on to Jacob's Ladder, where we had to wind waggon & teams up with a windless. Here we had to put in the extra lick with whip & hard words to the top of another beautiful slope to Battle Creek & the Devils Kanyan another ferry place above the crossing. High ledge of rock encloses the branch for over a mile with good grass on the narrow flat. We arrive upon the high ground & camp on the open plain where we see wolves walking about at their leisure looking at the boys. Get supper by dark the wolves set their pipes in order & howled loud & long until some of the mules began to bray. Then all was silent."

Lodisia Frizzell crossed this region the same day: "We drove about 10 ms. & encamped in the midst of volcanic hills, no water, not much grass, the soil is thin, the ground is covered with cactus, or prickly pear, the blossom of which is very beautiful of different colors, some pink, some yellow & some red. Here the earth has felt a shock at no very distant period, & by a convulsive throe, these enormous piles of volcanic rocks were upheaved; I went out and climbed upon the top of one of these mountains of red stone sat down, & looked with wonder about, & thought of the dreadful scene which it must have once presented. Then came the question, what has caused the earth to be to its center shook? Sin! the very rocks seemed to reverberate, sin has caused them to be upheaved that they may be eternal monuments of the curse & fall of man; viewing these symbols of divine wrath, I felt humbled; I took a small stone & wrote upon a flat rock beside me, Remember me in mercy O lord. I shall never forget this wild scene, & my thoughts & reflections here."

Illness struck the James David company in the Black Hills: "Taylor was here taken very suddenly and bad with cholera; procured medical aid immediately. Some of our teams left us not wishing to stay; not thinking him sick enough to lay by. We thought hard of them. Now only three teams of us. This was the first sickness we had and we were in hopes it would be the last. Some of the boys are badly scared. The whole theme is to get along and every impediment thrown in the way seems nearly to set the boys crazy. . . . Went into camp as tired as ever I was in my life. Taylor dangerous." David himself became seriously ill the next day, and his journal was largely discontinued.

"Frost. The Buffalo are feeding with the stock, but left on our approach," John Clark of Virginia wrote on June 16. "Just as we start Traxler & Doctor Ferguson died of cholera. We drive on . . . 7 mile. The plain here is somewhat roling, poor & sandy, some sage, but a few miles north appears dark with buffalo. Several of our boys are making for them while the teams are winding up to the top of Hurricane Hill. Desolate & barren looking, with deep & rocky gullies down to the river. Just draw out your glass here & look over the baren waste. For 30 or 40 Miles around not even a bush to be seen, but more Bison than you can possibly count in herds of one and two hundred or more feeding on the flats & sidling ground some few deer & small groups of antelope. Near by me is 12 large Elk, a part of which lies down, while the others watch & feed. The teams are now up & we drive down to Kinney's Run for diner, five miles. Here we find graves & dead stock. The hunters come in with one young antelope & three large sage hens, & we are off to the Diamond Spring, 4 miles. Then over a sandy flat to Dry Creek, 3 mile. Here we camp in good grass & wood. The last two days 9 graves, 3 waggons, & 11 steers."

Alpheus Graham was nearing Mormon Ferry on June 19: "Laramies peak in sight yet. 10 miles of sand today. About 10

[148]

o'clock we ascend a high hill from which I had a view of the Rocky Mountains in all their glory. Their snow peaks rising heavenward off to the north as far as mans eye could see. I now begin to think my boyish dreams are soon to be fulfilled. How often when a schoolboy have I dreamed of roaming amid the snow caped peaks of the Father of Mountains. Well, now I see them. Just befor me as it were but we are separated by 160 long miles, and I am so weak I could not climb the smallest mountain if I had the opportunity. This afternoon we struck the Platt river for the last time. Soon after we drove down to the river we saw a man floating down stream, Schuyler Fowler swam in and brought him to shore. He was dressed in a silk shirt and drawers. A whiplash tied around his body, the stok of which hung loose, has two brass rings on his left hand. one marked with the letters F.W. and a heavy gold ring on his right hand but his fingers were so swollen that we could but get one of them off, which we will preserve for identification. We are of the opinion that he has been killed and thrown in the river, his body and head having the appearance of bruises on them. We buried him on the bank of the river where we took him out." John Clark of Virginia, at the Mormon Ferry, reported that three men were drowned that morning, so the body found by the Graham party may have been one of the victims.

Reports of a murder reached Enoch Conyers on June 22, twenty miles west of Fort Laramie: "At this camp an emigrant, who with his wife was traveling with another family, murdered the man and his wife. He then took possession of the man's team, clothing and provisions and with his wife started on their return trip for the Missouri River. They reported to emigrants who inquired of them the reason of their turning back that he and his wife had become discouraged and concluded they would go no further. Within a day or two the dead bodies of the murdered couple were discovered in the brush near where they had camped. The officers at Fort Laramie were immediately notified of the murder. Suspicion rested on the couple who had turned back, and the commander sent a squad of soldiers in pursuit, who soon overtook and apprehended the murderers. We heard later that they were tried at Fort Laramie on the charge of murder, convicted and hanged."

Another murder was reported in the *Northwestern Gazette*, August 10, the news having been brought by a returned Californian: "An inhuman and treble murder is supposed to have been committed at a point about 60 miles above Laramie, on the north side of the river. On June 10, a lady, supposed to be about 30 years old, was found lying dead with her throat cut, and horribly mangled. Her hair was of an auburn color, her front teeth decayed, and upon her finger a gold ring, marked on the inside 'W.E.' and is now in the possession of E. Haway, formerly of Wisconsin, now in California, the gentleman who discovered and buried the corpse. She appeared to have been recently murdered.

"On the 20th, within a short distance of the same place, the bodies of a man supposed to have been 30 or 35 years old, and a boy eight or ten, both also having their throats cut, and the man had his skull entirely broken to pieces. The bodies of both were found in a slough, partially covered with logs and chunks. The man was of moderate size, sandy complexion and whiskers, heavy brown hair—was dressed in satinet pants, hickory shirt, dark vest and coarse boots. The boy sandy complexion, heavy red hair, had on a grey runabout, black cassimere vest, colored cassimere pants striped. No papers or other property to identify. All of them were supposed to belong to one family, and it is also supposed they were murdered by the men whom they were taking through, as a family of the above description, with good teams, taking three men to California, is remembered by some emigrants."

On July 2, Samuel Chadwick heard of this murder or one very much like it: ". . . there was another man and his son killed they had their throats cut and put behind a pile of brush it was a man that they Was taking through that did it he then sold the mans teams and waggon to the indians and french and started back east but the waggon was saw going back with the indians by some persons that knew it and then coming where the dead persons was and hearing of it the indians was followed and overhauled and they said they had bought the team of such a man and they followed the man back and found him before he got a great ways and fetched him back and hung him on a tree and left him there putting up a board . . . marked fresh meat to sell. . . ."

The rough stony road over the Black Hills was very hard on oxen's hooves, and Enoch Conyers described a means of curing them: "Quite a number of cattle in our company are getting lame by traveling over hot, sandy and stony roads, but we very soon cure them up in the following manner: we cut a piece of hide from a dead ox by the roadside; making small holes in the border of this piece of hide; through these holes we run a string or a narrow strip of hide for a drawstring; we then put this piece of hide on the lame oxen's feet, flesh side out, drawing the string tight enough to hold it on the foot, and then tie it fast. This completes the job. Two days' wear is sufficient for a cure."

Addison Crane, who had a wagon and a cart, stopped over on Sunday, June 13: "Packed our wagon and cart load together, and abandoned the hind axle tree and wheels of the wagon (which showed symptoms of giving out and have been running out of gear for some days) and put the cart axle and wheels in their place. This, with the work of packing and repacking—and remodeling the box of the wagon has made it necessary for me to work today, which I should much preferred not to have done.

"Completed this and at 5 P.M. went down to the river with soap and towel, clean shirt and socks, washed thoroughly and having shaved felt quite regenerated. One accumulates a great quantity of dirt about on these dusty roads. We all abandon here all our rubber clothes, and several other things, to make the load light as possible. Our rubbers have not been of much

[151]

use. We could have got along very well without them. I find the 'pilot bread' hard stuff very little nutriment in it, and we shall hereafter have warm biscuit when we can. Mr Merriweather (one of our Co.) gave me a sack of flour to day (100 lbs) he having more than he could use—He would take no pay for it—quite generous, as it could have been sold for $12 to $15. I believe however it is considered out of character for any one to sell any provisions to any person in the same train—but if he has any over it is considered common property."

The Cooke family laid over this same Sunday: "My dear husband had a bad toothache yesterday, and today his face is hidiously swollen and he feels miserably. So now it's my turn to be nurse. I let him have his breakfast in bed, and made him some cornstarch porridge. We have had quite a busy day in airing things in the wagons, for Sunday is the only chance we get for such work. The men mostly do their washing that day. We have just had supper, consisting of fish, rice, tomatoes and ham, with hot bread and tea.

"I drink chocolate since I have been sick; I enjoy it better. I am using a gargle now of sage tea, with borax, alum and sugar, and it is a great benefit. I wonder it never occurred to use it before, as the wild sage is abundant.

"We have been bathing today. 'Sissy' enjoys it so much, and seems ready for a dash whenever we see water."

Mrs. Frizzell was a day east of Mormon Ferry on June 16: "Where we nooned today, as we started out, we saw some men on the opposite side of the river chasing a buffalo, which on coming to the river, plunged in, & made for our side; the men gathered their guns, ran for the bank, stationed themselves by some trees, the buffalo coming to a sandbar in the middle of the river, halted a while, & those on the other shore, poured out upon him a shower of bullets. I looked for him to fall every moment, but they overshot him, for their balls struck the water on this side; a dog was sent into the river, he made for the buffalo, & seizing him by the tail, he made for our shore & as he neared it, the dog still hanging to his tail, & swimming, as

[152]

he rose upon the bank, he commenced to gallop away, when several guns were discharged at him, he halted, one lead entered the seat of life, the red blood spouted from his side; an ounce & a half ball from Georges double barrel shot gun, had done the deed; he walked on a little farther to some water, went into it, fell down, struggled & died in a few minutes. Twenty men with as many knives in as many minutes, had him in pieces ready for the stewkettle. One old mountaineer made choice of a *delicate* part, observing that no one would probably quarrel with him for his (part) piece. He was a fine male buffalo, eight years old (judging from his horns) hair short, & nearly black. I never saw a more noble looking animal, his eye looked green & firy in death, such strength did his enormous neck & great muscles exhibit, that all wished they had a team like him. All repaired to their tents, to have a feast. . . . we jerked most of our meat, baked, boiled & fried some; it was fine beef, some said it was better than any beef they had ever eat."

On June 14 Addison Crane received information concerning the number of teams on the road. In the afternoon he passed a company packing from Oregon, who said they had passed a large emigration ahead, and in the evening there was "encamped near us . . . a man with his wife & a child or two —horse team who had come through very quick from Council Bluffs—and has of course passed all the ox teams on the route. He reports the emigration in our rear as tremendous—Says he frequently passed solid processions of wagons three miles long —and often 3 wagons abreast—whipping their oxen swearing and scolding along—and expressed his belief that there are 15,000 wagons in our rear! At about 50 miles from here both the trails, (north and south side of the Platte) come together on this side and so continue for about 250 miles when the Oregon trail . . . leaves. During this 250 miles we shall probably have from 3500 to 4000 wagons—comprising perhaps 40,000 head of cattle horses and mules in advance of us, and shall no doubt be moving in and encamping with and near large trains

[153]

and processions, and I shall not be disappointed if we see some hard times for grass."

John Clark of Virginia passed the Mormon Ferry on June 19: "Here we found over one hundred waggons on the south side waiting their turn to cross. . . . The ferry men tell us the income per day during the emigration is from 15 to 18 hundred dollars. . . . This morning a difficulty occurd in crossing that led to a fight in the boat. One was killed while three were knocked overboard & drowned. One of the proprietors told me that over 2100 waggons had already crosd & he thought quite as many more had gone up our side, the north. Quite a number of indian lodges or wigwams are stuck up about the crossing. They are Crows. Men & women large & savage looking, big mouth & not dark, at that. Whiskey is selling here for six dollars the gallon. Bear & Buffalo meat one cent the pound from the tribe. We saw all round the encampment, bot our jug of whiskey, & followed up the train."

Jared Fox was at Mormon Ferry on June 10: "Fair—some wind. . . . Boys killed a buffalo fat as mud and some of the beef made me some broth which done me much good. Sick are gaining. The Elkhorn, Wisconsin Company passed. I saw Bradley of Elkhorn and wife. Had been sick but better now. Started at 10 minutes past noon. Went through mud where the river had flowed over the road. The wind blew a gale and had to stop and turn to it, deep sand in the road and the sand and dust blew so we could not go or see. Made 15 miles. 1 dead horse and 1 dead ox, 1 ox turned out to die, a large number of gun barrels, some waggon irons, a number of oxyokes and irons, etc."

Lewis Stout summed up the feelings of many emigrants on June 30: "Left the Platte River for good, none of us shedding any tears, for we were all tired of it. We have traveled up it 750 miles and longed for a change."

VI

FROM MORMON FERRY
TO SOUTH PASS

———◆◄●►◆———

AFTER passing Mormon Ferry the road divided—one trail
following a short way along the Platte River, the other
leaving the river and going over Rattlesnake Hill. The two
roads rejoined before reaching Willow Spring, and on both it
was a hard drive of thirty miles without good water. Addison
Crane took the river road on June 18: "The country through

which we have passed 12 miles to writing this is most barren & desolate Next to no grass at all The wagons cattle, horsemen and droves now form an almost continuous procession. There is no getting by them or around them—and no end to them as far as the vision can extend. Among this great crowd we are destined to move for the next 10 days and happy and thankful shall we be if our cattle do not famish for want of grass. The prospect now is exceedingly gloomy. . . . (Evening) The roads to day have been hard and good passing among and along the ravines of, and over the bluff hills—and the heat & dust in such a large emigration has been almost intolerable. In this heat and dust our cattle have been compelled to travel twelve hours without stopping, the distance of 27 miles without water. Many oxen in other trains dropped down in their yokes—our stood it through—but staggered towards the last. We took Platte River water along in our cans for drinking. Encamped tonight near Willow Springs—most excellent pure cold water —and from the waters of which our cattle satiated their thirst —but we could find no grass, worth the name for the poor animals—and they had to content themselves with the few scattering spears which could be found among the wild sage & other weeds. The country all day has presented a most desolate appearance."

Jared Fox went over Rattlesnake Hill on June 11: "A good deal of uphill but roads fine. Towards noon wind rose right in our eye and the dust flew thick to suffocation. Drove 30 miles without grass or water and when we got to water the wind blew a perfect gale. the spring small and 6 or 8 feet down the bank and 30 or 40 to dip out of it and dust drifting in from the top till it was thick and man and beast so choked up with dust we could hardly see or swallow. This was a lifter to our teams. Some 3 miles further we got a little grass making 33 miles in all today. I see that others had made up their minds here that times were hard for here were lots of waggon irons, stoves, and furniture, overcoats, bed clothes, 1 bed of feathers, hats, coats, boots, and all sorts. Bones and graves. Passed several graves today but to dusty we don't know how many."

Richard Owen Hickman commented on the abandoned possessions scattered all along the Platte River: "Along that stream there was old clothes of every description, and there was towels, gowns and hairpins strewed all along the road from the time we struck till we left the river, and books of every sort and size from Fanny Hill to the Bible."

On June 23, John Hawkins Clark made his way from the Platte to Willow Springs: "From this point to the topmost heights of the Rocky mountains is our next stage of travel; the road takes immediately to the high lands. We go up, up, up; for seven long miles, a dreary, desolate region, innocent of any kind of vegetation that can in any way be made available for food for our hungry teams; this is called 'rattle-snake hill,' but why so called I am unable to say; we saw none; it would be very hard on the snake if he was obliged to make this hill a home. After traveling eight or ten miles the road becomes crooked, rough and flinty; the face of the country a broken mass of natural ruins; colonades of stone from four to twenty feet in height, and six to ten feet square, dot the earth in a straight and continuous line for miles. What freaks of nature, or what time in the world's past history these rocks had been so placed, would be hard for the average California pilgrim to determine. 'Avenue of Rocks' is another curiosity; a range of rocks describing a half circle with a gateway through which the immigration has to pass on its way to what it hopes to be, a better land beyond.

"This is the land of the mirage, of 'delusions,' of the sage brush, and the alkali waters; a land of wonders and of hardships; a land to be avoided or left behind as soon as possible. Saw many dead cattle on the road; the poisonous water and the great scarcity of feed begins to tell on the poor brutes. Passed many graves on our journey of thirty miles, the biggest day's work we have as yet accomplished. Eleven o'clock P.M.

[157]

and we are in camp at 'Willow Springs' a name suggestive of a more cheerful outlook than any other place we have seen to-day. This is the first good camping ground since leaving the Platte river; there are a great many here and still they come, for come they must, as no good water can be had for thirty long miles over the road traveled; at least we could find none."

Caroline Richardson took the river road on June 19: "we traveled about eighteen miles and came to the mineral waters this water is thought to be very poisonous but we have seen no effects of it yet excepting a dog who was bathing himself in it he seemed to enjoy the bath but he soon commenced howling and panting most furiously the water looks clear temting the thirsty traveler to stop and take a cooling draught but no sooner it is disturbed than it turns black and becomes a deadly poison this after noon we have seen its effects quite a number of cattle that have drunk of it were left on the road to die as recovery is impossible. . . ."

". . . a great many are camped here to-night," Lodisia Frizzell wrote on June 19, "it had the appearance of a large town, & in a tent near by ours, they were fiddling & dancing, nearly all night; this was the first dancing I had seen on the plains. . . . but there had been so much sickness on the Platte, that perhaps they were rejoicing that they had left it."

The Hanna train laid over on June 22: "Two of our men went hunting, brought back 2 hares and a sage hen. . . . They are in every respect like our domestic hen, excepting the head is not quite the same shape, and the color is much the same as a pheasant. The meat is dark-colored and very good. The hare is delicious, as white and finely flavored as chicken. One of my neighbors has a churn and makes a quantity of butter. She kindly sent me a slice with which I dressed our game."

Camped a few miles west of Mormon Ferry on June 16, Richard Hickman's party received a gift of buffalo from a nearby train: "After getting supper ready we all sat down expecting to have a good supper off of buffalo beef, and indeed some were afraid they would not get enough and helped themselves to two pieces, but was soon satisfied that one was as much as they could get through with, for some of them run their fingers down their throats, but the old fellow had become sullen and refused to obey the call. It happened that the old veteran was of the masculine gender and in the possessive case, as the meat possessed the most disagreeable odor and taste of anything of the meat kind I have ever come up with yet; so after cooking some antelope we made out our supper. I made out to swallow some of the buffalo merely for the sake of saying I had eaten of buffalo. Some of the boys could not wait till they got through supper to throw it away, and it was not to be wondered at."

On June 24, John Hawkins Clark left Willow Spring: "While traveling over a heavy sandy road to-day saw immediately in front of us, a beautiful tree fringed lake whose tiny waves broke upon a shore of clean white sand, a strip of green verdure in front and on either side of this beautiful vision, stretching far and wide, were 'greener fields and pastures new' in beautiful contrast to the dreary plain over which we are now toiling. No pilgrim to the shrine of the Prophet. No crusader to the Holy Land. No prodigal son returning to the comforts of a distant home, were more eager than ourselves to enjoy the comforts, the luxuries and the pleasures so soon to be ours. But alas, the beautiful scenery before us vanished in a moment, and 'Like the fleeting spirit of a dream' was gone forever. A treeless, waterless waste, and a weary road, was now all that greeted our saddened eyes. 'That weary road' we followed to a cheerless camp, where water, wood and grass were conspicuously absent."

When the emigrants came to the Sweetwater River, they saw one of the most famous landmarks on the overland trail— Independence Rock, a huge granite outcropping covered with the names of thousands of mountain men, traders, and emigrants. The Cookes arrived on June 19: "Most of our party added their names to those already there. . . . My dear William, however, refrained, saying it looked too much like hard work to climb the rough rock barefooted for the sake of passing his name to the future."

"Rock Independence and the Sweetwater river are eight miles in the advance," John Hawkins Clark wrote on June 25; "some of us started on ahead to get a view of this celebrated rock. Saleratus lake lies on our way; it is merely a mud hole of some four or five acres across in extent. The water has fallen by evaporation and left a crust of four or five inches of crude saleratus of a yellowish color, and, like the desert around it, had a forbidding appearance. . . . The great rock lies just beyond us and we were eager to get upon its back. This great boulder is all in one piece. . . . It is oval on top and is of easy access; we were soon upon its back. The view from this elevation is a very extensive one; if we look toward the east we can trace our line of travel for thirty miles over an unbroken wilderness waste, a desert plain abounding in alkali lakes, poisonous unto death to whatever living thing may partake of their waters. The bones of hundreds of cattle lie strewn here and there over this pestilential district. . . . As there are generally two sides to the same story, so there are two different views from the top of this great rock, we will now look forward and as it is the direction we have to travel, may see something more cheerful to contemplate.

"Do you see yon huge range of mountains some four or five miles to the west? Well, do you see that it is split asunder from the bottom to the top, a narrow and perpendicular opening of some 400 feet through solid granite rock? that little opening is called the 'Devil's Gate.' By looking very closely at the bottom of that opening you can descern a little silvery thread of water issuing from it. Now follow it down as it winds from side to side through green meadows; as it approaches the great rock upon which you stand; it is now almost beneath your feet, but still follow it; is it not beautiful as it pursues its 'winding way' through the strip of green verdure which line its banks until it is lost to view behind that bare and rugged mountain which borders the head waters of the Platte. . . . I hardly know of a

[160]

Devil's Gate on the Sweetwater

[161]

more interesting spot than that on the top of Rock Independence. It is upon this elevation that one gets such a view of mountain, plain and river; such mountains, such plains and such a river are not frequently to be seen.

"There were many persons upon this rock when we visited it; some musician had brought a violin and discoursed sweet music to those who participated in a dance upon this mountain stone."

This same day Esther Hanna passed the rock and camped a mile beyond. There a member of the company died and was buried the next day: "This morning we consigned the remains of the departed to their last resting place close by the rock. We sang a hymn and Mr. H. offered up a prayer before the corpse was moved. He was buried with the clothes on that he died in, then wrapped in his bed and quilts. It seemed so hard for anyone to be buried so but it was all that could be done under the circumstances. The name of the deceased was James Briggs, 18 years old from Illinois. It wrung our hearts to resume our journey, leaving one of our little colony behind."

Near Independence Rock there was a crude ferry over the Sweetwater, although usually the river was low enough to ford. Jared Fox on June 12: "Crossed the Sweetwater on 12 old logs pinned together. Paid .40 cts. each wagon and done all the work ourselves. Swam and forded our horses. . . . Plenty of bones and irons of the other companies in other days which to me looked sorry but others did not seem to mind."

Enoch Conyers passed Independence Rock on July 2, and after adding his name to the multitude already there: ". . . one would naturally suppose that every man, woman and child that ever passed this way had succeeded in writing or having their names written on this rock. . . . came five and a quarter miles to the 'Devil's Gate,' which is something grand—perpendicular rocks of granite formation touring up 400 feet high on either side of the river, and the Sweetwater running between, having cut its way through this granite formation for about 1,000 feet in length, and about 130 feet in breadth."

"This morning after we started part of our company, myself included, determined to go to the top of the rock to have a better view of the Devils Gate," began R. H. P. Snodgrass' entry for June 8. "We soon found it necessary to haul our boots to make it anything like safe work to make the summit. We all arrived safe. Here for half an hour we amused ourselves tossing rocks down & hearing the echo. An adventerous Kentuckian lost one of his boots over into the stream, and as he was some ways behind his train he had to move along on one boot & one sock, much to the amusement of his companions."

"After supper last evening myself and a companion concluded to go down and get a closer view of the Devil's Gate," John Hawkins Clark wrote on June 26. "After walking a mile, fording the river and floundering over great rocks and small ones, came to the great gap, which is in the neighborhood of fifty yards wide, 400 feet in height and one-third of a mile through. The low tide in the river at this time enabled us, by leaping from rock to rock, to reach the center of the passage. Weird, grand and gloomy rose the huge walls on either side, while the little river, mad and furious, went tearing, hissing and foaming between the great angular rocks that had from time to time fallen from above and which now lay partly submerged beneath the angry waters, producing a noise, confused and tumultuous that would have rivaled pandemonium itself. . . . It was only by the light of the friendly moon that we found our way out of this misnamed wonder—the Devil's Gate.

"Why this great opening should be so called I cannot comprehend; the very name suggests something uncomfortable, and an uneasiness that many do not care to contemplate. While we were within those walls no odor of sulphur was perceptible; no grumbling or suffering humanity was heard; the master of the house, if there was any, was conspicuously absent; no inscription over the door warning all who would enter to 'leave hope behind.' On the contrary, the air is cool and refreshing; the establishment well ventilated; a full supply of water; with a healthy drainage of all the surplus. No power, but the power of the rod with which Moses smote the rock in the wilderness, could have sundered this great mountain and made it one of the wonders of the great American desert."

Independence Rock

On the day he passed Independence Rock, Addison Crane: "Met the mail from Salt Lake on our drive. It goes in a very light wagon, drawn by 4 mules and one mule in the lead. Two men. They move in a trot, and I suppose have fresh teams about once a week, at the Forts. They average over 40 mi. per day. . . ." And later in the day at Devil's Gate: "At this point we found a traders tent and express office where a man could be relieved of money for quite a small consideration. They charge 50¢ per letter upon the pretence of taking them back to the States—but all they really do with the letters is keep them until the Salt Lake mail comes along and then hand them over to the driver, to be deposited in the nearest P.O. according to

[164]

law. This I ascertained is the course they take—one of their men unwittingly remarked that they sent of[f] their letters last night, & knowing the mormon mail must have passed there then, we having met it early this morning, upon being questioned he admitted he sent by that. Of course they got no letter or half dollar from me, as I did not wish to entrust my journal to any such jockeying concern."

John Clark of Virginia camped near Devil's Gate on June 22, and the next day was enough to try any man: "Just before day we thought from the noise that the devil & the rocks were upon us. Our stock, with two or three hundred others belonging to other trains, took a stampede & made a thundering rush right for our waggons & tents. But accidently they took a shear & mist us all. But one waggon & tent broken down. It was late in the morning before all was right. We took two wheels from the broken waggon & made a cart for Young & his mohala. This morning a difficulty arose between the passengers, and this Mr. Young & lady from St. Louis belonging to our train was thrown out and left to join another Company. One of our men, a Mr. Sidney, is very sick—mountain feever. Two of our wagons lay by for him while the rest drive on for better feed. From this to Mudy Run, 8 miles. Here we broke down one of our waggons; however we draged it 2 miles to a grassy flat where we dine & leave the waggon for the next train just behind us. In driving across the Mudy Run, or slew where we broke down, the driver of Dunmore's wagon broke the tongue. This agravated Dunmore so he drew his pistol & shot Dunbar dead. He was tried & hung on our old waggon at sundown."

Devil's Gate may have been more aptly named than John Hawkins Clark believed, for only five days later, June 28, it was the scene of another tragedy to which Dr. John Dalton briefly alluded the following day: "This day came to two graves where Horace Dolly had killed Chas Botsford yesterday by shooting and for which the Company killed said Dolly today, by hanging. Said Dolly had a wife and two children along in the train and was the principal owner of the train."

Lucy Cooke, along with "Ma, Lillie, William . . . and two or three of our young men," visited Devil's Gate on June 19: "When we left the 'Devil's Gate' it was about noon. We had to walk a distance before we overtook our wagon, which was awaiting us. Many tents were pitched on the banks of the Sweetwater, and we expected our company to be there. But not seeing them, we enquired at different camps, and each told us our folks had gone past between eleven and twelve o'clock, so were ahead. We therefore drove on and on, looking eagerly this side and the other. Meantime our appetites admonished us that it was a long time since breakfast, and seldom did we carry food in our wagon, and this was the first time we had wandered away from our food supply. Well, on and on we rode, till we felt pretty certain our folks must have turned off the road, and consequently were behind us. But each company we passed said, 'No, they were ahead.' . . . Well we drove about ten miles in all, and saw no signs of them. Had nothing to eat, and it was now near five o'clock. So we made our case known to and accepted the offer of a company called the 'Bull Heads' (which sign was painted on their canvas covers) to camp with them that night, though it seemed a strange experience to be lost on such a journey. But so it was.

". . . Well you may be sure we were glad of our suppers, and they freely gave us of their fare. I ate biscuit, rice, stewed apples and tea, then felt refreshed and better. The young men seemed a fine set of fellows, and enjoying their trip. One of our young men concluded to make further efforts to find our company, . . . and at length reached Perrin's company, and on entering camp found Pa there and our cook, eating supper, but most dead with fatigue. All were astonished at thus meeting. It appears Pa and the cook had visited 'Devil's Gate' early in the morning, and then they followed along the road, and each time they enquired for our company they were told, as we had been, that they were ahead. . . .

"Then they met a man who said our tents were two miles back, so back they trudged; but at length they stumbled on

Perrin's camp, which they had not seen for two or three weeks, and here it was our young man met with them, and then it was found in distance only about a mile from us to the 'Bull Head' company. So after supper Pa walked over to fetch Ma, Lill and Richard to share Mrs. Perrin's hospitality. But William, myself and the two young men remained till next morning with our new friends, who at night amused themselves with dancing, in which William joined as heartily as any. Their cook on the previous day had found a bundle of woman's clothing, which he put on and had worn it all day, sun-bonnet and all, which had caused considerable merriment all along the road. So when dancing came off at night there was a grand demand for this lady partner. So William came to where I was gone to bed (on the ground, by the way) and took my saque, dress and sun-bonnet to wear. What guys the two did look. But they all seemed to enjoy it, and I was amused till after dark looking at them."

After passing Devil's Gate, one of the oxen in the Conyers train died from drinking alkali water, and they made the acquaintance of a French trader named Schambeau: "About fifteen minutes before old Dick died, this man, Schambeau, stepped up and inquired: 'Who does that ox belong to?' On being informed that he belonged to Mr. Burns, he said: 'Well, had I been here twenty minutes sooner I would have saved that ox for you. He has been alkalied.' Then he added: 'When I was with Fremont, we lost quite a number of our oxen before we discovered a remedy, but afterward we never lost a single head by poison or alkali.' The following is the remedy he gave us: 'Take one-half pint each of lard and syrup; warm just sufficiently to mix good, and if the animal is bloated, add to this one-half pint of good vinegar and drench them immediately.' This recipe proved a sovereign remedy, and we lost no more cattle."

Schambeau, who was building a trading post near Devil's Gate, told them there was good grass and water in a small valley four miles to the south: ". . . we found the very best of grass, over knee high, and a creek of splendid ice-cold water. Here we camp and intend staying until after the glorious 4th. This is a beautiful little valley, almost surrounded with mountains, with a rich fertile soil, and room enough for four or five good farms."

On July 3: "Several of the boys started out this morning for a hunt in the mountains for the purpose of obtaining some fresh meat, if possible, for our Fourth of July dinner. Those who remain in camp are helping the ladies in preparing for the banquet. A number of wagon beds are being taken to pieces and formed into long tables. A little further on is a group of young ladies seated on the grass talking over the problem of manufacturing 'Old Glory' to wave over our festivities. The question arose as to where we are to obtain the material for the flag. One lady brought forth a sheet. This gave the ladies an idea. Quick as thought another brought a skirt for the red stripes. Now we have the white and the red for the stripes, but where will we get the blue for the field? Another lady ran to her tent and brought forth a blue jacket, saying: 'Here take this, it will do for the field.' Needles and thread were soon secured and the ladies went at their task with a will, one lady remarking that 'Necessity is the mother of invention,' and the answer came back, 'Yes, and the ladies of our company are equal to the task.' Some of the boys were gathering wood to cook the dinner, and others went after a liberty pole. In fact, every member of our company took hold with a willing hand to make our celebration on the plains a grand success. The boys who went out hunting early this morning returned to camp about 3 o'clock in the afternoon, some loaded with antelope, some with sagehens, and some with jackrabbits. Others brought a huge snowball, inserting a pole through the center the easier to carry it. The game was quickly dressed and made ready for the cook, and the cooking was carried on to a late hour in the night. All being in readiness for the morrow, we retired to rest.

"July 4—Sunday.—The day was ushered in with the booming of small arms, which was the best that we could do under the circumstances, so far away from civilization. Although the noise was not so great as that made by a cannon, yet it answered the purpose. Just before the sun made its appearance above the eastern horizon, we raised our forty-foot flagstaff with 'Old Glory' nailed fast to the top, which waved as majestically and graceful as though it had been made of the best Japan silk. After the flagstaff was raised to its position our company circled around the old flag and sung 'The Star Spangled Banner.' Then three rousing cheers and a tiger were given to 'Old Glory.' The question came up, To whom should the honor be given to deliver the oration? This honor fell to the lot of Virgil Y. Ralston, a son of Dr. J. N. Ralston, of Quincy, Ill., and an old schoolmate of your humble servant. Unfortunately he, with several other young men of our company, went this morning to the Devil's Gate, where they obtained a little too much 'firewater,' and by the time they reached the camp were considerably under its influence. But this was the glorious old Fourth, therefore the oration we must have. The Declaration of Independence was read by R. L. Doyle, of Keokuk, Ia., after which several of the boys gathered around Virgil, lifting him bodily upon the end of one of our long tables, where they steadied him until he became sufficiently braced up, and then let go of him. He spoke for over half an hour, and delivered, off-hand, an excellent oration. Just after the oration there came up a storm that threatened to spoil all our fun, but fortunately it lasted only a very short time. All gathered around the tables loaded with refreshments, beautified and decorated with evergreens and wild flowers of the valley, that speak volumes in behalf of the good taste displayed by the ladies, both in the decorative and culinary art. The following is our bill of fare in part:

MEATS

Roast Antelope, Roast Sagehen, Roast Rabbit, Antelope Stew,
Sagehen Stew, Jack-Rabbit Stew, Antelope Potpie,
Sagehen Fried, Jack Rabbit Fried.

[169]

Irish Potatoes (Brought from Illinois), Boston Baked Beans,
Rice, Pickles.

BREAD

White Bread, Graham Bread, Warm Rolls, fresh from the oven.

PASTRY

Pound Cake, Fruit Cake, Jelly Cake, Sweetwater Mountain Cake,
Peach Pie, Apple Pie, Strawberry Pie, Custard Pie.

DRINKS

Coffee, Tea, Chocolate, and Good, Cold Mountain Water,
fresh from the brook.
The snowball was brought into use in making a fine lot of
Sweetwater Mountain ice cream.

"No person left the table hungry. After our feast patriotic
songs were indulged in, winding up with three cheers for
Uncle Sam and three for Old Glory. Of course, the ladies were
not forgotten, and three rousing cheers were given for them.
Take it all together, we passed an enjoyable day—a Fourth of
July on the plains never to be forgotten."

Mary Stuart Bailey, two days travel east of Conyer's company, wrote this day: "It is windy cold & somewhat inclined to
rain—not pleasant—rather a dreary Independent day—We
speak of our friends at home. We think they are thinking of us
—'Home sweet home,' I dare not think of it while so far away.
the hundreds of Dear Friends, so dear to me from whom I
have been a long, long time separated—they now find an easy
access & a gratefull admission into my heart—It is so sad to
think that every day takes me farther from them."

The region around Devil's Gate seemed to have a special
affinity for violence. On July 5 the Conyers train left the site of
their celebration: "At about 11 A.M. we passed the camp where
on Saturday, July 3, some emigrants hung a man for murder.

We did not learn the names. The company chose a judge to preside over the trial, and a sheriff, who empaneled a jury of twelve men, who heard all the evidence, after which the judge charged the jury. The jury retired a short distance from camp, under the charge of the sheriff chosen by the company for the emergency, for their deliberation. In about twenty minutes they returned and informed the court that they had decided on a verdict. The foreman then handed their written verdict to the court, which read as follows: 'We, the jury, do find the defendant guilty of murder in the first degree, as charged.' Signed by all the jurors. The court immediately passed sentence on the defendant, to be hanged by the neck until dead, dead, dead, and may God have mercy on your soul. The company ran two wagons together, elevating the tongues in the shape of a letter 'A,' tying them together. On this improvised gallows the defendant was hung until life was pronounced extinct. Near by two graves were dug, one for the murdered man, the other for the murderer. Their burial being completed, the company started on their way."

The Mormon Council Point Emigrating Company, traveling along the Sweetwater from August 20 to 26, recorded an unhappy time of dying cattle and dissension: "August 20th Friday. After the wagon of J. W. Vance had been repaired we moved out and had not gone far before a Cow belonging to F. J. Daves gave out and died. As soon as we camped this evening an ox of James Porter died. This afternoon while traveling over a heavy sandy road one of the boys of David Nelson fell out of the wagon and the wheel went over him but inconsequence of it been in the sand he was not hurt so bad as was supposed to be.

"August 21st Saturday. This morning another ox belonging to Phillip Armstead died supposed by partaking of Saleratious. Captain Tidwell solicited help from the people for William Clark in the lone of an ox for a few days until his got better which is sick but no one rendered help. So we put out and traveled some short distance when William Clarks sick ox was not able to work. Capt. Tidwell seeing this stoped the company and again solicited help for W. C. some tried to raise a contention but was sharply reproved by Captain Tidwell but when the request that was made came to the ear of Phillip Armstead he nobely said they might have his ox although his team was almost unable to haul himself. We had not gone much farther before Captain Tidwell had to leave an yearling heiffer which soon after died. . . .

"August 22nd It froze so hard the previous night that large junks of [ice were] found in some of the pots this morning and another ox was dead. . . .

"August 23rd An ox was found dead belonging to John Eldredge and also a stag belonging to Martha D. Howland. . . . as soon as we arrived into camp the first thing that saluted our ears was that Captain John M. King had deserted his Ten and the company and had gone an head. It was said by W. C. Dunbar that he came out and said that he was going upon his own responsibility and would not be answerable for another mans sins. It is well known unto most of the company that he has been harping with a contentious spirit ever since we was reorganized at the cold springs the other side of the Missiourie River

"August 24th Tuesday. . . . The Second Wing then went out and left on the ground two dead oxen. . . . About an hour after we also put out and left one ox dying belonging to William Clark. . . .

"August 25th This mo[rning a] meeting was called and the following arrangements was made respecting the hauling of freight for William Clark as one of his oxen was dead and the other sick so he had nothing but a yoke of cows it was so managed for the brethren to haul his freight and let his own wagon go to brother Armstead as it was lighter than his own. . . .

"August 26th Thursday. . . . also this morning a cow of Martha D. Howland died of partaking of saleratious. . . ."

Although the Council Point Company had a harder time of it along the Sweetwater than most, the poor grass and the dangers of alkali poisoning the stock told on everyone's nerves. "About noon we passed a train that had stopped for lunch by the roadside," noted Enoch Conyers on July 6. "Just as we came abreast of them we observed three men seated on the tongue of one of their wagons, when a large-sized woman, weighing something over 250 pounds, with sleeves rolled up above her elbows, stepped out in front of the three men, smacking her fists and shaking them under the nose of the little man seated in the center, as though she intended leaving nothing but a great spot after she got through with him. Then she commenced a harangue of abusive language that ought to shame the most profane person on the face of the earth. This little man she dominated was her husband. She berated him for everything that was good, bad or indifferent, charging him with bringing his wife and children out to this God-forsaken country to starve and die. To the honor of the little man, I will say, that he sat there like a bump on a log, seemingly taking it all good-naturedly, without making any answer whatever. Perhaps he was afraid to open his mouth in self-defense, and that silence was the better part of valor. This much I have learned since I started across the continent. That if there is anything in the world that will bring to the surface a man's bad traits, it is a trip across the continent with an ox team. In honor and justice to our little family, I must say that we have thus far gotten along together splendidly, without any display whatever, more especially since scenes as we have witnessed by the roadside today. And the school of experience which we are daily passing through, witnessing scenes so repulsive and disgusting, would almost drive one to believe that the whole human race, with but few exceptions, were hypocrites."

Along the Sweetwater the emigrants encountered new Indian tribes. The John Kerns train, on July 5, passed a band of nearly 500 Shawnees and "they all possess a good countenance, both as to intelligence and neatness. They lack nothing considering their station." Three days later the party went hunting and shot six antelope. "While out enjoying our hunt,

Snake Indians of Utah

some 300 or 400 Snake Indians came and pitched camp 200 or 300 yards below ours on the same branch, alarming the few at camp very much. We soon all were in camp, however, and watched the motions of the rascals close. . . . All well, but somewhat uneasy with, or on account of so many Indians near."

The John Lewis company had traveled as far as the Sweet-water without ever having posted guards at night, and on July 18, seven of their horses were missing—run off by Indians, they feared. They were wrong, and the horses were found ten or twelve miles from camp; but they decided they should have guards from then on: ". . . so when night come lots was cast to see who should stand the first night & it fell on me & N. R. for another just the one I wanted for I knew that an Indian co[u]ld not git to camp without us nowing some thing about it but for the first thing we got a wagon wheele and laid it on some pices over a ditch then piled the hub with dry pine & set fire to it & you better believe we had a fire we spen our time in hawlowing about the fire & when we got sleepy we set the watch ahed to 12 oc & then we called the next watch & went to bed."

Addison Crane started up the Sweetwater on June 22: "Our road today has been generally level and sandy, in places deep which has rendered our progress slow. About noon the weather suddenly changed from the most intense heat to almost winter coldness, and this sudden change was accompanied by a gale, thunder, lightning, and hail, which lasted about half an hour, and which cooled the atmosphere and laid the dust. Thunder among those 'rocky mountains' has the most singular rever-brations and tones. One clap had the sound of the twang of a base viol string. The bluffs each side our road rise almost per-pendicular from 200 to 600 feet high, are of solid granite, and present themselves in every iminginable form. Indeed we are now . . . among what are properly termed the *rocky mountains* and are fast approaching the summit the south pass not being more than 80 miles distant. The country is barren and sandy covered with wild sage, and other shrubs intermingled with a great variety of most beautiful flowers. The grass is only found in patches, and mostly on the banks of the River. The scenery is of the wildest and most magnificent character, and anyone who would seriously attempt its description would only make a fool of himself and a greater fool of the reader who should take his description as a true representation. . . . We are now en-camped near the river—distance to day only about 17 miles. Our company have changed their notion again and are now for Cal. via, Salt Lake—news having come (very authentic) that a new route has been opened avoiding the desert entirely. We can reach the city of mormons in about 12 days travel— now distant about 260 miles." The following day: "Met a company of 20 packers who were returning from Cal. They left Hangtown May 15. They report plenty of grass after we

[175]

pass Green River, now distant 150 miles. Say they had no trouble from Indians."

Mrs. Sawyer was not far from the Crane company when the hailstorm struck on June 22: "The stones came down thick and fast, and they were as large as walnuts—none smaller than bullets. The wind blew so hard and furiously that all the animals within our hearing stampeded. All hands had a hard time getting them together again. Some escaped entirely, but we had the good fortune to recover all of ours. Some of our men got bruised heads and hands by the heavy hailstones striking them. I was badly frightened, and thought the wind would surely blow us away." Like Crane, the Sawyers also changed their plans at this time. "We have concluded to go to California instead of Oregon, as was our first intention. I am greatly pleased by this change of intentions, as I had much rather go California. My brother B. B. Lamar, is there, and to see him is a greater inducement for me than the whole of Oregon can offer."

Stampedes were common along the Sweetwater. Mrs. Cornelia Sharp wrote on July 6: "About noon our team, with some others, became frightened and ran away, and killed one of our work oxen." Her son, Joe Sharp, recalled: "All at once the teams broke into a run—something started them, no one seemed to know what. It was a regular stampede as to our team. Father and mother were walking; I was walking, also, and some of the children were in the wagon; away the team went, the hardest and wildest running I ever saw. When they stopped and we caught up with them, we found the children were not hurt, but the two wheelers were down and one of them was dead. It took our team a long time to get over the scare."

In the vicinity of the Ice Springs—a marshy area with saleratus resembling ice just below the surface—Lewis Stout wrote: "The busiest day since we left Iowa. Quite a trying time. We left our camping ground as usual. Got along well 'till about ten o'clock. Nothing serious then, only a little preparation for war. Indians traveled along with us all day. Once in a while some rode on ahead. No alarm till a man came back and told us we had better look out and have our guns ready, for the Indians were collecting in great numbers on ahead and that trains were waiting for back trains to come up. In the course of half an hour some twenty wagons were collected. Drove on two or three miles and came to their town and passed through without any blood shed. Then the whole town moved along with the emigrants. Traveled five miles in the afternoon. Came to the ice swamp and crossed over. Cattle got scared and ran off, which is called a stampede as it is represented to me. It was an awful time, I was never so struck in my life when I came up. I stayed back at the swamp to get some ice. There was a man who came back and told me that there was a wagon upset. I knew it was one of our company. I lay whip to my mare. Saw Fisher's team running like a streak. The next thing I saw was our two wagons upset and torn in a wonderful race. Mother and my sister was badly crippled. Six teams in company. Represented to me that 100 men could not have stopped the teams."

There were nine crossings of the winding Sweetwater River before the emigrants left it. Some of the fords could be avoided by traveling over the bluffs, and on June 27, John Clark of Virginia was approaching the last ford over a rocky ridge: "This is more like a day in January than the latter part of June. We now travel on this cold ridge 6 miles to a small drain & great snow bank just to your left. Here we dine on the cold & rocky Sumit. Draw out the brandy keg fill our cups with sugar & snow turn it down. Then begins our fun with run round & snow ball, until another cup was cawld for & drank in a hury. While the teams put forward down a good road & gradual slope, I bore off on the ridge to the right 2 or 3 miles just to see the poor & raged looking hills that is quite destitute of grass or vegitation save the broken benches of granite rock, then a low flat that streaches away north to the very base of that great mountain covered with snow. I could see with my glass many curious looking places, besides some deer & wolf on the flats & bare ground."

The last crossing of the Sweetwater was, early in the season, the most difficult. On May 31, in the forefront of the emigration, G. A. Smith forded the river: "Got up this morning and found the ground covered with snow drove on and forded 2 bad streams the last one was very swift the water turned the waggon over and came near drowning 2 men before we could get them out but swam in and rescued them the waggon lost all of its provisions by getting wet."

Richard Keen's company reached the ford a week later on June 7. "Crossed Sweet Water for the last time there was several trains here waiting for the Water to fall we concluded to cross at any rate Raised our Wag beds to top of the stakes and lashed them fast Swam our horses over (i e) all but the larges[t] pair which was left to the wagons then fastened a line to the end of the wagon tonge and hitched a team on the opposite side of the River. In about One and half hours Our train was Over in safety 6 of us stood in the water up to our Waist until all was Over. another train then undertook to ford after us up set One of their Wagons and lost all their provisions. the brandy keg was then brought forth and all indulged More or less." The same day Jay Green "was obliged to ferry with my wagon bed this occupied a good part of the night."

Between June 7 and 10, a rude ferry was set up which George Short used on the tenth, but the Snodgrass-Riker train decided to ford on the following day. "Early this morning we were at the Ford and found it the worst stream we had yet attempted to cross," R. H. P. Snodgrass wrote. "The melting snow had brought it up swimming high. Some men have gone into the mountains and brought down some logs and made a raft & were preparing to swing waggon across on that but as there were some hundred waggons standing there waiting, we determined to ford. Our waggon-beds were soon hoisted on blocks we had brought along for the purpose. Just as we were getting ready some one drove a light two-horse waggon in

[178]

without raising the bed, and away went man, waggon, horses & provisions down stream. The second waggon they tried to ferry backed off the raft & with its load followed suit with the two-horse waggon. An immense amount of property will be lost here. I was in the cook waggon about the middle of the stream, Riker was driving and one of our horses had balked when the water began to strike his side. I was looking on very unconcerned, but just then the waggon slid off the raft and came floating towards us. I snatched the whip & lines from Riker & raised a yell at the balked horse. That sent him end-ways a little the quickest, but only just in time to save the bacon. We got all over safe, and rose the hill & started on, for we have to cross the South Pass today."

John Riker described the event: "Already one of our teams has entered the angry waters, but the current proves too strong for them. With many efforts they approximate the shore, when a new and unlooked for incident threatens their complete destruction. The raft above has been sunk by the violence of the current, and its freight, a heavy wagon, is precipitated into the stream—down comes the drifting mass.

"These ill-fated animals are urged to do their utmost; with one final effort they succeeded in gaining the shore. They are safe. The remainder of our teams, being stronger, were crossed with safety."

Although safely across the Sweetwater, they had further troubles before crossing South Pass, as Snodgrass related: ". . . when we are about half way from the ford to the Pass there came up all of a sudden a hail storm, and before we could get our waggons turned round and our horses unhitched it was hailing none of your easy hail storms, but a regular mountain storm—hail stones as large as Partridge eggs, and blown till they came at a slant of about 45 degrees. It was impossible to hold the horses still. Occasionally we could hear Bailey's voice calling to us to hold on to the horses for a moment, at times I could see the waggons moving in every direction—the horses perfectly crazy as the storm increased in

[179]

The Road to Utah: Dome Rock on the Sweetwater

fury. Happy for us it was soon over and our stock became quiet. Some of the men were completely exhausted and could not have held out much longer. That day's work will not be forgot while I live."

"Ma and I have just been to bathe in the Sweetwater," Lucy Cooke wrote on June 24, "but, oh, it was cold! We could only take two or three dips and then run out. What a strange country we are in. Here we are bathing alongside snow banks and in sight of mountains covered with it, whilst at the same time grass is green and gooseberries growing in abundance. I picked some to stew, but they were pretty small." The next day: "William and I amuse ourselves picking gooseberries. What a task it was. We gathered about a pint. I made two pies of them, and gave one to Ma. I had to roll my piecrust on the wagon seat; rather primitive style, you'll think, but it seemed good to do even that bit of cooking. I just long to be housekeeping again."

The same day, June 25, Addison Crane stopped to rest near Strawberry Creek: "Morning cool, and most delightful. I have rode on 10 miles and must have gained an hour, and am now seated in a wild gorge near a little rill called Strawberry Creek, using a rock for my writing desk, and within 6 rods of me is a bank of hard solid snow—probably 20 Rods long and from 2 to 3 Rods wide—4 feet deep at the deepest places, of which I have eaten as much as my appetite craves. . . . Babbitt the M.C. from Salt Lake passed us this P.M. in a buggy drawn by a large mule. He crossed at Kanesville 6th June and has come this far in 20 days! I was off the road and did not see him—but he reports the death of Henry Clay. Met a man from Cal. with newspapers for sale at 50¢ each dated May 22d at Placerville—bot. one at 35¢ encouraging news from the mines and the new pass thro. Nevada mountains has been opened and travelled. at the Branch of Sweetwater is a blacksmith shop and trading post—charge for shoeing a horse $6. an ox $12! Bacon 40¢ per lb! and other things in proportion. . . ."

The trading post was near the last crossing of the Sweet-water, which Emily Adams reached on July 30: "We passed a station here today. We saw plenty of Indians. They seem very friendly. They were engaged in dressing some prairie dogs. They had several little papooses who looked very cunning. Some of the Indians were making moccasins for sale. They trim them very nice with beads. Went on a little farther and came to another camp. Here there was a blacksmith shop. We saw but one white lady here. The men were engaged in gambling and playing cards."

Seven weeks earlier Richard Keen wrote of the white woman at the trading post: "there is a black-smith here a french man who has in his possession a white woman (American) she wished us to take her to California. her story was quite affecting She stated that she started to California in 1850 in Company with some young Men who left her here would not take her any farther she had remained with these Frenchmen for 2 years had been bought and sold three times and was used worse than dumb brute notwithstanding all her entreaties none of our Company would consent to take her."

Esther Hanna was near the last ford on June 30: "Last

[181]

night we had our wagon cut in two and had a cart made of it. Put in the hind wheels, left the fore ones and made firewood of the remainder. It was too heavy for our oxen. Two have given out, poor brave beasts! We have but two yoke left and our two cows. They work well in the yoke. . . . We have snow all around us today. The mountains are covered with perpetual snow. Came near a large snowbank. I went to it and found it about 3 feet deep, solid snow mixed with ice. When we scraped the top, we cut out lumps of it, pure and white. I carried some of it nearly a mile as our train had gone on and I had to walk! My hands were almost frozen by the time I got up with them. But we had a drink of snow water!"

The Sawyers, while at the trading post, also made changes in their outfit: "We passed a trading post to-day. The keeper is a Frenchman. Mr. Sawyer exchanged his wagon for a lighter one, as ours was too heavy for four mules to pull over the mountains. The wagon he got in the trade is not as good as the one we had, but when you trade for anything on this trip, you usually give double value for what you get in return. He, also, exchanged the wild mule, that he bought at St. Joseph, for an Indian pony. The pony is not half as valuable as the mule, but we never could break the mule to work or ride well."

From the last crossing of the Sweetwater it was ten miles to South Pass and another two to Pacific Spring. "The Pass is quite level; so much so that it is hard for the traveler to locate the exact spot he can call the summit," John Hawkins Clark wrote on June 30. ". . . We were now upon the Pacific slope and felt rather lonesome. Took a walk upon a rising mound and from there bid farewell to the Atlantic. We have thus far traversed the water's course from the Missouri to the Rocky mountains; we now bid it adieu to follow the water's course from the same great mountain as it speeds its way to the great ocean of the west. It has been a hard task to climb to the elevation we now occupy. We were elevated on more ways than one. To say the great mountain is beneath one's feet, and to have it there, is something; we felt a kind of proud satisfaction

[182]

in walking to and fro, gazing at what we had toiled so hard to overcome."

Alpheus Graham reached South Pass at six in the morning of June 28: "Here I threw away my old boots which I had worn since last September. . . . Here is now the great wonder of this pass, a person does not know they have been climbing a mountain although they are 7000 feet high, but soon after passing the summit it can be seen by the water from the Pacific Springs which runs to the west."

A man in the E. S. Carter train had bought a small brindle cow a few days before reaching South Pass: "At last she got sullen and lay down and the only way we could get her up was to get off our horses and get in front of her; then she would jump up and take after us. As soon as we would get on our horses she would stop and then we could drive her several miles before she would lie down again. She kept this up for several days. One day one of the boys and I were driving her along behind the train. We were ascending a long hill and had nearly reached the summit when she laid down. Looking back I saw two men coming up the hill on foot, and further back was a wagon drawn by four yokes of oxen. The men soon overtook us and said: 'Is your cow sick?' 'No,' I said, 'she is only tired. Will you please kick her in the head and make her get up.' One of the men stepped around in front of her and raised his foot. When she saw him raise his foot she jumped up and ran after him. He made for a wagon which was about one hundred yards away, and the race which followed was one of the most exciting I ever witnessed. The cow was about three feet behind when the man jumped into the wagon. A woman was sitting in the front end of the wagon. She laughed heartily when the man jumped into it. At last he raised his head above the wagon box and commenced to 'te he' and we all roared with laughter. 'Look yonder,' said he, pointing off to one side of the road, 'I think he is as badly frightened as I was, for he is still running.' That night Mr. Duncan had the cow shot. He was afraid she might hurt some one."

South Pass was looked upon by the California-bound emigrants as being halfway on their journey, to some a discouraging thought. Lodisia Frizzell wrote on June 24: "I felt tired & weary, O the luxury of a house, a house! I felt what someone had expressed, who had traveled this long & tidious journey, that 'it tries the soul.' I would have given all my interest in California, to have been seated around my own fireside, surrounded by friend & relation. That this journey is tiresome, no one will doubt, that it is perilous, the deaths of many will testify, and the heart has a thousand misgivings, & the mind is tortured with anxiety, & often as I passed the fresh made graves, I have glanced at the side boards of the waggon, not knowing how soon it might serve as a coffin for some one of us; but thanks for the kind care of Providence we were favored more than some others."

VII

FROM SOUTH PASS TO
THE CITY OF ROCKS
VIA SALT LAKE CITY

———◆◗◆►———

"THE pacific spring is the clearest and coldest spring
water I ever tasted," Addison Crane wrote on June 26.
"An endless number have pitched their tents about us—and
there is but very little grass about—the vast amount of stock
which has preceeded us having made pretty clean work of it.
. . . Met this P.M. a very good looking young man on a mule 6

days from Salt Lake—sent out as a runner to turn emigrants that way—he distributed a large hand bill setting forth the advantages of that route and promising good usage to all who should come to see them—signed by the Governor & other principal men—we shall see how well these promises be kept.

"This day being the Sabbath," Crane continued the next day, "we had looked forward to it as a day of rest, both for ourselves and teams—but Pacific Springs were thronged to repletion and more constantly coming—indeed an almost unbroken procession driving in. I suppose there were at least a 1000 head of cattle, pastured near that point last night—that 20,000 head had been over the same ground before us, and, as may be readily imagined, there was but a poor chance to recruit our cattle here, so we pulled up stakes and moved on. At this point the trail turns off to Salt Lake, and we took it, glad to escape the monstrous throng in which we have been moving for two weeks past. There is another trail some 15 or 18 miles beyond which also leaves the California route for Salt Lake—but this was thought to be the best. It goes down the valley of Pacific Creek to its entrance into Green River—we found comparatively few emigrants on this route—but enough for protection." Crane learned the next day why the road was little used. "Found that the trail down pacific creek was quite indistinctly marked & full of roots—hence we concluded to wheel back—about a mile on to the regular California & Oregon trail, until we came to the regularly traveled Mormon trail."

While camped on Pacific Creek on the twenty-seventh, Crane, after first having "refreshed myself by shaving—washing all over with warm water and soap, and finishing with clean shirt and socks. . . . Went over to Mr Cooks camp—½ mile off, this P.M. Himself and lady are well educated (English) and the family in every way accomplished. She being a music teacher. They have 6 children with them—the eldest son being maimed is also accompanied with his wife (quite a lady) and one child He has 4 wagons & 9 men who work & pay him

[186]

$100, each. Mrs. C. told me that she frequently walked 15 miles a day—preferring it to rideing. She expresses herself highly pleased with the journey—and says they have all had excellent health." Lucy Cooke stopped keeping a detailed diary at South Pass, so her opinion of Judge Crane, who thought her "quite a lady," will never be known.

John Hawkins Clark approached the junction of the Salt Lake and California-Oregon roads on July 2: "Have traveled seventy-five miles without seeing enough grass to stay the hunger of a lame mule. Those who pretend to know say it is forty miles yet to where an ox could get a living if he had nothing else to do. Wild sage covers the whole country, and for what purpose I cannot imagine. Some say it is more for ornament than use, but where the ornament comes in is a question with most of us. A crooked gray stick about four to five feet high, with some branches and a diameter of one to two inches; in the absence of wood we manage to cook with it. It is about ten days' travel to Salt Lake, where it is said grass grows plentifully.

"Passed the forks of the road to-day. . . . A man stationed at the forks of the road is trying to pursuade the emigrants to take the right hand trail. 'Gentlemen,' says he, 'men, women and teams are starving on the Salt Lake road. There is no grass for a hundred miles, the water is poor and poisonous, and if by chance any of you should live to see Salt Lake the Mormons will rob and steal everything you have got, take your women and send you out of the country as bare as you came into the world.' The grand secret of this man's persuasive eloquence was that he was the proprietor of a ferry and wanted as much travel over it as he could get. As we were not of the number he could persuade we proceeded on to Little Sandy river, where we went into camp."

From the Little Sandy—a small, shallow stream—it was eight miles "to Big Sandy—a good sized stream 50 yds wide—good ford—sandy bottom—little muddy," Edward Kitchell noted on June 29. "After we crossed this creek we found in amongst the sage & a stunted under brush what is called wild oats, alias Barley—alias Rye, alias Wheat. Cattle did not suffer at noon for feed—The Big Sandy lay off to the left of the road at points running near the road—so there is no scarcity of water, nor feed between this Camp & at the point we crossed—Camp tonight is on banks of Big Sandy—$\frac{1}{2}$ mile south of road—near 5 cotton-wood trees—(trees on an Island) Sage brush for cooking. Move cattle across river & got tolerable good feed—Country is not handsome, only as you view the white peaked mountains—Soil sand & clay—Dust intolerable At noon it blew a perfect hurricane for an hour. The dust was around us, over us, under us, in our eyes & mouthes, our coffee & what not!"

Caroline Richardson was on the Big Sandy the next night: "our place of encampment is a bed of sand to night our supper was seasoned with sand our beds filled with sand our eyes even mouths and our teeth are filled with sand in fact it is becoming an almost indispensible item with us." To add further discomfort, "the sage brush which we use for fuel is covered with wood ticks which annoy us very much," in spite of which she visited a nearby camp and "was agreably entertained with conversation and singing."

Addison Crane arrived on the Big Sandy the same day as Edward Kitchell: "While we were stopping for noon to day three quite respectable men came up leading a horse on which was lashed a carpet bag and some other packs. They had been in the employ of a Mr Brown from Ohio, and he had so abused and maltreated them that they were forced to leave, and so took their blankets, bought the first horse they could find and left him. Among them I noticed quite a gentllmanly appearing young man of 22 or 3, and who evidently was seeing the elephant. I walked with him a piece and he gave me a short sketch of his recent history. His name is Davis, & his father he told me was a wealthy wholesale merchant at Zanesville O. He said he had never been accustomed to any labor harder than clerking in his fathers store—but for two months past had been compelled to drive oxen all day—chase & water cattle nights until his life was worn out of him, and after doing his best, working 18 to 20 hours out of 24 had been scolded and sworn at and found fault with—until poor human nature could endure no more. 'Oh!' said he 'I should have listened to my father—he foretold all these hardships but I did not . . . and came off against his wishes, and now here I am, almost begging my way to Salt Lake—where, if the Good Being above allows me to arrive I shall feel thankful & hope to get some way of finishing my journey from there' He told me his father offered him $3,000. cash to stay at home. 'Oh what a fool I was.' Such are some of the many incidents constantly occuring here."

Leaving the Big Sandy, the road passed over a barren, desolate region for ten miles to the Green River, where there was a ferry and, farther downstream, a ford. The evening of June 13 John Riker was "encamped on the banks of Green River, a deep rapid stream. When within its banks it is sixteen rods wide. At this time it is so swollen by the recent rains that it is near half a mile in width."

The next morning they prepared to cross: "Drove down to the ferry (kept by Mormons). They refused to carry us over for a less sum than eleven dollars per team, or eighty-eight dollars for the train. This our captain refused to pay, offering them fifty dollars, which we all considered a sufficient compensation. After a little delay, the teams were all crossed but one, which they refused to bring over until the full amount of ferriage was paid. At this the captain became angry, and immediately the company were ordered a short distance to camp, when nine of the men, well armed, returned to the ferry, determined to bring over the remaining team at all hazards. The captain then demanded their charter, which was reluctantly produced; and upon examination it was found that they were allowed to charge but three dollars per team. Then the captain drew his revolver, and threatened them with instant death if the team was not immediately carried over. They

[189]

seemed to think the latter preferable, and acceded to his request.

"We left them, under the full impression that Ohio boys are not to be swindled." The sequel was told by R. H. P. Snodgrass while the party laid over at Salt Lake City: "They sent their Sheriff out and he has just got back with the Green River ferry men, and they are putting them through for charging more ferriage than their charter allowed. They notify emigrants now in the City that what they paid over rates will be refunded." The action of the Riker-Snodgrass company may

Emigrant's Rock Twenty Miles From the Green River

have had a salutary effect on the ferrymen, for none of the following emigrants paid more than $3.

Sixteen days later, June 30, Addison Crane described the ferry: "We found quite a number of wagons ahead of us awaiting their turn, and were detained on that account some 4 or more hours. We drove our cattle into the River & the[y] swam across, thus saving ferriage. . . . The ferry here is constructed to work on a cable stretched across—and is propelled by the current, and runs over in one minute so swift is the current." The river which John Riker found to be half a mile wide in flood was, by the time Crane reached it, no more than 300 feet in width. Once over the river, Crane continued: "Here we saw quite a number of Snake Indians—some of whom appeared very well. Here was a miserable whisky pedlar and I am sorry to say that some of the boys of our train patronized the concern and one of them (Paschal Buford) got intoxicated, and in attempting to get into the wagon while in motion he fell and the two wheels passed over his thighs." However, ". . . young Buford proved not to be injured at all. So much for the luck of a drunken man."

John Clark of Virginia had something to say about the Indians at the ferry the next day, July 1: "Here we see the first Indians belonging to the Snake Tribe that inhabit the Rocky Mountains. They are generally small in stature, dark & spare in the face. There are several lodges here on each side of the river. The men are good riders & use the lassoo eaquealy with the bow & lance. The Squaws are very small & filthy looking. They slip in the smoky tents, or hide in the grass or small willows to keep from being seen by the paleface. The urchins are all naked & kite through the weeds like minks on the run. Just ask Giles & Sturgeon what spared them catching Squaws at the ferry. . . . We camp with the tribe & visit the skin-covered Campoodies for the purpose of seeing the brown or leather colored Mohalas that give us a shear look & slipt from our sight, & we to camp."

The Crane company moved two or three miles beyond the ferry and encamped on the bank of Green River: "Here a denoument occured which I knew must come and for the comeing of which I had most earnestly prayed than for anything else. I have heretofore refrained saying any thing in my journal about Lovejoy—and it would take more time and paper than I am prepared to spare, to say all or even a part of what would be necessary to a full understanding of his character, and I will therefore content myself with saying that I have found him the lowest and most degraded human being I have ever met with. All his language was of the most licentious, blasphemous and profane character. Added to this he was insolent, lazy, and malicious in his disposition, constantly complaining of his work, (which was easy in comparison to what I myself did) and in every way the most disagreeable man I ever knew. After we had been together about 10 days on our journey & only 130 miles he became so insolent and profane that I told him to quit—that I would not travel with such a man any longer. He promised to reform and I relented and kept him. Since then he has been a little more reserved in his language when he thought I could hear him—but has appeared to owe me a spite, and he & Lane being constantly together has took his revenge by attempting to prejudice him I had fully determined to discharge him at Salt Lake, and having told some of the boys I intended to pack through from there—he took the hint and Lane and him announced their determination to leave after we encamped. To me and Albert it was most joyous news—I willingly gave him all he asked for his third interest in the concern, one yoke of oxen and the pair of cows—keeping three yoke—the wagon, and all the provisions (which I bought myself) We have plenty of teams for our light load after we get rid of them, and I shall certainly pass along more pleasantly than before. We shall leave this train—because these men are to keep with it, and we will not longer associate with them. Trusting to the kind care of a good Providence which has thus far been over us, we entertain no doubt of working our way through."

Of the next day Crane wrote: "This is the only really peaceable day I have had since we started. . . . To night at camping time fell in with three brothers named Ingram from Ohio —who are traveling with ox teams—and have also some 20 head loose cattle & cows—two of which they milk. They have two wagons—7 men. 1 wife (Mrs I.) and a boy 14 years old, and were quite willing that we should camp & travel with them which we conclude to do for the present. We find them very fine intelligent people—no bad language about the camp

[192]

and everything moves on with as much order as in a well regulated family."

Over the next several days Crane kept up a running litany of complaint against his former driver Lovejoy: "Have enjoyed myself well to day—& I find my work not half as hard as before—while I am no longer subject to the company of low vulgar profane men. . . . I *can* rest now I have got rid of the two *creatures* I have been cooking and working for, during the last two months . . . I cannot but constantly think what a fool I have been to have washed and cooked for and been at the expense of victualling two men . . . for doing nothing. It is a mere amusement for Albert and myself to take care of our cattle and drive them along in the wagon—and yet these two worthies were constantly complaining of it as most prodigious hard work, when in fact, the work is very little. Lane was naturally a well disposed man, but had very little physical endurance. He would tire out at what I should think nothing of. But after all there are but few commendable qualities about him. While there are very many bad ones. He was very profane passionate, fault finding, & peevish—just such a person as would render himself and all about him unhappy. The only enjoyment I had was out of his & L.s sight, and I have made it my business to get away & keep away from them during the day while the team was moving—but at night and in the morning I was necessarily subjected to all the unpleasantness of fretfulness profanity and vulgarity. Now however I am delivered for which I am most heartily thankful. They and our old train are encamped . . . about ½ mile back of us, but we pay them no attention."

John Clark of Virginia was approaching Fort Bridger on the Fourth of July, but the day was far from a festive one: "I am very poorly. This afternoon a tremendous gale of wind springs up with snow squall. Hail & gravel fly & one of the waggon covers gives way. The tents blow down, & we are all in a horid condition. Some are crying & others, no doubt, thinking of home & the friends they left. This day will long be remembered by our Company."

Edward Kitchell was eight miles beyond the fort the same day: "This is Independence morning—what a contrast 'tween here & the States where all is hustle & commotion—bright faces & happy hearts—strains of music & cheers & loud hurrahs—booming of cannon & what visions of roast turkey—chicken, pig—of pies & cakes—of lemonade and all that makes the stomach glad. rise up before & mock my golden dreams of California. I wonder what people are doing in Ft Madison, in Hillsboro & in Olney today! If there was a Spiritual Rapper, I should consult—I should like to see what some *other* folks of my acquaintance were about. I should like to know what was the real cause of my going to California. I do know but shall keep it to myself.

"Well here I am on the morning of 4th of July 1852, nearly 1300 miles from home over 900 from California & within 100 of Salt Lake City. I have not left camp yet—The waggon has been gone an hour—My black horse Tom stands patiently at my feet (save switching his tail at the musquitoes) while I am lying on the ground scribbling—The morning is cool—the sun shines—beautiful (not hot & sultry like in States) A gentle breeze stirs the air (what is a breeze but air stirred up) the snow capped mountains glisten in the rays of the Sun The valleys sparkle with flowers & wave with luxuriant grass—now let us look at the other side of the picture—We have to trudge along with an ox-team—dust in our eyes & mouths & oaths upon our lips—Jerry's feet have given out—Frank's are pretty near so & Old Buck is lame—Crackers mush & coffee—sleep on the ground & get up by daylight—No Sunday here, nor 4th July, nor holidays of any kind—My face is covered with hair & dust—my hands are dirty & chapped—my lips are sore—my nose is peeled—my clothes are ragged & I dare not shake them for the dust arising from such exercise is akin to that of shaking a carpet. But this wont last long because in four days more we will be at Salt Lake & there 'we put on' good clothes

Fort Bridger, Wyoming

& cleans up our hands & faces—(my good clothes are reduced down to a pair of corderoy trousers.) I must close this & go on my journey—"

From the Green River there were several crossings of Blacks and Hams forks of the Bear River to be made before arriving at Fort Bridger, where the famed mountain man, Jim Bridger, had been living for the past nine years.

"Today we ferried Black's Fork at Bridger's ferry," R. H. P. Snodgrass wrote on June 15. "Bridger was at his ferry, and went with our train up to his place." They came to the fort the next day. "Some of the men are buying them suits of buckskin, full suit 25 dollars. The following of a mountaineer life suits some men, but not me. Bridger has been here 25 years. He looks to be 55 or 60, has plenty of money and no mistake & a Squaw wife." (Despite his appearance, Bridger was forty-eight at the time.)

John Hawkins Clark arrived at Fort Bridger July 7: "The residence of the colonel [Bridger] is of logs and forms a hollow square, the doors and windows opening into the court, to which we were admitted by a massive gate. . . . Clothing, powder, lead, tobacco, whiskey and many other articles of merchandise are kept for sale within its walls. Horses, mules and cattle run at large and come and go as they choose, but make the fort their headquarters. . . . Our stay was short, but while there had the curiosity to examine his premises close enough to learn that the colonel was lord and master of two yellow skinned ladies and the acknowledged father of any number of boys and girls whose tawny complexion and intelligent look forbade the idea that they belonged exclusively to either the race of white or Indian. The family rooms of these ladies differ but little from the regular wigwam of the wild Indian. Dried meat, the horns of an antelope and a tomahawk garnished the walls; buffalo robes, bear skins, dirt, ashes, dogs and children were scattered promiscuously over the dirt floor."

Marriett Cummings was at the fort on June 30: "Major Bridger is a man considerably advanced in years. Has had several squaws of the different tribes for wives. Is now living with a Root Digger which he brought from California. Has in all six halfbreed children by three different wives. He lives in the fort in one room in the most Indian-like manner, but is immensely rich. Has a Mexican grant of ten miles square around the fort, stock in abundance, and gold without end, and yet is much of a gentleman but lives like a hog."

Another emigrant, Godfry Ingrim, wrote: "Col. Bridger had two large log houses; in one he kept a store, carrying such things as the trappers needed, which he exchanged for furs and skins. Bridger had two squaws and several half-breeds. I saw him there and he reminded me of one of my neighbors who always went with his shirt unbuttoned in front so he could move the gray-backs when they became too familiar. He was really an odd genius. He called the trappers the free men of the mountains. They came in twice a year, he said, for supplies. After buying what they needed they would have a high old time getting drunk and gambling. They would stay around until they were dead broke. At times they would gamble away their supplies and have to get trusted for an additional supply.

When they were forced to buy supplies on tick, Bridger told us, they always came back and paid up. There were quite a number of the trappers at his quarters when I was there. I fail to see where the pleasure comes in for a man to go away and isolate himself from all comforts for six months then come in and spend it for forty-yard drink."

Addison Crane was camped a mile from the fort on July 3: "Two men (an old man & his son) are staying in our camp to night who have come all the way so far on foot. They . . . depend on the emigration for their food. They sometimes find hard times. There are great numbers of emigrants travelling here very ill supplied with food & heat that I doubt not is the cause of much of the sickness." A week later: "There has been for a week past travelling with our camp, two footmen—Mr. Russell and son from Defiance Ohio, and we finally consented to carry their baggage and provisions say (100 lbs.) and they were to drive half the time & help do all camp work—the arrangement to be terminated at any time when they don't suit."

Later Crane went into more detail concerning the Russells: "By way of a specimen of what happens to persons on these plains I will give a short statement of the history of Mr. Russell and son . . . They left their home at Defiance under an engagement to be taken over in a horse train (or wagon) from their neighborhood, and went on expecting to meet their conveyance at Kanesville—but could never find anything of it. They there bought one mule packed their provisions upon it and started on foot driving their mule. Three days out the mule broke a leg and died, and then they were forced to pack all their luggage on foot. They threw away almost all their things—retaining only absolute necessaries to support life. On they came day after day, over the burning sands, until the young man sickened and had nearly died. Recovered and again went on—until they reached our camp. We find them to be kind & obliging—willing to do all that we ask them, simply for our hauling their little baggage. They are worth 4 times as

[197]

much as Lane & Lovejoy, & cost us nothing. They never think of riding at all. They have both been in Cal. before—this is their second journey over the plains."

Just beyond Fort Bridger, John Hawkins Clark was "visited by a lone pilgrim, a jolly, rolicking, pleasant faced young man of about twenty-five years; a good talker and, according to his story, a fast traveler, born and brought up somewhere in York state. He had taken a notion to visit California and Oregon, and having no money and being impatient of delay had started without it and beaten his way over steamboat and railway lines; reached St. Joe, Mo. about the middle of May; there he borrowed a small boat, worked his way over the river as a deck hand and landed on the high road leading to the great west and the Pacific ocean. From camp to camp, from train to train, he borrowed, begged or appropriated a sufficient supply of daily grub to keep him in running trim. His hat had fallen by the way; his coat, too warm to wear and too heavy to carry, was laid aside; shoes ground to dust and scattered to the four winds, and here he was, active as a cat and as fresh as an Amboy oyster, hatless, shoeless and without a coat, sunburned, travel stained, his long black hair wrestling with the morning breeze."

West of Fort Bridger the trail crossed over a summit, 7,320 feet above sea level, then descended 14 miles to the Bear River. John Clark of Virginia stood on the summit the morning of July 7: "When I look through the glass & see all the ground we have traveled on the last eight days. The very South Pass bluff & Fremont Peak, the Mamoth Mound are all visable now near by, but lower down is dark & cragy & broken points, even fearful to look upon. The caves & caverans belonging to the grizzly & wolf of the Mountain. . . . I am now cold & go down a long broken steep into a kanyon of good water. . . . The country here is very wild, broken & romantic. One mile more brings you to the Bear River, deep & rapid, some 60 feet wide. Some few trees on the margin & brush at the ford. We had some trouble in crosing, as the stream was rapid & our stock poor & light; so we had to place

James Bridger (1804–1881)

a man on each ox to keep him down, or the current would bear him away. The water cold & men mad until we got through. Then a difficulty arose between ourselves & an Irish train that had like to clean us out. After a knock-down between Giles & one of the others in regard to the ownership of a cow we made up with the Irish emigrants."

The next day, just as they mounted the top of a hill, "Frank Johnston & I saw three large Elk cross the road just before us. We gave chase along the ridge for some distance. When near the point a short stop. Just to our rear was several indians on the same trail following up the Elk. We of course withdrew & returned to the road at the head of the Utah gully. Met over 200 of the tribe, mostly mounted, with many loose horses loaded with dried meats & peltry for Fort Bridger. We were in a narrow flat, Johnston & I Alone, surrounded by such a band of savages, made us not only fear, but tremble for the safety of our lives. As the crowd came upon us we began giving to one then another some little present in the way of a cap, bucket, little powder & other trinkets in the pouch which we always kept for the purpose. We soon found them to be our best friends. The Utahs gave us in return dried meat. . . . They soon made way & bid us begone. We soon got through the crowd, gave our horses the spur. With a loud yell from the crowd our frighted steeds made the dust fly until we caught up with our train. . . ." Later in the day, following down the narrow defile of Echo Canyon: "One of our devils Bill Morton made an ascent of several hundred feet up the rugged point but in coming down, by several slips, found not only a little blood but the rear of his pants entirely gone so that Giles had to meet & give him another pair before he could come into camp with safety."

The next day, July 9: "Roll on down the rough & dismal Kanyon with a small streak of sky above you to the Webber, 8 miles. Here is a mountain stream for you. Clear & rapid, 60 feet wide enclosed by grizzly looking hills, the sides of which the sun never shines on. The tops are white with snow. Fish in the stream & a few cottonwoods on the bank. As we sat here

[200]

Ute Mother and Baby

taking our cold bite some one below us set the dry grass on fire. With a breeze it ran up upon us & had like to burn our waggons before we could hitch up & get away." That night the Clark party camped at the ford of the Weber River: "Our tents were scarcely set before forty or fifty ragged Squaws and naked urchins were about us beging bread & clothing. We gave the poor beings all we could spare. A little later after this came three braves on horseback. We also gave to them. In return, gave us a part of their wild sheep & venison which lay across their ponies with their bare hips up on it they told us they were friends to the emigrants & always gave them good meat if they had it. We shook hands & seperated for the night."

Robert Laws reached the Weber River on July 15: "I think that we begin to see the Elephant in full Uniform & I dout but we may have to ride him to water: I dont regret my going to California for I believe it to be the best thing that I ever done: A young man knows nothing about this world till he goes the overland route to California."

The last mountain to be crossed before entering Salt Lake Valley was the worst. Addison Crane on July 8 and 9 struggled up Canyon Creek to a summit of 7,245 feet and then lurched down the mountainside to the valley: "The road would come to the brow of a precipice, 200 or 300 feet deep, $\frac{1}{3}$ or $\frac{1}{2}$ mile long. Down these chasms would frequently occur 'jumping off places'—or perpendicular drops of from 2 to 5 feet, where the wagon would have to drop square down—in doing which the whole load wagon and all, would fall directly upon the open. But the cattle would soon crawl out again and on we rolled. To add to the difficulty these roads for miles run through a forest of small timber, and the pathway is only cut wide enough for a wagon—the track often crooked. But we came through as hundreds had done before—safely. Chain the wheels—drive carefully—get one or two men in the sideling places to hold on to the upper side, & you have the whole secret. It is astonishing what roads a wagon can be hauled over."

John Hawkins Clark crossed the mountain on July 12: "Twenty miles from Salt Lake City, but the hardest road, we are told, on the whole route, a part of which lay up a small creek with seventeen crossings. I had never before seen such a road; rocks to the right and left of us; rocks big and little, but by careful management we got over the road without an accident. Another mountain between us and Salt Lake City. It is not four miles long, yet long enough to take our teams nearly all the afternoon in reaching the summit; then locking the wheels of our wagons we began to descend the steepest, roughest and most unchristian-like road that man ever traveled. Good luck attended us and we alighted in safety and camped at the foot of the hill, where we had a full view of the tide of immigration as it came tumbling down the steep incline. Sometimes the wagons would take the lead and drag the teams after them until brought up by some great boulder, when wagon, oxen, women and children would tumble together in one confused mass, amid the wreck of which would soon be heard the cries of women, the screams of children and the swearing of men."

Mary Medley and her family were caught on the mountain by darkness: "We were on a mountain, overlooking the valley, about four o'clock in the afternoon. The valley looked lovely to our tired eyes and seemed so near. Some one said, 'Shall we camp here or in the valley?' The captain was sent for as he always selected our camping places. The captain said, 'In the valley, by all means.' He, too, was deceived as well as the rest of us, for the valley was further off than we imagined. We soon started down the mountain, which was heavily timbered. It was soon pitch dark, and the road was so rough and dangerous that we were afraid to ride in the wagon. An old man with a lantern walked ahead and the women and children followed behind, and there were some mothers with young children in their arms carrying lanterns. Brother John with his broken leg was carried on a litter.

"Very few words were spoken, as we had to look where we were stepping. Eight o'clock and nine o'clock passed and we were all exhausted, but we had to go on, for there was no place to camp. Every able-bodied man was needed with the teams and wagons. Several men had to walk on each side of the wagons to keep them from turning over. At last at ten o'clock at night we found a place where we could turn out of the road, but with not room enough to pitch a tent. Most of the travelers went to bed supperless, being too tired and sleepy to think of anything to eat."

Weber River—Entrance to Echo Canyon, Utah

Once down the mountain, the emigrants traveled on through a long, narrow canyon to the edge of the valley, and here they found a quarantine station, of which John Hawkins Clark noted: "Quarantine ground lies at the gate of this canon and here is a hospital, or what pretends to be one, established by Governor Young, where all, both great and small, Jew or Gentile, are obliged to report. Those who are well are privleged to continue their journey, but what they do with the sick or disabled I am unable to say. I saw none, and as the hospital building is barely large enough to hold the doctor, a barrel of whiskey and a few decanters. I can safely say there were no sick or disabled emigrants within its walls. The doctor was busily employed in dealing out whiskey and appeared to have a good run of custom in that way, but how many sick emigrants he attended to I did not stop to inquire."

Salt Lake City was a welcome sight to weary travelers who had been two months on the plains. John Clark of Virginia "saw several ladies burst into tears at the sight of houses & white inhabitants." "I visited the city this morning," Edward Kitchell wrote on July 9, "it is really a beautiful place—laid off with a great deal of regularity & taste—The houses are of adobes or sun-burnt brick—make a good warm house & most of them look as well as kiln-burnt brick—They have good gardens—fenced with poles principally. . . . The city is well watered by the mountain streams that flow through every part of the city. . . ." John Hawkins Clark arrived on July 13: "The first thing I noticed was the little canals of water traversing every square, or nearly every square, in the city. The water is clear and cool and of sufficient volume to supply all the wants for which it was introduced. Every family has a good, large lot, and this water is mostly used for irrigation. . . . The city is clean, snug and cosy; the people plain and very common kind of folks."

Edward Kitchell: "Everything is reasonable in this a far off country but in trading of cattle & horses—Their horses are very fat & so are their cattle. They have the finest looking cat-

[205]

tle I ever saw. Their beef is the richest & best I ever tasted.

"For two yoke of oxen, that have been brought from the States, you can only get one fresh yoke—Two horses will bring one fresh one—A good fresh yoke is worth from 60 to $80. Good horse $100. a pony from 40 to $70 mule 75 to $100. Cow 15 to $30. Stock recently (this summer) brought from the States will not bring near half this in cash."

Caroline Richardson reached the city on July 10 and "stoped at a boarding house kept by a widow we pitched our tent in the potatoe patch which was quite a privilege as it had been so long since we had seen one there were several other camps there turned our horses out below in pasture found a fiddler at the house and some of the neighbors hired the room and to night we celebrate our entrance in the city by a social round of cotillions we had enough for two set and danced until eleven."

R. H. P. Snodgrass noted: "In passing through the City we stop at any house that we see fit—public or private—and go in & have a social chat with the inmates, male or female, young or old; ask and be asked a thousand questions. I was lucky enough to have a supply of newspapers of late dates, which are considered invaluable by the Saints, especially the females, & I have a very considerable circle of acquaintances already formed by my old newspaper presents. And I have reserved a few to win favors with as we pass through the settlements up the valley."

John Clark of Virginia: ". . . this morning met friend Babbot from Council Bluffs. This gentlemans acquaintance I had made on the plains. It appeard he was a Mormon in good standing, & soon gave me an introduction to his honor, Brigham Young, whom I found to be a gentleman in every sence of the word. He was standing & in conversation with some grandees of the town, who soon joined us in our walk to the storehouse, printing press, court & plaza. Then great pains in showing the outlines of the new temple now under construction. . . . We next made a call on the widow Green, an

First View of Great Salt Lake Valley, From a Mountain Pass

accomplished lady from the East. We were soon joind by three others, two of middle age, the other young & of rare beauty. This was in the afternoon of the second day, & towards the close, when the table was spread, and notwithstanding my imbarisment & dusty garb, I took my seat amidst the mormon bells, for such they were in manners & appearance. After a sumtious repast & when about to leave had a pressing invertation to call again, am of course agreed to do so before leaving."

He visited the widow Green the next day, "where I had the offer of a brilliant outlay, not only a handsome Ranch but fine Cotage well stowed with gay fixens, a large garden, fine walks well lind with varigated flowers, two shade trees in front, where we sat for some time in quiet conversation until the dusk of the evening when I returned to camp." Other members of Clark's party also formed attachments in the city: "I had to be on hand as a part of my young had been lasoed the evening before by dames near the plaza & were not yet disentangled from the facinating clutches of the Mormon pulletts."

On July 17 it was time to leave: "It was now I felt timid to make the last call on those whose kindness I never shall forget.

With a fluttering heart I approached the cotage where I found all quiet and the lady at home. After a short conversation I was told I had acknowledgd not only the kind reception but the beauties of the valley, and there was no cause for journeying further, as I had been offered a Mormon medal whose motto would be confidence with lasting care. In return I could only say my heart was at home and ambition abroad."

The subject of the Mormon faith was a source of great curiosity to all the emigrants. Many attended services in the tabernacle and reacted to Mormonism, especially polygamy, according to their own lights. William Lobenstine wrote: "One of the precepts of their faith, Polygamy, although generally used as a reproach to them, I personally admit as a true natural one, being consistent with nature."

"I took a lounge in the bar-room—sat in a real chair & read a reply to remarks on Mormonism, and came very near being a convert," Edward Kitchell wrote. "Orson Pratt talks like a book—The mormons are not such a bad people after all—They are a remarkable tribe No other set of people from the United States, would have made the improvements that now are made in ten years—They seem to thrive under persecution—It is true they believe in 'plurality of wives,' but did not Solomon, & many more good old fellows that we read of in the Bible? It is true that they believe Joe Smith to have been a great & good man & a Prophet & one who could work miracles—And do we not read of just such things & more improbable ones in the old Testament? If I should stay here long I should join the church & fish for an office—the Apostles & 'chief priests,' live like fighting Cocks—They stand & receive the 'tenth of the increase,' just as if they had a right to it."

On July 11 he attended services: "At 10 O'clock went to Tabernacle—crowded—was a perfect sea of heads & bonnets —Heard one good Sermon & some infernal slang & rant from Kimball & Brigham Young—my idea is (& 'I know it,') that the leaders of the 'Saints' are a regular organized set of scoundrels. The Governor said that all would be d—d unless they believed Joe Smith a Prophet & that the Book of Mormon was true—I felt like pulling his ears—There were 7 or 8 hundred Emigrants present—& his subject was the persecution of the Mormons."

Caroline Richardson attended the same service: "sermon delivered by Rev Daniel Tyler he was succeeded by another rev which was not slow in battling the states people of which a greater part of the congregation consisted Gov Brigham Young also addressed the audiance he spoke easy and lightly recounted his history . . . the music was delightful being of vocal and instrumental."

Addison Crane was also there: "There were three speakers, —the first of whom I thought mainly idiotic, the second evidently insane—and the last (Brigham Young) a knave. They preached mormonism instead of Christianity—and Jo. Smith instead of Christ. . . . Ten of Brigham Youngs *wives* attended church—the balance being detained at home by domestic cares of one kind and another."

The subject of Brigham Young's wives was one of endless and inaccurate speculation among the emigrants. Godfry Ingrim reported he had fourteen, Mrs. Cummings believed the number to be between thirty and forty, and Mrs. Bailey put the total at seventy-three. R. H. P. Snodgrass gave up trying to find out: "I dont think any of them knows for certain how many Brigham Young has. They tell us all numbers from 13 to 50."

If Addison Crane disliked the service, he approved of the tabernacle: "This is a large and commodius edifice, capable of seating about 2500, and was crowded to repletion. . . . The Tabernacle on the inside is built quite in the form of a theatre —benches rising one behind another until the outer row is a great way above the pulpit. The building is excavated on the inside so that it is one story under ground, and in entering it steps decend."

"The Tabernacle is the most supurb building of the kind I ever saw," thought Mariett Cummings. "It is built of adobe,

160 by 60 feet in length, one story in height and arched, with Gothic windows in the ends. The altar is in the middle of one side and is an elegant affair. The seats at the end and side are elevated from the altar to the doors one above the other, so that a person has a perfect view from any part of the house.

"There are no posts or columns to obstruct the sight. On the front of the building is an elegantly carved cornice and a gilded design of the rising sun."

"I think the Mormon people have been very much misrepresented, and that injustice has been done them by travelers," was John Udell's opinion. "I have not a doubt that, if travelers would manifest towards them a spirit of kindness, they would receive kind treatment in return, at all times. They have as good order in the management of their temporal and religious affairs, as I have ever seen elsewhere. They are polite in their manners, and very well informed on general matters."

Udell published a letter in the *Deseret News* of August 7, stating the above views, and in the same issue, another emigrant, George M'Cune of St. Marys, Ohio, also came to the defense of the Mormons:

"MR. EDITOR—SIR:—Permit one who has been surprised at the ignorance of some, and the cupidity of others, in relation to the inhabitants of your valley. . . . Upon starting from home, notwithstanding the misrepresentations and endeavors to dissuade me from doing so, of many who profess a knowledge of the Mormons' character, I had determined to pass through your city. At almost every point upon the route through the States, and beyond the junction of your road, these endeavors were repeated, in order to prevent any of the emigrants from passing this way. We were told that the ferriages, tolls, tithes and exactions of the Mormons for passing through their territory, would amount to the enormous sum of more than one hundred and fifty dollars per waggon, besides the great danger the emigrant would be subject to of having what little their exactions left, stolen from him. . . . Now sir, my whole outlay in the Mormon territory has been $4.25. I

Street in Great Salt Lake City Looking East

paid $3 for ferrying my waggon, and 25 cts. a head for my horses over Green river, which is the only expense I have incurred in your territory, . . . and as to the treatment I have received, I have no cause for complaint. Indeed I have never traveled where the people appeared more disposed to attend to their own business and let other people's business alone than since I have come among you. Nor have I ever received more courteous treatment, in all the dealings I have had with them, than I have experienced amongst the Mormons. . . ."

James Carpenter and his partner arrived in Salt Lake on June 28: "My Partner was not well so we put up at a private house and I looked for work as my Partner said he was not able to go on through that season. I got work in a Blacksmith shop and got 25¢ a day. the Bosses name was Lampson. he was a mormon had two wives. I boarded with him. His first wife was a very nice Lady, they had two nice children, a girl of 10 and a Boy of 6 years of age. His second Wife was a Norwegian Woman about 29 years old. she didnt live in the same House the other did. she had a House at the back end of the Lot and she done the feeding of Calfs, hogs, milking, Hoeing in the garden, washing & shopping and such rough work and the first Wife done the fine sewing and overseen the Cooking. . . .

as my Partner was sick I had to make some other arrangements about going on. So I found a man that said he would take me through for a 100 dollars and I took him up at that offer and left Salt Lake City on the 13th of July. Our train consisted of about a dozen wagons all Horse teams."

"At noon today we left the City and went up the valley 8 miles and camped," R. H. P. Snodgrass wrote on June 25. "This evening I made my first effort in making Chicken pot pye, my favorite dish, and I succeeded far beyond my anticipations. The boys say it tasted very well and eat first rate. We catch some fine trout in the mountain streams that run through this valley. We got the joke on Butler today, he was driving along close to our teams & coming to a nice Spring of water he determined to give his ponies a drink, so out of his waggon he jumped and stepping into the edge of the water he dipped up a bucket of scalding water; he dropped the water got on his wagon & drove on without being told. The boys are trying him tonight for insanity before Squire Skinner—rare sport. This is the first hot spring we have found that did not emit a strong vapor and sulphurous smell; this has neither."

Passing through the Mormon settlements beyond Salt Lake City, the road came again to the Weber River, where Mariett Cummings went fishing on July 10: "Fished all day faithfully and caught 17 fine speckled trout. But as we were doing up our fishing tackle preparatory to a start home they floated off into deep water and sank past recovery and we went home crestfallen indeed—fishless." But the next day: ". . . went fishing again with better success. Caught fifteen large trout and gathered a fine lot of ripe service berries."

Twenty-seven miles beyond the Weber River was Box Elder Creek and the last of the Mormon settlements. "We can see at least 30 miles up the valley, which is very wide here & without timber," John Clark of Virginia wrote on July 22. "A more beautiful spot would be hard to find. To big Elder 5 miles. Here is the last of the Mormon settlement &, we think the most beautiful portion of the valey & the mountain. Scene grand even beyond description. Under a small tree on the bank of the stream was a smith busy shoeing oxen at $12 the yoke. Several Indians were standing by to see the work go on. Just after crosing the creek the road passes around, & near the base of Louise Dome, one of the most grand & rocky Towers bordering on the lake." (Clark gave his own names to many of the sites on the trail.) "It is nearly perpendicular & must be 25 or 2600 feet high. The road keeps near the base of the mountain for 3 miles to the Kinsey Spring. Here fill your water cans. Here the valley is some ten miles wide, high grass and most beautiful to look over. The mountain to our right continues the same high & is romantic in the extreme. To the hot & cold Spring, 10 mile. Here we camp and boil our supper by setting the camp kettle in the hot spring. Within six feet of this same boiling pool comes out water cool enough to drink, but rather brackish. No fire is wanted here for boiling purposes. The valley still continues very wide, but the water in this arm of the lake that we came up is about gone or nearly so."

The next day brought the Clark company to the Bear River with a ferry and a rather dangerous ford: "Long before sunrise our teams, in Company with a long line of others, were on the road hurrying up towards the Bear River that emties itself & sinks in the head of the valley, 10 miles. Here we had to ferry the waggons at $3 each, & swim the stock. The river is rather deep & 80 yards wide. Sinks a few miles below us. . . . Some teams are crossing at the ford above the ferry. Some lose their waggon bed, grub & clothing. Most of our boys are swiming in to save a portion of the floating donage, while women & children are standing on the bank crying as the plunder floats down."

Near the junction of the Salt Lake-California roads on July 27, a quarrel forced a reorganization in Clark's train: "This morning in getting up the stock Giles & Morton fell out because the grub was nearly gone and G always thought M took more than his share. To get rid of Giles proposed to give Morton the last five dollars he had to leave his mess & join an-

[213]

other. He accepted and barefooted Bill fell in with us for the balance of the journey. The quareling was now about over, the donage thrown out & divided, Bill recvd for his share one tin cup, a dinged coffee pot, leather belt, & a part of the old burnt quilt. This with his satchell & day book was neatly stowed away in the hindmost waggon of the train, for all the others had gone forward on the road. . . ."

The road approaching the junction of the two roads was a desolate plain with a scarcity of water, and on July 21 the Addison Crane party began to suffer: "The sun rose burning hot—no water but salt, and prospect of going 13 miles which will take until noon or after before comeing to the spring of good water. Took Kate & rode on alone ahead—found the spring at 10 A.M. and also found myself quite thirsty—having no fresh water for 24 hours. Filled two small rubber bags—6 qts in all, and started back to meet our suffering company—Met 6 or 8 men before I got to our teams and could not resist their supplications for a little water—met our Co. 3 miles back from the spring, and the little water I brought afforded great relief. . . . Road very good Passed on this P.M. over a very good but excessively dusty road about 7 m. to deep creek where we made our camp. Took a wash in the creek & got rid of a vast quantity of dust. . . . From here we have no more water or grass fit for use for 23 m. and shall endeavor to take a supply of the element." That evening: "Young Davis of Zanesville—one wagon & 6 men joined us to day & also 4 other young men . . . with their wagon we have now 5 wagons—34 cattle—21 men 3 horses—train & force large enough to meet the bloody Indians reported ahead, on the Humboldt."

The day of July 24 brought Crane to the junction: "The night was cool and this morning early it was quite cold enough to freeze—but old sol came up bright & fiery, and made a very hot day of it. Snow lays all about us on the mountains—and I will here remark that we have not been out of sight of snow since we came to Ft. Laramie, and yet the days are burning hot, with snow banks within often a mile of us high up on the mountains. Left camp at 6 A.M. in 5 miles passed a beautiful clear cold stream, and in 2 miles further another large one in which I bathed. 7 miles further brought us to the junction of the Salt Lake and here as we expected came again into the crowd—but not so large a crowd as we had left. all the Oregon emigration are now gone, & this P.M. have not seen over 20 wagons ahead and behind."

The junction was near a natural formation known as City of Rocks, which John Clark of Virginia saw five days after Crane: "Here is wild & rocky wonders to gaze on until you reach the junction of the Lake & Fort Hall road, 2 mile. We are now amidst the numerous pyramids of white & gray-looking granite that is scattered over the ground for some dis tance. They are in lumps, some resemble the trunks of old trees, others that of a furnace-stack from ten to 70 feet high. There is but two so very noted & they are close together, nearly white & tolerably high. Upon the whole they much resemble the white chimneys of a ruined city or tombs & spires of a gigantic graveyard. Here we meet with some of the same old dusty crowd we left at the South pass four weeks since."

VIII

FROM SOUTH PASS TO
THE CITY OF ROCKS
ON THE CALIFORNIA TRAIL

EMIGRANTS not going to Salt Lake City had two choices at the junction of the California-Oregon and Mormon Trails. They could take the right-hand road, Sublette's Cutoff, across a fifty-one-mile desert to the Green River, or they could take the Mormon Trail as far as the Green River to the south and then turn northwest on Kinney's Cutoff to rejoin the main road. Kinney's Cutoff was a new road, and its main advantage was that the longest drive without water was seventeen and a half miles.

Four miles from the junction Sublette's Cutoff crossed the Little Sandy, where Esther Hanna laid over on July 4: "We have cold high winds today, blowing the sand and dust in every direction. Even our victuals are covered with it before we can eat them! . . . This morning we had another division of our company. Our captain and two other families left us, making in all 4 wagons and a carriage. They wished to travel on the Sabbath. The company took a vote on it. All the rest wished to remain, so they left. Our captain was not a professor of religion, nor any of the others excepting his wife. We are still a Presbyterian colony! The owner of each wagon left is a Presbyterian." Francis White was one of those who remained: "Three wagons, those of Captain McCullough and two others, left us on Sunday morning and drove on, thinking that they would lose more in time than they would make by recruiting their teams. We were sorry to part with them, especially those with whom we had been acquainted for years. But we knew we were about to enter a desert of forty-five miles on which we should find neither water or grass. And, moreover, we believed the Sabbath day should be observed on the plains whenever possible to do so." The reduced company then elected White captain of the train.

On the same Independence Day, Eliza Ann McAuley drove to the Big Sandy, the last water until the Green River: "Hitched up and went ahead two miles and found a little dry grass and stayed to get breakfast and let the cattle feed. Four miles brought us to the forks of the Salt Lake and California roads. We took the Sublett cut-off, leaving Salt Lake to the south. Made eighteen miles today and camped on Big Sandy. Had to drive the cattle about six miles towards the hills for grass. It has been so windy and dusty today that sometimes we could scarcely see the length of this team, and it blows so tonight that we cannot set the tent or get any supper, so we take a cold bite and go to bed in the wagons. The wagons are anchored by driving stakes in the ground and fastening the wagon wheels to them with ox chains. . . .

"We came near losing our pet antelope this evening. As she was frisking about the camp, a man from another camp was about to shoot her, thinking she was a wild one. She ran to another camp where a woman got hold of her and held her, and would scarcely believe that she belonged to me, though the poor little thing was struggling to get away and bleating piteously for me. Finally she got away and came bounding to me and followed me home."

That night the wind did considerable damage to the Hanna company: ". . . we had a perfect tornado! It commenced about dark and continued until 11 or 12. Several of the tents were torn from the pins and hurled away whilst the owners were in bed inside. They were obliged to take shelter in their wagons. One or two tents were rendered useless and were left; even the wagons were in great danger of being blown over. We had to have our carriage tied down with rope. Our company have been lightening their loads as much as possible as our cattle are getting poor and less able to haul our wagons. The good trunks were broken up and burned, carpet sacks, tinware, baskets, axes, shovels, chains and many other articles of value were left behind."

The Hannas reached the Green River ferry on July 6: "We travelled hard all day yesterday and all afternoon in the desert. A little before dark, we stopped an hour to rest our cattle and get our supper. Started again at dusk and travelled all night, stopping at 12 o'clock an hour and a half to rest again. I had my bed made down and then lay down but could not sleep much. We had good roads, most of the way until about 2 o'clock, when we came to a very steep and dangerous hill descending from the table land. I wrapped a blanket about me and walked down it. . . .

"We stopped at about 5 this morning to rest again and get breakfast. We have a considerable distance yet until we reach

Green River. We were forced to leave another oxen last night not able to go any farther. One of our men left two yesterday morning. My heart aches at the thought of leaving these noble animals behind! They have been so brave and uncomplaining, all through this heart-breaking trip. Their staring eyes, their moans at night, and their gaunt bodies haunt me continually. It is almost more than I can bear!

"Have had very bad roads this afternoon. Some terrible hills. Once we had to let our carriage down with ropes after taking the mules out of harness. The oxen succeeded in getting down tolerably well with the wagons. We reached the river

Giant's Club and Giant's Tea-Pot on the Green River

about 3 o'clock. There is a rope ferry here. Paid 6 dollars apiece for our wagons, and 50 cents a head for horses and mules. . . . The scenery about Green River is very beautiful. The rocks and bluffs are beyond description! Whilst we were at the river a heavy thunderstorm came up. We had to go a mile to camp through the pelting rain. It was almost dark when we reached it, cold and wet and hungry. We found no fuel without going a mile farther, so we went to bed supperless!"

Holmes Van Schaick was camped on the Green River the

same day: "Some of our men during the day made a raft, on which we are to float our waggons and provisions across the river. Some spent a portion in baking, others in prospecting for gold along the bank of the river. They found gold, but in small quantities. I spent the most of the day in mending our tent." The next day: "Our raft not being made right, we spent the day in remodeling it, and rafting our waggons and provisions across the river. This was the most difficult task we have had to perform on our rout. The current of the river was strong, and rapid, & our raft was floated across it, only by hard labor & good management."

An all-night drive brought the Alpheus Graham train to the Green River on June 30: "They charged $6 per wagon and we swam our cattle over a little below the ferry. Got all over about 2 o'clock. We had the coldest rain I ever felt, I got wet as a rat being down the river with the cattle, but I had to leave them and run to keep from freezing, pulled off my clothes as quick as I could but was so cold I could not wait to put on dry ones but wrapped up in our blankets and laid down after taking a big horn of brandy. After I got dry I put on my clothes and wrapped up again to get warm."

From the Green River ferry it was about forty miles to the ford of Hams Fork over rough, hilly country. Jared Fox, who had been taken ill at the ferry, made the last eighteen miles to Hams Fork on June 22: "Had a most distressing night. Did not eat, sleep or rest. Have not eat since yesterday morning. Charles is down in the mouth, poor fellow, can't eat. At 8 o'clock I have a bed fixed in the wagon and Charles get up the team and we start. Very warm but snow banks all around us. Soon came to some most tremendous hills or mountains. Wind rose and it thundered and lightened, rained and hailed and snowed and was very cold. I was chilled through covered up in bed, except now and then I peeped out to see Charles drive straight up or straight down. We found more mud today than in a month before caused by the snows melting and running down the hillsides. Some of these were very bad—deep and steep. In one of these we got the team in till I did not know how we would ever get Jerry out—he was all under but his head. On some of the hills today we could actually see the clouds below us. We made 18 miles and forded what is called Hams Fork of Bear River. We had to raise our box by putting things on the bolsters to keep our things from getting wet. We broke out one stake of our waggon. Here we camped after crossing and I feel better than I did this morning notwith-- standing our hard day's work, but I feel poorly at that. Plenty of snow close by. Passed 3 graves. Saw some of the mountain flax today and it reminded me of ours and resembles it very much. Has a blue blossom. Feed is getting better. When we came to comb Jerry we found he had a bad wound just back of his forelegs—a large hole cut deep. I suppose that he cut it in the mud when down."

Two of the three graves mentioned by Jared Fox were of members of the Jay Green train which had left the Green River ferry on June 12: "There was a division of one of the teams belonging to my train this morning. Two men who ware partners in a team seing fit to seperate Did so without hard words. The principal owner in the outfit Mr Balsley took the wagon two mules and a hors accompanyed by two young men and set out on his journey erly in the morning leaving his partner Mr Beel behind with two mules Beel applyed to Mr. Gray my partner for conveyence to California wee took him into our wagon and traveled on pasing Balsley about two O'clock of the same day—about one mile from the grove Balsley rode up to my wagon and shot Beel in the left breast [causing] instant Death—There being an ox train band by a company of thirty men wee concluded to await their arival they came up buried the murdered man and after a short counsil took the murderer into custody Wee then traveled on about six miles and encamped. . . .

"June 13 A council being held upon the best way of dispos- ing of the prisioner and it being agreed upon that wee travel on about thirteen miles to a large crick (hams fork . . .)

whare we expected to overtake a large train—in doing so our object was to get more council— . . . Wee arrived at Hams fork about one O'clock P.M. Here wee found a large ox train from Iowa a mule train from pennsylvania and some packers making in all about one hundred men After dinner the trains and companys were respectfully invited to meet and attend the tryal of Balsley for the murder of Beel—About three O'clock the companys met for the investigation of the matter A [jury] of twelve men ware chosen one of whom was an elderly man who acted as fourman of the joury The witnesses ware caled and sworn by the fourman—And gave in their evidence all of which the prisinar did not deny. The jeury gave an ascenting voice as to the prisinars guilt but could not agree on the punishment seven being for amediate punishment and five for delivering him to the authorities of California The company was then caled together and a vote was taken on this question and the majority of the company ware in favor of amediate punishment The jeury again assembled and after a short consultation returned with the verdict as follows Leanadas Balsley arise and receive your sentence Wee the Jeury find you guilty of willful murder and sentance you to death by shooting tomorrow morning at six O'clock The prisioner retired to his tent for the purpos of writing to his friends A strong gard was posted over him during the night. . . .

"June 14 The time has now come and a file of twelve men ware drawn from the company by ballott to execute the prisinar Twelve guns were charged six with ball and six blank and placed in the hands of these men under the command of the fourman of the Jeury marched about four rods to the place whare the prisinar awaited them under a strong gard The prisinar was then marched about eight rods to the road side with a blanket about his shoulders, by command the procession halted The commander with the prisinar steped [off] twelve payces in front of the file The blanket which hitherto had bin about the prisonars shoulders was then spread on the ground upon which the prisinar knelt down with his back to the men This was his chois This being done the prisinar then caled for a man who had conversed with him upon his future destany and requested a prair of foregiveness This man was one of the twelve who the prisinar had knelt before for execution—He laid down his gun and with a bended knee did offer up the Almighty God a prair in behalf of this retched man The executioner then steped into his place and these words ware given (by the fourman) make ready take aim—the prisioner gave the signal for fire by raising his right hand this was his request One sharp report of twelve rifels and all was over."

The El Dorado *News* supplied more details of the murder and execution. The two men, Leonidas Beasly and Matthew Beal, were brothers-in-law from Barren County, Kentucky: "In the division Beasly got the weaker team, and had a sick man in his wagon. Immediately after the division he hitched up his team and proceeded on his journey, leaving Beal at Green river. In a few hours after, Beal started, and on the course of the day overtook Beasly on a hill, where he had stopped to rest his mules. The former turned out of the road and passed by, the latter asking him if it were his intention to leave him [Beasly] with the sick man. Upon Beal's answer being given in the affirmative, Beasly stepped to the front of his wagon, drew out his rifle, and deliberately shot Beal down, killing him instantly."

After the trial, the newspaper reported, one of the guards offered to let Beasly escape, but he refused: "In the morning Beasly displayed a great deal of braggadocio—swearing at the men, and telling them that it was then six o'clock, and that they had set that hour for his execution, they ought to be punctual. (His conduct at this time, together with that of his refusal to leave the train, went to show that he did not believe they intended to shoot him.) . . . He requested permission to give the signal, which was the raising of the right arm. He now gave directions as to the disposal of his property, and taking leave of some of his friends, knelt down and seemed to be engaged in silent prayer for about five minutes, when he raised his right arm, and in an instant every gun was discharged, five balls entering his body in the region of the heart, and he died almost without a groan. He was then buried, and a board placed at the head of his grave, with his name, the cause of his death, the names of the jurors who tried him, and also the names of his executioners. . . . Both men leave families who were dependant upon them for support."

A few miles before Hams Fork, the Kinney Cutoff rejoined the main road. D. B. Andrews, on June 28, came into Sublette's Cutoff: "Late in the afternoon we commenced the ascent of the mountain on our right, the road being crooked, steep and in many places covered with small round stone. From the base to the summit is upwards of a mile. From its summit Ham's Fork of Green River with valley first present themselves the valley being skirted on its western as well as its eastern side with mountains. The descent to the ford of river was crooked, steep and stony in places. Forded Ham's Fork late in the afternoon. The river at this point is not far from $2\frac{1}{2}$ rods wide, 2 ft. water with a brisk current. Speckled trout abound in this creek."

Samuel Chadwick reached Hams Fork on July 13: "we have had some fish to day and stued gooseberrys for supper there is good fish in the crick and plenty of gooseberrys along side the crick." The following day he wrote: "this morning we got all [h]itched up ready to start out when an affray took place with D Dunmoore and Holmstead both from Illinois when Dunmoore undertook to pound Holmstead and they had a few minutes scuffel in the tent when to our alarm Dunmoore was stabed in the belly with a butcher knife . . . he began bleeding out of his mouth and died in a half hour he was burried right off and then the train started out and the murderer along and he [is] to have a trial tomorrow after the excitement [is] over he has left a wife and 3 children at home we traveled from hams crick to bear river to day it is 31 miles it took us till 10 or 11 clock at night and to day we have traveled over the biggest hills I ever saw almost straight up and down. . . .

[224]

"Thursday 15 we laid up all forenoon and part of the after-noon when we started out with the Oregon train which left Condys company and went about 3 miles and camped and some of the Oregon company stayed behind to hear the trial of Holmstead for stabing D Dunmoore they had a jury of men out of another train and witnesses out of our train and the Jury dismissed him as he was fighting in his own defence."

From Hams Fork the road led up over steep mountains be-fore descending into the Bear River Valley, a distance of twenty-five miles. "This is a lovely stream," Esther Hanna wrote of Hams Fork, "with gravel bed, beautiful trees, flowers. Here we found our first strawberries! There is an Indian camp here, about 30 wigwams and trading post. . . ." The next day: "Passed through a beautiful grove of fir and quaking aspen trees. I have never seen anything so lovely as these aspen trees in motion with a delicate trembling of their leaves. This is the first shade we have come through since we have been on the route. Got some beautiful roses, pinks and honey-suckle. . . .

"Began to ascend the Bear River Mountains, some of them are very high and rocky. From these mountains the scenery is most delightful. From the valley of the Big Bear River, which is 4 or 5 miles wide, there is the most beautiful view. At a dis-tance beyond the river is a range of high mountains, stretching far as the eye can reach. Their tops glimmer with snow. The mountains on either side of the road are very rough and bear a singular but beautiful appearance. The earth is of many col-ors, black, white, red, yellow and intermediate shades, with an occasional grove of trees or bushes, which adds to the variety and beauty of the scene."

Stephen Gage left Hams Fork on June 20: "we was attacted by a new adversary big innumerable herds of musquitoes they were indeed Blood thirsty The way they poured their venom upon us was surprising we at first bore it well but soon we got tired of their co. we brushed them with our hdfks. until it had no efect we then pushed them off & ran & plunged into bushes but this did not rid them still they were there & soon drove us from our supposed protection we then proceeded on until we could go no further stoped & kindeled a fire & lay down in the smoke this seemed to check them. . . ."

Alpheus Graham camped the night of Independence Day four miles beyond Hams Fork: "A little before sun down it began to snow, very cold the snow freezing to every thing and covering the ground to a depth of 2 inches, this 4th will be remembered by all of us while we live."

Jared Fox crossed to the Bear River Valley on June 23: "Started ½ past 7 went right up Jacob's Ladder two miles and could see the teams descending on the other sides as we did yesterday with 2 wheels chained and all due diligence at that to keep from ending over. After we got on top of the hill we had some 10 miles of good road and began to see a sprinkling of small timber. Some little poplars and balsm. Passed through a grove of some 20 rods wide—the most timber we have seen in a thousand miles and in this grove there is I suppose 5 or 10 thousand, for ought I know names cut in the trees. Some printed with chalk of waggon grease, red paint and anything and everything. . . . In the afternoon we had the worst road that was ever made and this was not made, but people tumbled down the hills neck and heels with all the wheels chained mile after mile and then up and down again. Made 22 miles and got within two miles of Bear River."

G. A. Smith entered the valley on June 9, so early in the season that there was considerable flooding in the valley. "Bear River this afords good and a kind of grass called bunch grass it resembles our red top some but the seed is as large as millet which makes as good feed as oats we have traveld in water all day as the River is over its Bottoms saw hundreds of Antelopes and cranes to day Shepherd cooked an cranes egg but had to call 3 men to help eat it."

More than a month later, on July 13, Eliza Ann McAuley wrote: "Here is splendid feed, the cattle wading in wild oats up to their eyes, while we have fun making pop corn candy.

Margaret is baking cookies, but the boys steal them as fast as she can bake them."

Two days earlier, it being Sunday, the Hannas laid over: "Rev. Mr. Yantis and train camped near us last night. He preached at this camp. We all went to church. It is so pleasant to have a tabernacle in the wilderness. They had 2 or 3 large tents put up together and seats placed so as to accomodate all. Our sermon was from Christ's sermon on the Mount,—'Rejoice and be exceeding glad for great is your reward.' I trust that we all enjoyed hearing a sermon so full of instruction and hope we may profit thereby. Mr. Yantis is a Presbyterian minister from Lexington, Missouri, also going to the Oregon country."

"This being the Lords day we did not leave camp," Holmes Van Schaick wrote the same day. "Our company spent the day in various ways. Some were fishing. Some hunting, others in reading, conversation, & meditation. Indians passed and repassed nearly all day. We were troubled considerable by their calling at our tents and urging for something to eat, to traid &c. This has been the most solemn day to me that I have seen since I left home. Nothing but experience can teach any one my feelings. Surely the western plains is the place to try mens souls. The fatigue and length of the journey, the exposure to a variety of weather in a strange climate, and the absence of civilized society, all tended to iritate, and begat within the human heart partial inhumanity and desperation. But God, the Author of the Universe who knows many hearts can comfort the weary traveler; even in this land of desolation."

A few miles up the valley it was necessary to cross Smiths Fork three times in 110 yards. Mrs. Francis Sawyer forded on July 2: "It was a very rocky and dangerous ford. We went into camp on the bank of the river and thought we would fish some, but the mosquitoes were so thick, so brave and so resolute, that all our time was occupied in fighting them off. I never saw the like before, and we thought that they would surely eat us up. The grass is good here, but our mules could not eat any until 8 o'clock, or after, when the mosquitoes left us."

The McAuleys, beginning July 15, made an improvement in the trail: "Traveled ten miles today and camped on Bear River. Just before coming to the River we had the hardest mountain to cross on the whole route. It was very steep and difficult to climb, and we had to double teams going up and at the summit we had to unhitch the teams and let the wagons down over a steep, smooth sidling rock by ropes wound around trees by the side of the road. Some trees are nearly cut through by ropes. . . . Mosquitoes very bad. The boys fished awhile and then took a ramble around the country and discovered a pass, by which the mountain can be avoided by doing a little road building."

They decided to build the road, and on the eighteenth: "Notwithstanding it is Sunday, the boys continue their work and have hired some men to assist for a day or two, to cut brush." William Hampton was paid $4 for two days' work: ". . . hot and sultry working at the foot of the mountains and the mosquitoes verry thick. We can hardly eat for this nights."

While the boys worked on the road, Eliza Ann and her sister "settled down to regular housekeeping and this being Monday it is of course washday. In cutting a way for the road, the boys find thickets of wild currants. There are several varieties, the black, the red and the white. The boys cut the bushes, some of them ten feet long and . . . loaded with ripe currants, which we strip off and make into jelly, currant wine and vinegar, dried currants and currant pie."

Two days later, July 21: "We have met with a sad loss today. Our pet antelope, Jennie, was playing around the camp and the dogs belonging to a large group of Indians espied her and gave chase. The Indians tried to rescue her, but could not. They then offered to pay for her in skins and robes. We told them it was an accident and they were not to blame, but they were afraid the men would shoot them when they came.

[228]

"At dinner time a very inteligent Indian named Poro, came to our camp. He says he has been to the Missouri River and seen steamboats and explained by signs what they were like. He seems to understand the customs of the whites very well. In the afternoon he came again, bringing his little boy, four or five years old. He interpreted a number of Indian words for us."

In the next few days the McAuleys became well acquainted with Poro and asked his wife to make moccasins for them. "Old Poro came along about ten o'clock and stayed a long time, teaching us his language. It pleases him very much to see us try to learn it. . . .

"Ironing and baking today. Poro brought our moccasins. They are very neatly made. His little boy came with him. I offered a gay plaid shawl in payment for the moccasins. Poro was quite pleased with it and inclined to accept it, but refered the matter to the boy. He talked to his father, who explained to us that he thought it was very pretty, but he could not eat it. He wanted bread and sugar, so we gave him what he wanted. . . .

"Poro came again today," Wednesday, July 28, "and brought a nice mess of service berries. He has been counting the 'sleeps' before we go away, and regrets our going very much. he said today, 'One sleep more and then wagons go way to California,' and we have parted with white folks that we did not regret so much."

On the following day: "Poro came twice today to bid us good bye and feels very sad about our going. After dinner we started on, leaving Thomas and Mr. Buck to remain on the road a week or two to collect toll and pay the expenses of making it."

John Lewis was a day's travel from Soda Springs on August 10, when he decided to leave his train. His decision might have been motivated by a series of entries which began at Pacific Springs on July 25: ". . . thare was about 100 wagons here & we got the girls together & had a fidle & catarrh & (hi

u girls) & another sutch a party was) never got up all for Oregon this is the first party in Oregon & this is one of them as we
had no house to dance in we took it on the ground the moon
was shining very bright & the dust cold be seen rising over the
party for 2 hundred yards for I tried it got———lost———
from the rest by some accident." The train laid over the next
day. "I wood not care if they wood lay in camp all the time";
then on July 27: "this day we left camp and d.m. the difference how far we got but I wish this day had bin as long as
from here to the states for it has bin the happest day in my life
if every day in oregon is like this I want to live a thousand
years this day was the begining of life to me all rite if it is not I
will make it so, so, so. . . ." Lewis crossed the Green River on
July 31 and camped beside the stream: "here we found plenty
of curens this was fine but I got some thing———elce that was
finer than this I wish that such days was as long as a yeare or
that the yeare was made up of just such days—we had some
rain today but I do not care if it rains all of the time & corne is
4 dolars per bushel its all rite———if it is not we will make it
so when we kill our hogs O that I cold all ways be on the
plains—" Then on August 10: "this morning had rather a bad
afect on some of the party thare was three of the boys that got
it in them to leave the train & myself was one of the three this
rased quite an excitement among the crowd some of them
tried to pursuade us to stay by coxen others by swaring but all
for nothing they could not git us out of the notion of leaving
but you may think thare was some of the old coxen dun but
Boy like we went our way inspite of all the train they don all
they knew with tears in thare eyes but just like Boys we went
our way we set out our things in the open plain without wagon
or tent horce or mule bread or meete."

Esther Hanna arrived at Soda Springs on July 14: "This
morning came in sight of Soda Springs. The location of these
springs is known by the two white mounds almost 35 or 40 feet
high, the size of one still increasing as the water oozes out at
different points, producing a crust that becomes quite hard.

There are some 9 or 10 of these springs in this place. The water is clear and sparkling, boiling and bubbling, swelling at times almost to the surface. It is strongly impregnated with soda, and by putting a little acid in it and adding sugar, it makes an excellent drink. It will compare with any soda as it foams and boils up in the same way. It will also raise biscuit equal to saleratus. I tried it and found it to be very good. There is in this place what is called the Beer Spring. The water is the color of beer and tastes a little like flat beer. The rocks for miles around are of soda formation. We encamped at this strange and interesting spot. Thursday, 15th: This morning we visited the several springs in this area. There are small holes a few inches in diameter, where the water is boiling up to the surface. This is very good drinking water and is considered wholesome. Whilst we were at the springs tasting each of them, an old Indian came up. We handed him a cupful. He tasted of it and spit it out, saying, 'No good, no good! . . .

"We next crossed a stream, passed a trading post and blacksmith shop. Came to a very large soda spring on the bank of the river. This one was much more strongly impregnated with soda than any of the others. We mixed up a drink of tartaric acid and sugar, which was excellent and foamed nicely. About a quarter of a mile down the river bank we came to the famous Steamboat Spring. This is certainly one of the curiosities of this western world! The water has formed a cone of about $2\frac{1}{2}$ feet high and an orifice in the rock of about 8 or 10 inches in diameter allows the water to discharge itself to the heighth of several feet with a kind of puffing motion, producing a sound similar to the puffing of a steamboat, only not so loud! The water is milk-warm, and has a white milky appearance, but when taken into a cup becomes quite clear and transparent.

"We next came to the junction of the roads or what is called Myres Cut-off. The principal part of the California emigration leaves us here."

The Sawyers traveled all day the Fourth of July to reach Soda Springs and decided to lay over the fifth by way of cele-

Crossing the Desert

bration: "We went fishing this morning. then came back and cooked a good dinner. We had canned vegetables, fish, rice cakes and other little dishes. We see lots of Indians now, and some are at our camp most all the time. They usually want to trade fish for fish hooks and something to eat. We found ice on the water in camp this morning, so you can see how cold it sometimes is here on the glorious Fourth. We were glad to get the ice water to drink."

Richard Keen was at Steamboat Springs on June 16: "there

are about 50 frenchmen here they have Indian Wives and appear contented there is a large Village of Snake Indians here they are horse racing I have witnessed several races 8 or 10 run at a time they have splendid horses and hundreds some of the finest horses I have ever seen. Some of the Boys are buying buckskin suits (ie) Coat & pants 14 dollars the pr the frenchmen appear very Anxious to buy all the Powder they Can get One of the Boys Doc Humly traded horses with an Indian and gave him an Accordean to boot the Indian was well pleased with the Accordean Anthony Rogers Fish and Myself went into his lodge he gave the Accordean to Rogers to play lit his pipe and smoked Awhile then handed it to the next Indian who did the same and so it passed all around I thought it would come my turn soon so I left."

Four miles west of Steamboat Springs was the junction of the California and Oregon trails. California-bound emigrants no longer went by way of Fort Hall, so here the emigrants parted. Jared Fox, John Lewis, Esther Hanna, Enoch Conyers, Emily Adams, Lewis Stout, Dr. Anson Henry, and many others took the road to Oregon.

Another who took the Oregon Trail was seventeen-year-old John Dodson. When he reached Fort Hall, he was hired by a man named Owen to go to his brother's post, Fort Owen, in what is now Montana. Dodson reached the post on September 4, and on the fifteenth another hand made the last entry in the boy's journal: "The poor fellow was killed and scalped by the Blackfeet in sight of the Fort."

Beyond the junction, the California road went over hills and mountains some sixty-five miles to Gravel Creek. There was a stretch of desert twenty-five miles without water after this stream, so most emigrants laid over to the recruit. Dexter Hosley rested there August 10, and on the eleventh: "were awakened this morning by a new voice the first thing I heard was come boys get up it is time to be on the move we want to make a big drive to day some roust out and get breakfast ready well we did not know what to make of it but we all soon got up to

[233]

see what the stir was and by looking about we found that our head men had left us the night before about 3 O clock with 3 horses they had concluded to pack it the rest of the way and had put their property into the hands of henry davidson a young fellow that had traveled with us for some time from Michigan we asked him the reason of their going away in that flight he said they told him that they were aware that they had not provided for the company as they had agreed to and said they had no money to get any thing with thought they could not get through without a fuss with the company and took this way to get out of the scrape and left what provisions they had for us to get through with well we hardly knew what to make of it but finaly thought it best to harness up the teams and go on as fast as we could as we all feel anxious to get through and be earning something for ourselfs and familys as for we have already been 3 months on the way."

Dr. John Dalton was traveling through the Raft River Valley when, on July 24, there was a revolt in his train: "Seven of the Drivers this morning refused to drive any longer; asserting that Mr. Stephens promised to take them through to Cal. in 80 days, and that length of time being up, their labours were ended—Four waggons, ours among the number, started out at $\frac{1}{2}$ past 6 & drove on about 6 miles, one mile beyond the West Branch of Raft River & stoped. The Capt went back & got hands to drive the other teams up to where we were, and carilled [corralled] A proposition was made to divide all the provisions giving to each mess its proper share of everything; which was put to vote & carried without opposition from any one except the *Captain* and his boys. They were then accordingly divided; each mess taking its share—Several of the men refused to stand Guard for the cattle any longer—and many others declared that they would not stand Guard unless all the others did—Stayed here from 9 A.M. until next morning. . . . A vote was passed that no team should drive out without the consent of the majority of the Co."

The Keen train crossed the West Branch of the Raft River

June 21, and there began a mystery which would preoccupy Mrs. Brandon, the captain's wife, for the next two weeks: ". . . very bad crossing on account of the Mud this River is about 30 yards Wide and deep some of the Boys Wished a little Brandy and when The[y] opened the Keg they found it to be near all gone or Out. Some fellow or fellows had been drinking it up. Mrs. Julia Brandon our Lady had taken the precaution to Nail a bit of Leather over the bung of the Keg some 4 Weeks previous. as we were all passengers it was Considered a grand insult. We were all strangers to her with the exception of Vader who is her Brother. At any rate the Leather was torn off and the greater portion of the Brandy gone no one knew where Mrs. Brandon told her brother (Vader) that she knew he did not take it. Well I supposed there was not a Man in Company that would be guilty of such an offence unless it was Vader. As I never drank any they cleared me. Our Lady by this time procured a bit of tin and nailed it Over the bung of the Keg Remarking that if it was disturbed again she would throw it out and our Melee ended."

Three days later: "O Yes the Brandy Question Was agitated to day When We stopped to noon Our Would be Empress Julia looked up the Brandy Keg When LO, the tin was torn off and Our ears were saluted with a Volly of Curses that would shock the Modesty of the roughest sailor. she procured a bottle and filled it and locked it up in her Carpet bag her husband then proceeded to pour the remainder out on the ground When Doot Weatherby interposed and after some hard Words the Keg was placed back in the Wagon but no tin nailed upon the bung."

On July 1, the keg was found entirely empty, and on the Fourth of July, on the Humboldt River, the mystery was solved: "We were Just starting to day at noon . . . when the news came to me that Vader had a fit. I was driving they brought him and placed him in the Wagon. two men had to ride in the Wagon to hold him he appeared to be dreadfully Alarmed and Kept grasping after a gun that was in the

[235]

Wagon exclaiming there they Come dont you see them And when Asked What he saw he answered Indians Devils &C. I thought it a queer kind of A fit. . . . I ventured to ask Doc Hinkly if Vader had not the Delirium tremens. he told me that he had and that would account for the Brandy disappearing so mysteriously."

The road came to the western junction of the Fort Hall road a few miles beyond the West Branch of the Raft River, and from there it was a drive of only twelve or thirteen miles to the City of Rocks. "Traveled eight miles when we entered Pyramid Circle," Eliza Ann McAuley wrote on August 9. "This is one of the greatest curiosities on the road. In some places a piller rises to a height of one hundred and fifty feet, with smaller ones piled on the top and sides, looking as though a breath of air would hurl them down. These pyramids are of various colors. The sides have been washed by the rains in all manner of fantastic shapes, giving the place a most romantic and picturesque appearance. The circle is five miles long and three miles wide, level within the wall around and entirely surrounded by these pyramids or cliffs except an inlet at the east end of about fifty yards, and an outlet at the western end just wide enough to permit the wagons to pass through. The rocks are covered as far up as one can reach or climb, with names of emigrants. We left ours with date in a conspicuous place for the boys behind." Another five miles and they passed the junction of the Salt Lake road.

IX

FROM THE CITY OF ROCKS
TO HUMBOLDT SINK

———◆◄◉►►———

ON July 13 Dr. Wayman wrote: "We this morning left Granite City and commenced our daily toil. drove to Mountain Spring Creek say a distance of 14 miles & nooned. Some d——d Indians sneaking around beging. As usual McT & Loring were conjureing around the Squaws. I saw them give her (the Squaw) some victuals with a great [d]eal of care, & solicitude without receiving any thing in return in sight. they were seen going in the direction that the squaw indicated and return with out any explanation."

On July 20 Peter Hickman, before crossing the mountains from City of Rocks to Goose Creek Valley, "was promoted from Ox herder to Ox driver, & had the worst road to drive that we have had since we started." That road was described by John Hawkins Clark on the twenty-ninth: "Our pathway down to Goose creek valley was so steep that many persons attached small trees to their wagons as a help to let them down easy. We were in too big a hurry so let our wagons slide with the two hind wheels rough-locked; we gained the bottom as soon as the best of them, but our drivers and teams got mixed up somewhat and a great deal demoralized. One driver started downhill on the wagon box but landed at the bottom on top of the lead mule; another slid off his box sideways but kept going down, down, until the bottom was reached."

". . . before we extinguished our light last night," Caroline Richardson recorded on August 4, "our teams came up bringing news of breakdown and bad luck it was very dark when they reached the hill and one of their wagons (their luggage wagon) turned over and was percipitated to the first landing being a distance of thirty feet or more almost perpendicular this was rather a sad sight flour bacon lard vinigar cans cooking utensils all lay in one common pile lost about a hundred weight of flour spoiled a large water can and sundry articles though the wagon was not injured much only bending an ex which was iron and tearing of[f] the cover."

After this accident the company moved four miles up Goose Creek, where they "found plenty clams and caught enough for supper they are very good and make an exelant change."

R. H. P. Snodgrass camped on Goose Greek the night of July 3. "We had calculated to lay still today, but early in the morning we found that we were camped just between two large droves of cattle, Baker ahead of us, and Pomeroy close behind. About 3 o'clock in the morning we heard Pomeroy's cattle coming, and in 15 minutes we were out of bed and under way, as we were determined not to take the dust and leavings of two droves of stock, and it is almost impossible to pass a drove on the road; and to be behind they raise such a dust you can hardly live, and they muddy every spring & branch. We had the satisfaction of getting ahead of Pomeroy and of passing Baker before he started, if we did have to do it on empty stomaches. We stopped for a short time and got dinner at 1 o'clock. Baker swore he would pass Pomeroy again or kill every ox he had."

Richard Owen Hickman was driving cattle into Goose Creek Valley when he met a party of packers returning from California. "One of the men came up to us and said, 'Ah, boys, you ought to have women in the place of cows, for they are the scarcest article in California.'"

While moving up Goose Greek Valley on July 27, Addison Crane had word of his former companions: "The Capt. of our old Co. came ahead of his train and told over their troubles. They are already heartily sick of Lovejoy, and regard him as only a beast in human form, and from what I could learn I think they will turn him off quite soon. Lane goes swearing & cursing and fretting along as usual, and he & Lovejoy have fell out—and indeed from his description the whole Co. are in a constant turmoil and quarrell, haveing since we left, drawn knives & pistols upon each other! We were quite fortunate in getting clear of them." Two days later, he related further details: "Yesterday fell in with David Ayers formerly in the company which we left, but who abandoned them about a week ago. He represents the state of things among them to be a perfect hell upon earth. Him self & Lovejoy had a regular fist fight before he left them. He says L. got beastly drunk at bear river when he begged some whiskey of an Indian trader. According to him L. is to be turned out of the Company, upon

[239]

the Humboldt—a few days from now, and I hope yet to have the pleasure of seeing him footing it with a pack on his back—and it would be hardly what he deserves."

John Hawkins Clark, on July 30, wrote: "The main road of this valley is with but few exceptions very good; the exceptions, however, are the most miserable we have as yet encountered; especially at the crossing of tributary streams. At some of them had to leave the main road and travel miles to avoid getting stuck in the mire and slush of the valley. A mule we purchased in Salt Lake has a habit of lying down on every damp spot he travels over. In passing through a mud hole this afternoon he took it into his head to lie down and rest; a wagon standing in the middle of a great mud hole with one mule before it standing up and another with his head just above the surface was a scene not often witnessed in Goose creek valley. What good feeling the mud and water gives the brute is a mystery known only to himself."

By the time John Verdenal's company reached Goose Creek Valley, August 26, the grass was nearly gone and water was low: "Started at 7 o'clock road level camped a few hours at a small spring where grass was very scarce. we hitched on the cattle and it being moonlight we travelled on in search of water and grass. I and many others went on ahead we passed many trains and many cattle we saw some by the side of the road fatigued broken down and staring, we that were on horse back reached the water full 2 hours before the train. we lit a large fire with sage brush to warm ourselves the weather being rather chilly. here there was no grass the train came on but the cattle had nothing to eat two had been left behind it was midnight. laid by till five oclock I slept not a wink. the cattle were flying in all directions in search of something to appease their hunger we at last succeeded in huddling them together and at five oclock again passed on. the cattle could hardly be made to go they were dreadfully cut and whipped by the merciless drivers. and no one rode within the wagon. all that had not horses were forced to walk we camped at noon there was no water and not much grass. here we left the cattle roam far from camp with guards. Elsworth said there was no water for 8 miles ahead. some who had horses went back to the last camp a distance of five miles and watered their horses. but this was too much for the cattle, we dug a well and got a little dirty water for 125 head of cattle. it would not do. . . . (Saturday August 28th.) Started at 5 had not porceeded more than 1 mile when we found inumerable small springs of clear & cold water. this proved that Elsworth was unacquainted with the road. here we unhitched the cattle. our horses drank about 4 buckets of water each & might have drank much more had we not restrained them. the cattle dirtied all the springs in their hurry to drink and some also got stuck in the mud after they had enough we again hitched on and went on a few miles near some more fine springs and camped, where grass was in abundance."

On July 14 Richard Owen Hickman camped at the head of the valley: "Soon after stopping a young man came up on a mule and spoke to us. He was from the city of Memphis, Tenn., and had come up on the same boat that we did to Independence and had got pretty well acquainted. His name was William W. Johnson. He stated that he left the Mo. line on the 10 of May and passed Biddle, Constant and Dr. Henry at Kaw river. . . . On the next morning we were off soon after daylight, having to travel 17 miles to water and 25 to grass. Wm. Johnson passed us before we got to Thousand Spring Valley, bid me goodbye and said he would be in Sacramento City in fifteen days." Two weeks later on the Humboldt River: ". . . whilst we were filling our vessels with water a company of packers came up. One of the men I recognized as having seen him in company with Mr. Johnson. I went up and inquired where he was and also how they came to be behind us. He told me that on arriving at the head of the Humboldt one of their men was sick and they laid by for him to get well and whilst they were laying by Mr. Johnson was taken with the cholera and after an illness of only 13 hours, died. Thus it

The Palisades on the Humboldt

seems like a man has no assurance of his life, for only three days before his death I saw him and he told me he was in better health than he had been for years."

Caroline Richardson was nearing the end of Thousand Spring Valley on August 9: "there are a great many packing through some with horses and mules others on foot but the most novel way we have seen was a boy packing through with a cow he had come all the way in that manner and his prospects of getting through were indeed fair."

The trail from Thousand Spring Valley went over a small ridge to Hot Spring Valley. The hot springs were a famous landmark, where Eliza Ann McAuley, on August 14, noted: "About ten o'clock we came to the boiling springs. Here several large springs boil up in the middle of the valley, forming a large stream at a temperature of one hundred and seventy degrees with a nauseous, sickening smell. A distressing accident occurred here about two hours before we arrived. Two brothers, who had been out hunting, stopped here to wait for their train. As they were sitting on the ground, they heard a gun fired off across the stream, and thinking there were Indians about, one of them sprang to his feet, at the same time catching up his gun, which was lying on the ground before him, with the muzzle toward him and it went off, the ball passing through his lungs. He was still alive but sinking rapidly when we left. We gave them all the fresh water we had, which was all that we could do for them, as their train had come up."

Stephen Gage camped near the Boiling Springs the afternoon of the Fourth of July: ". . . then commenced operations for a 4th supper which in due time was prepared & ready to commence depredations Our supper consisted of Oysters Oyster soup fine Biscuit Good Boston Crackers & tea Preserves & some fine Fruit Cake 'c. &c. . . . This was the Glorious Anniversary of the 76th year of our American Independence celebrated by our company And long will it be remembered by each & evryone."

George Short, ahead of Gage on the headwaters of the Humboldt, spent a dour Fourth of July: "another Christian Sabbath has arrived i am thankful for a Chance to rest from labor and hold sweet Communion with God Crocker and Root are doing their washing some are fishing some are shooting at a mark and serving the Devil but there is a day coming when all shall receive their reward both the Christian and the bold blasphemer and the miserable insulting Hypocite not every one that saith Lord shall enter the KM of heaven."

The Richard Keen train had been traveling for several days with an Illinois company. The two trains camped, June 26, some twenty miles past the Boiling Springs: "this morning Mrs. Ward breathed her last she died about 2 Oclock She leaves three small children a little boy of 7 and two little girls 5 and 3 years this is the first death we have had it fell upon me to prepare a head board which was done in as short a Manner as possible cut the letters With a small knife it read. Mary Ann Wife of Dr. D. Ward died June 27th 1852 Aged 26 years, from Adams County Illinois. we burried her on an eminence close the side of the road so that her friends who were coming might know that here rested the Mortal remains of an early friend was a member of a church and died a Christian. she requested a hymn to be sung over her Grave. we had no Coffin so she was Wrapt in some blankets and consigned to the earth Dr. Hinkly performed the duties of Chaplain read a chapter from the Bible the funeral numbered 42 persons."

A friend saw her grave on July 3. "passed the grave of Dr Wards wife," George Short wrote. ". . . they Came on the boat with us down the Mississippi and up the Missouri she left 3 Children and a drunken father."

William Lobenstine passed the springs on July 24: "Friend and companion Logan died this morning at five o'clock. Logan, a partner in our team, took sick very suddenly about noon this day about two miles this side Hot Springs. Driving on some few miles after noon, the disease came on in a very serious manner so that we were obliged to stop and camp. His strength failed rapidly and cramps in all his parts caused him very aggravating pains. Getting worse and worse and medical help having no effect on him we finally concluded that although unsuspected and however sudden he would go home to his Father. Living on till sunrise next day, he died about five o'clock in the morning after a sickness of seventeen hours. This then is human life—to live, to eat, to propagate and die."

The emigrants had heard much of the Humboldt River and had steeled themselves for the worst, so their arrival at the headwaters of that river was a pleasant—albeit short-lived— surprise. Typical was D. B. Andrews, who reached the headwaters on July 19: "Instead of finding a stream filled with filth, poison water and very sluggish, found a beautiful creek about one and a half rods in width with clear water, lively current and fine gravelly bottom. The water is not unpleasant, tasted but a little warm. The valley about the head of this stream is very beautiful being surrounded by high mountains. Crossing the creek continued down on its north side some 12 or 15 miles. Camped at a fine piece of red top meadow. Thus far on the river there is hundreds of acres of red top grass and other grass of the finest quality. The bottom is much cut up with slues which in a time of high water are filled with water preventing emigrants from reaching grass without considerable trouble. At this time the river is very low & most of the slues are dry or impassable."

"The stream at this point is neither wide nor deep," John

Death on the Trail

Riker wrote of the North Fork on July 9. "The banks near the margin of the stream are covered by a dense growth of small willow bushes; the branches from either side unite above the stream, and in many places form a beautiful shady arbor, through which the silent waters pursue their onward course. On the east side of this stream are large quantities of alkali and some saleratus. In many places the ground is made white as snow by this coating, which, when reflected upon by the rays of the sun, forms a scene beautiful and grand." But the region lived up to its reputation in one respect: "Our journey to-day has been very unpleasant; the air being constantly filled with clouds of sand, carried before the wind, and filling our eyes to such an extent as to cause us much pain and suffering. Our persons, too, did not escape the general conflict; for when we entered camp, we are at a loss to know one from the other."

Eighteen fifty-two was a year of good grass in this upper meadow of the Humboldt. Mrs. Sawyer noted on July 18: "We came to Mary's river, or Humboldt, as some call it, to-day. All the emigrants dread this river, but we found some grass, which is more than we expected, as Mr. Sawyer says there was very little here when he came out in '49." On August 3, Dr. Dalton thought: "This certainly is one of the most beautiful valleys I ever beheld The large, luxuriant green grass near the water resembles Oats just heading; very thick & rank—While the large rank wild wheat grass over the bottom looks precisely like wheat, just before harvest when begining to turn its color. There are hundreds of thousands of acres of this kind of Grass." But on August 20 John Udell said that "the herbage is fairly eaten out."

Tosten Kittlesen Stabaek, one of a company of Norwegians from Rock Run, Illinois, recalled his first night upon the Humboldt: "In the evening we drove the cattle over to the brook, which ran a little distance from the road; here was such an abundance of grass that the cattle had a feast such as they had not enjoyed for several days past. The animals settled down near the wagons, and all but the watchman went to bed as usual.

"The next morning five of our draught oxen were gone. A careful search revealed their tracks and those of four horses, and we no longer doubted that the Indians had stolen them. In the dark the Indians had spirited them away under the noses of our guards. Twelve men set out on foot in pursuit of the thieves, but after a march of some four or five miles without a trace of the oxen, a council was held to decide what should be done. It was decided to continue the pursuit. But as it promised to be a long search, I was sent back for provisions. I returned and managed to collect the necessary food, but was not allowed to carry it back; for Søren Knudsen and Nels Nelson insisted on going in my place. They returned, however, at sunset, without having found the others.

"Fearing more visits from the Indians we made an enclosure with the wagons and herded the cattle inside it; in this way it was easier to mount guard over them. . . . Our search party returned the next morning. They had found the oxen, slaughtered. The Indians were nowhere to be seen, but were no doubt near enough to see what was going on. All that the men got out of the oxen was some meat which they sliced off and roasted at a fire which they kindled. They were famished after having tramped all day without a bite to eat. . . ."

The Indians were a harassment all the way down the Humboldt, but not, as the emigrants accused them, so much from hostility as from hunger. G. A. Smith, on June 25, noticed: "On rising a bluff this morning we looked back and saw our camping ground covered with digers Indians thay swam the River and dove into camp like so many hungry wolves after the rines and crumbs."

The Indians were also blamed for many thefts for which they were not responsible. "We now learned of others who had also lost cattle; the Indians always got the blame, even though white men might be the ringleaders," according to Tosten Stabaek. "At Stone Point a company of emigrants lost some cattle and sent out four men to search for them. At length they found the cattle, but were attacked by the band of robbers, consisting of five white men and a number of Indians. The four emigrants were well armed, and the Indians, who shot their arrows from a safe distance, could do them no harm. Thus they had the upper hand and got their animals back.

"Many others who lost cattle followed their tracks and thought they were hot on their heels, but nevertheless failed to

[247]

get hold of them. A certain man lost twelve horses by Stone Point one night. In the morning he followed their tracks until they began to point towards Salt Lake; then he turned back, for he knew where they were gone and that his pursuit was in vain."

John Udell camped for dinner on the Humboldt on August 23: "While here, Campbell Drury, who had parted from us at Salt Lake City, came up with a band of ruffians. They presented their pistols, demanded our provisions, and threatened to take them by force, if we refused to give them up. They were prevented from carrying out their threats, however, by a large train, encamped at a little distance from us, after I had appealed in vain to their sympathies, telling them that we had barely provisions enough to carry us through, and representing to them the cruelty of leaving us to starve on the plain. But the Lord in whom I trusted, sent deliverance!" Udell, wisely, joined a large train the same day.

"Sabbath morning fine but warm day," Thomas Lewis wrote on July 18, "saw some indians (root diggers) Prowling about for to steal . . . the men in our camp did not think it safe to stop anny Longer than noon in camp but to move off. I did not want to move on the Sabbath. they left us at 1, 0. Charles and me thought we could stay by our selves. in about 1½ hours, I went up on the rise of ground above the [camp] I saw 2 indians on the river a short distance above us and 1 on horseback a little below them. I Looked about me I saw on the hills above us 5 or 6 miles off the smoke of their fires. I did not think Prudent or safe to stay by our selves, I went back to camp told Charles it would be most Prudent for us to move off, for we were Left by our selfs and but one gun, so we geared up started about 2 hours after our company started, caught up with them before sun down."

There were two roads out of the first valley of the Humboldt. One, up over the bluffs away from the river, had to be taken in times of high water, but was often traveled to avoid four crossings of the river. The other led along the river at low

[248]

water through a narrow canyon. John Hawkins Clark, on August 5, took the bluff road: "The terminus of the first valley of the Humboldt river is reached to-day. This, the eastern section of the valley is said to be seventy-five miles in length. . . . Our road this afternoon is up a steep mountain side seven miles long; the steepest, roughest, and most desolate road that can be imagined. The mountains that border this valley are looking very old. I think they must have been the first created, bald and hoary headed, ragged and torn to pieces, have a decrepit and worn-out look, suggestive of old times and old associations. It makes a man lonesome and homesick to contemplate their forlorn, deserted and uncanny appearance. Stunted and scattered cedar trees, broken down by the snows and wild winds of the winter season, gives them a sort of ghost-like appearance that makes one shudder to behold. The mountain we are crossing to-day stands at right angles with our road and cuts the valley of the Humboldt into two separate divisions, making an upper and lower Humboldt valley. We camp to-night on the summit of this great mountain; tired, hungry and disappointed, we pitch our tents beside a spring of good water, but of so scant a volume that we can give no drink to our thirsty and half famished animals. This has been a hard afternoon to ourselves and teams; seven miles of a continuous rise and many places so abrupt that it took all the strength of men and teams to overcome the difficulties of the way. We were more fortunate than many of our neighbors; we lost no stock in making the summit of this difficult road; we counted eight or ten horses and two or three mules that failed to make the journey. The scenery at this place is wild, desolate and forbidding, without a spark of romance to enliven our spirits. Everything about us has a look of stubborn fact that is easy to realize as to count one's fingers. No wood, no grass and but a scanty supply of water; all is rock, rock, rock, as bare of vegetation as a sterile rock can be; some little sage brush grew near the spring; these we gathered and warmed our coffee."

The next day the other John Clark took the river road:

"Before day we was moving down the Saleratus flat. Brush along the creek. Tom Alexander kills a very large sandhill crain, Robinson the ducks, Price the sage hens & the Sturgeon boys several hares & gophers. We saw some Indians along the stream, & one large band of mounted men just coming out of a Canyon. But seeing so many men & waggons on our side of the river they wheeled about & put back for the bluffs, while we drove on down to the first crossing, 20 mile. Now the hills close in & makes a deep narrow canyon. A more wild & savage looking place I never saw. I am really affraid to go ahead of the teams. Great presapes [precipices] on the right & Mary's high point to the left, & the Canyon before is dark & fearful. A narrow gorge for 2 miles, then 2 more brings you to a steep bank. Here we camp on the narrow flat to the left. No fire is made for fear of being discovered. The stock is all tied, & we sleep in the grass & brush, out from the waggons. Just after dark a large band of Indians made their crossing above us. The wading, & splashing of the horses in crosing the stream lasted near half an hour. We lay close & still for some hours before we would venture to let the stock loose to graze just before day. This was truly one fearful night to me, as well as others in the company."

By the time the emigrants had traveled eighty miles down the Humboldt to Stony Point, the river was beginning to live up to its reputation. "Today again we had 22 miles without water," R. H. P. Snodgrass wrote on July 13, "and now we begin to suffer in earnest. Our lips bleed almost every time we speak, and our mouths and throats are sore from the effects of the dust, heat and bad water. Close off to our left the mountain is covered with snow, while here in the valley we are suffering from heat and dust in the longest days of summer. The water in the valley is growing worse."

Three weeks later Addison Crane experienced an unseasonable storm. It had rained on August 4, for a time, and then on the fifth: "Rain! Rain! rain! During all P.M. yesterday the black clouds in the W. & low distant thunder betokened show-

[250]

A Chief Forbids the Passage of a Train Through His Country

ers ahead. After encamping (which we did not do until sun set & after) we got a very hasty supper & at about 9 commenced and continued for over 2 hours one of the most terrific thunder showers I have ever witnessed. The rain came down in torrents,—floods—the thunder fair shook the earth, and the wind blew little short of a hurricane—the whole lighted up almost every instant by the deep red glare of the burning lightening. Albert had been complaining during the day of head ache & other pains came into camp very sick, and during this terrible storm we were in our wagon with a lighted lantern, curtains tightly fastened, and some of the rain (very little) driveing through our hitherto water proof cover; he writhing with pains in the head back and bones, almost screaming with agony under a burning fever & a hard pulse—in short a very critical case of some acute fever, requiring the best care of a skillful physician, & the comforts of civilized life—but instead of that he had neither but was cooped up in a $3\frac{1}{2}$ by 9 box—dependant only upon me for medical aid—& I without the skill of a doctor and with a very small variety of medicines was forced to 'take the responsibility.' First got down cathartic—pains increasing gave during the night repeated small doses morphine—in morning an emitic—to day pains gone & much better—but no appetite & much nausea. To day we have moved 15 m. down the Humboldt—through & over very muddy roads—sometimes for $\frac{1}{2}$ A.M. mud 2 ft deep. All caused by said shower Hope it wont rain any more on the Humboldt! for dust & dirt are preferable—& even heat."

If Addison Crane expressed a desire to see no more rain on the Humboldt, John Hawkins Clark would have welcomed it eight days later: "A desert of twenty-five miles has been traveled over to-day and under a hot, broiling sun. Its scorching rays appeared to penetrate through our hats. Our feet coming in contact with the hot sand felt like burning up. Our great want now, is: water! water!! water!!! good spring water, good well water, good snow water, good river water. Our dreams are of water, clear and cold, spouting from the earth like a geyser; the mountain streams that come tumbling over the great boulders, making a noise like the rush of 'many waters,' are a part of our midnight visions. Our ears are sometimes greeted with the groan and grumbles of the old ancient well sweep as it lifts the 'moss-covered bucket' full to overflowing with the sparkling water. We remember every good spring we ever visited, whether away back in the old home in the Jersey's or in more recent years, while wandering among the lakes and dells of the far off Minnesota's. It must not be inferred by reading the above, that we are destitute of water—far from it. We are somewhat like the cast away sailor when he had 'water, water, everywhere, but not a drop to drink.' We have a river to draw from, but such water—warm as fresh milk and impregnated with alkali and a taste of salt to such a degree that we cannot use it until after the poison is killed by heating. We boil all the water we drink, and then it is barely fit for use. Sometimes we find a spring near the river's edge and among the tall wild grass, and if it is full of snakes, frogs and other reptiles, it is all right. We drive them out, and take a drink ourselves; but if the water looks black, and we can find no water varmint, not even a snake, we let it alone."

The next day, August 14, Clark continued: "In passing through a long, deep mudhole to-day our Salt Lake mule, as usual, laid down to take a rest, and as it happened the wagon to which he was attached was a long way behind, and consequently no help at hand. How to get the mule out of the mud and water and proceed on our journey was a question with the driver and myself hard to solve. However, we had but little time before a young and sturdy-looking chap rode up on a big strong mule and made inquiry as to what we were doing in that kind of a fix. Our driver gave him all the necessary information as to the habits and antecedents of our delinquent mule and wound up by telling him that the captain had purchased the brute at Salt Lake and that he had been a trouble to us ever since, and for his part he wished the d——d thing was dead. The young stranger laughed at the young man's ca-

[253]

lamity but promised for a drink of good brandy not only to help [him] out of his present difficulty, but to cure our tricky mule of the bad habit of laying down on every soft spot he met with on the road. It is needless to say that a bargain was soon struck; our festive mule was stripped naked, one end of a lariat belonging to the stranger was passed around his neck, the other end to the horn of its owner's saddle and away he went, dragging the unfortunate mule through the slush and water almost at a 2:40 gait. However, that kind of locomation did not suit our delinquent friend; he soon began to hunt for his feet and in spite of the rate of speed he was traveling was soon up and on all fours, alongside his tormentor. The fun was now up and our friend had the mule back, hitched him up and drove him through a stretch of a half mile mudhole without any further difficulty. A good swig of brandy from the big jug and our bargain concluded; the stranger went on his way rejoicing and our driver drove into camp a happy man."

Clark continued: "A mule is a mule, the world over I guess; their peculiarities are many and so different from all other animals that man is often at a loss to comprehend them. At what period in the world's history he made his advent upon earth it would take a better historian than myself to say; 'no pride of ancestry and no hope of parentage,' a living phenomena of man's inventive genius; good to do the bidding of his master, hardy in the performance of his task, easy to manage and not expensive to keep. As a rustler I have not seen his equal; he can strip a cottonwood in less time than a truant school boy can shed his trousers at the edge of a swim pond; very particular about water, would rather go dry all day than touch water that a horse or an ox would delight in, but when hungry will eat anything within reach; tear the roots of grass from the astonished earth after the blades have long since disappeared; have known him to attack a half worn-out boot belonging and attached to a weary and sleeping pilgrim. Except the grease wood and sage brush there is nothing edible that I know of that he will not eat; in some respects he is an ungainly and rough brute, his ears out of all proportions to his heels; head rough and ungainly but with an eye as mild as a lamb and twice as innocent, except when he is out of humor, when they are dangerous even to look at. It is said that a 'mule never dies'; I do not know how that is as I never saw a dead one, but have seen his heels very lively when I thought their owner half dead with hunger and hard work. Take him all in all, the mule is a peculiar animal, good and bad, according to his whims; 'but, with all thy faults we have thee still.' "

Death, both for men and for stock, was ever present on the Humboldt. "We are begining to find lots of dead stock," R. H. P. Snodgrass wrote on July 16, "some by the road side, some stuck fast in sloughs, and the most in the river. The carrion crow is here croaking his harvest song, & so full of meat that they will hardly get out of the road as the train comes along. Coming down this stream we have seen the skulls of a number of persons who have been buried in '49, '50 & '51 and have been dug up by the wolves, and their bodies left to whiten the plains. And we see a great many fresh graves of the victims of this year. The well and hearty suffer intensely along here, but the sick are soon taken to a bourne where fatigue and suffering are no more known—here the sick have no soft bed, no mother & sister to watch over them, none of the little delicacies of life, and too often not even the necessary supply of rough camp fare and attention. Few trains make any calculation for sick men."

"it is disheartening to endeavor to travel with so many of the boys are sick Lolas is getting very low," Richard Keen wrote on July 6, "the Physicians gave him Calomel which has salivated him very bad and they cannot stop it this Humbolt water is so strongly tinctured with Alkali it makes all our Mouthes sore. Lolas will not endeavor to take any care of himself says he will die anyhow this humbolt Country never was made or intended for Man the water even effects the horses and Mules and if we have to stop on this Accursed stream long we Will all die the Majority of Our Co. are sick at this time."

The next day: "Lolas is past speaking he is truly an object of pity he can yet walk around his face swelled very much his lips and tongue are eat off poor fellow we will soon have to put him under the sod."

"July 8: held a Council last night to Consider the propriety of stopping with our sick. after a lengthy discussion it was left to a vote. which was given in this way or taken at least. Whether we stop with our sick until they die or recover Or should we pursue our Journey and get off this terrible river as soon as possible it was a hard and sad question. On the one side was the pitiful sight of A man that was suffering the bitter pangs of death he had but a few hours or days at most to live and his suffering appearance when moved. Was mutely pleading for a few hours rest until his weary spirit might wing its flight. And on the Other side was sickness and probably death staring us in the face the longer we stayed the worse it would be for us we could not save the lives of those that were sick by stopping and those that were not too far gone probably might recover when we reached good Water the vote was taken and we are to pursue our Journey. We Rolled out very early this morning . . . we traveled until noon when humanity again triumphed and we are to stop this afternoon at 4 Oclock poor john ceased to be numbered with the living Death the King of terrors now reigns in Our Midst Johns Pilgrimage is Oer . . . he is to be buried at sun set. I had to guard our stock at that time so I could not attend the burrying Our horses were grazing about One half mile above Camp I ascended a bluff or eminence from where I could see the funeral procession. it was a sad sight to behold that little band of Emigrants slowly wending their way to what was to be the last sad resting place of One of Our Comrades. he was buried in the middle of the road this was done to keep the Indians from digging him up. . . .

"He was an Orphan Boy . . . when quite a small boy he was adopted by a quaker family residing somewhere in pennsylvania They afterward Moved to Indiana Laporte County

[256]

John remained until he was 21 years of Age the Old Gentleman had also two daughters near the same age of John. John and the Oldest daughter formed an attachment when quite young at length the Old people Appraised them selves of the fact it did not meet with their approbation and they forbade John ever coming into their house again. John Obeyed and left and went to work in the neighborhood the young lady also left home and lived with a neighbor where they often met time ran on for about One Year When they were engaged to be Married the time and day was set for the Wedding. About this time emigrants were starting to California, when some of our Co. insisted upon John to accompany them a short distance for a day or two John Complied he would go a short distance with his young friends this was Monday Morning and on the thursday following he was to claim his bride. Well they traveled two or three days and finally pursuaded John to go on with them as far as St Joseph at least and before they reached St Jo. he had paid 100 dollars for his passage to California he was a man that was easily expected or stimulated and in his thoughtful moments he was reproached he knew he had done wrong he would sometime think of his oft repeated vows of constancy. When they reached St. Joseph he received a letter from the Girl he so wronged. which informed him that if he went to California he need never return with the expectation of Marrying her but if he would then return she would forgive him for the past. this broke the spell and his finer feelings gained the Mastery he concluded to return drew his money that he had paid for his passage and was going . . . but before the steamer Came the Boys had encircled John taunting him about backing Out &c. telling him that he ought to be independent and not submit to being led by the nose telling him what fine times he would have &c. Johns resolve was broken he paid his money and swore he would go I could see that all was not right with John from the time we started until his death there was something weighing heavily upon his Mind he was in trouble he would take no Care of himself life was no

Lassen's Butte, Sacramento Valley

object and When he was taken sick he would expose himself and on being told that if he expected to reach California he must take care of his health he replied that he did not care to live he wished to die Which wish I am sorry to say was eer long granted. . . . And now the question arises does not these young Men who prevailed upon him to go to sacrifice his honor and eventually his life do they not even feel the pangs of Remorse for they have been Accessory to the dead. this should and will serve as a warning to these men at least to never persuade a man to do A wrong action Knowingly I think it has taught a lesson that still never be forgotten by some of the party at least but poor John is no More peace to his Ashes his troubles are Over he has crossed the River and is now realizing the Realities of a future world."

At Lassen's Meadows, some fifty miles above the great Humboldt Meadows, there was a new route—opened this year—Nobles' Road, which followed the old Lassen Trail to some extent and led to the northern mining town of Shasta. Solomon Kingery's company reached Lassen's Meadows on

July 28: "Here three teams of us concluded to take the Shasta or Knobles rout. This is a new rout across the Siera Nevada Mt & leads into the northern mines & has never been traveld before this year. [July] 29th. Three teams of us made a ford & Crossed the river, 4 rods wide, 4 ft. deep. The rest of the company preferd the old rout. We traveld 15 miles. Encamped on Marys river at the Junction of the roads. Here we found another Company of 11 teams that are going the new rout. This follows the Lawson rout 54 miles."

Addison Crane neared the junction on August 10: "This is our last encampment with our friends Ingrams whom we have travelled with since July 1. . . . *they* taking the right hand road from this to Shasta City . . . while we keep on the old road to Sacramento. Our acquaintance & association with this company has been every way agreeable & pleasant, and we part with them with regret—but our interests compel the separation. I shall always remember them with pleasure. . . . They are from Western reserve Ohio and every one of them gentlemanly. Mr. Russell & son remain with us and work well & faithfully—indeed they do nearly all the work & no growling about it."

The Kingery train covered thirty miles on their first day on the new route, and on July 31: "Traveld 24 miles acrossed the Dessert. Road good. Weather warm. This Drive Should be made after night. we Suffered very much for the want of water as the water at the wells is not fit to drink. . . . Encampd at the Black Rock mountain & Boiling Spring. Here is plenty grass but no Cold water. . . . We passed upwards of thirty waggons to day that were left on this desert in 1849 & Bones of hundred of Cattle & Blacksmith tools, saw mill Saws & Different kind of machinerys &c. Here we leave the Lawson rout & turn to the left."

On August 12 the train was in the mountains beyond Honey Lake Valley: "Before daylight this morning the Indians got four of our oxen and out of another team, out to themselves Some way and drove them of. . . . 4 of the boys well

[259]

armed followed them about 2 Miles. They found the Cattle: three of them were Killed & partly Skind & had a large peice of Stake on a fire Cooking it. . . . No Indians could be Seen or found near the Cattle. . . . Encamped on a Small Creek. Grass tolerable. We Saw Some Indians drive a cow away from here when we Come. 6 of our boys followed them about 6 Miles or near to where they had Killed the other Cattle. They Saw a Smoke in a thicket. Our boys got around on a hill & Killed three of the Indians, 4 more run. They had Killed the Cow and were Cooking Some of the beef. . . .

"[August] 15th. Traveld 20 miles. . . . We passed the black Bute or volcanoe; this is a great Curiosity. Road very heavy, Sandy. Encamped on a Small Lake. Grass mostly Clover. To our left is the Lawson or Snow Peak Coverd with Everlasting Snow. Here we met five men that are Sent out by the Citizens of Shasta City to Pilate us through. . . ."

When John Clark of Virginia passed Lassen's Meadows on August 16, he found many emigrants sick and dying: "Here was many emigrants in camp. Five had died during the night, & one man just drowned in bringing his stock over. Here we came up with Stambaugh & Coulter's train from Columbus. Some of them are sick, & near dying. Graves are very plenty all along here, & the dead stock make you sick, the stench is so great. . . . To the head of the Great Bend, 4 miles. Here the Lawson Trail bears off to Shasty, but we keep down the bend to a low, ashy bluff, 5 miles. Now pass over a poor saleratus flat to the creek again, 6 mile. Here we camp near Coulter's train. Doctor Stambaugh from Columbus is about dying. This day we have seen 18 graves, 87 burnt waggons, dead cattle, 104. The road is dusty, great whirlwinds, & in spots the dry gras in fire."

All along the lower Humboldt the emigrants met men who had come from California to meet their families. The McAuleys were nearing the Humboldt Meadows on August 29. "After traveling about six miles we met Father. Oh wasn't it a joyful meeting. He had been waiting at a trading post."

The Great Humboldt Meadow gave the weary emigrants an opportunity to rest and recruit both men and stock before moving on to the Sink of the Humboldt and the long trek across the desert to the Carson or Truckee rivers. "There is three trading posts at these Meadows," Richard Keen observed on July 11, "they sell flour at 25 cents pr pound beef the same tobacco One dollar pr pound and Whiskey 50 cents pr drink I bought none but some of the Boys did and got considerably Alkalied." Mary Bailey arrived at the meadows on September 11: "We had thought that some of our profane men were bad enough but the Cals are so much worse that we will not compare them. A man here that had come out to meet his wife & she was married to another man before she got here he says that he shall shoot her father before morning."

"last evening we were called upon to sit with a lady in camp who was not expected to live until morning," Caroline Richardson wrote on August 29, "we made haste to her camp but when we reached it she had just breathed her last she was a Mrs Grigsby from Mo who had started in co with a brother in law to join her husband in California her husband who apprised of her coming came out and met her here but oh that meeting he had heard of his sisters death his only sister and felt as if the blow was hard but he had come on to feel a sader his wife did not know him until a short time before she expired when on being asked if she recognized her husband she grew restless puting her arms around his neck while large tears rolled down her cheek she could not speak. thus they met and thus they parted he was nearly distracted and his cries could be heard full a mile."

Nearing the meadows, Dr. John Dalton struck out ahead of his train: "About 10 o'clock I started from the waggon; saw ahead the point of a low mountain running down from the North and Capt. Stephens told me that we passed over that hill, and that when upon it we could see Humboldt Lake, which, & the meadow, lay right beyond, on the other side of it. The Guide mentioning a spring of good, cold, water at the head of a slough, supposed to be not far ahead; & getting *very tired* of the River water, I pushed ahead, bearing to the left & in about 3 miles struck the slough; & the water looking very bad, went up to its head in search of the Spring, across decidedly the *worst* spot of ground over which I ever traveled—It was baked & cracked on a magnificent scale—the cracks being from 12 to 15 feet deep & nearly a foot wide; and to make it worse, the fire had burned over it, leaving ashes & cinders at least a foot deep so that a person would slump in nearly every step half way to his knees; and on I trudged about five miles, sweating like rain; and getting most *tremendous thirsty;* and when I arrived at the head of the slough, there was a first rate place for a spring, but *not a drop* of *water* could be found; saw a road 2 miles ahead, passing over the bluff; went up on to the high part of the hill; saw Humbolt Lake which looked but a little ways ahead; pushed on & traveled about eight miles; when concluding I had taken the wrong road, I turned square to the left & in about 2 miles came to an other road—went up one mile & *suffering intensely* with a *raging thirst,* I broke across for the river; & after going *on, on & on,* through the rushes, I found there was no river, nor a drop of water there; it having sunk above; returned to the road; went up one mile & met some Packers, who told me that this road came down on the North side of the river, that it was about 14 miles to the head of the meadow up that road—It was now nearly dark; pushed on & in 5 miles came where two waggons had camped, but had no fire for want of wood—got of them a drink; which though Humbolt River water, warm and slimy; yet under the circumstances, I thought it the *best* I ever *tasted*—went up one mile further & found others camped with a fire got of them a cup of coffee; & a blanket; after drinking the coffee, wrapt myself in the Blanket and laid down in the open air; but I was so *tremendously fatigued* that I could not sleep a wink all night; rose early, and after getting a little breakfast & paying them one dollar, started up the road and after traveling 7 miles came to our train; right *glad* to get at my *old quarters* again—I thought I had heretofore suffered from fatigue & thirst; but never before did I ever suffer so much in any one day; nor the fourth part of it, as on the 14th of August, 1852; in tramping through the Humbolt valley in the manner above described."

"We are now at the end of our journey of the Humboldt river," John Hawkins Clark noted on August 16. "Here she sinks beneath the sands of the great desert, but before she is lost in sight of forever, her waters spread out into a lake some six or eight miles in length by one and a half in breadth. . . . The grass is coarse, tall and heavy; what it lacks in nourishment is made up in abundance. We cut this grass and load our

Humboldt Wells and Ruby Mountains

nearly empty wagons to furnish feed for our teams while crossing a forty mile desert stretching from the sink of the Humboldt to Carson river."

"This morning we started without breakfast and traveled 8 miles to the head of the Slough or Big Meadow as it is *'Miscalled,'*" R. H. P. Snodgrass wrote on July 19. "Here we stopped and burnt our cook waggon for fuel to cook grub to last us over the desert to the Carson River. After we got through cooking we moved down the slough 15 miles and camped for the night. Here we had to wade through water from six to two feet deep into where we could get water fit to use. The water is a mixture of salt, sulphur, iron, alkalye, mud, dead horses, mules and oxen. Very palatable indeed."

John Riker said of this day, "All are now busily preparing to cross the desert; some are over-hauling their goods and casting away everything that is deemed useless, while others are busily cutting grass for their stock. The cooks are preparing 'grub;' all is bustle and anxiety, as all are anxious to shorten the distance as fast as possible; and the opinion is very prevalant in our camp at last, that we will soon bid adieu to these plains forever, as few, if any, harbor the opinion that they will ever again try the sad realities we all have experienced since leaving our peaceful and happy homes."

X

FROM THE SINK OF THE HUMBOLDT
TO CALIFORNIA VIA THE
TRUCKEE RIVER

ON AUGUST 21 John Clark of Virginia began the
arduous fifty-five-mile trek across the desert to the
Truckee: ". . . long before sunrise our teams were on the trail
marching forward on the desert. Very little of note save the
dust & brightness of the glittering sand. Now & then a grave,
little donage & dead stock. One low bluff, & not a drop of

water or spear of grass to the Boiling Spring. . . . This afternoon I was some distance forward of the train, my poney became faint & lay down in the road. I thought it was gone in, but I had near a quart of water in my gun pouch, stove in my hat crown & gave it the drink. This soon releavd the suffering beast so that it was able to get up & go on with the train to the spring, where we found the water in a tremendous boil. It was now sundown. There were lots of kegs, buckets & large tin cans laying about & we soon had a number of them fild in part, so the water would cool for the stock. As they stood bawling at the sight of water we had to drive them off some distance to keep them quiet for a while. Some of the party during the day killed a couple of grouse. They were put in the camp kettle, set in the spring, & in a few minutes boild to pieces. The principal spring is four or five feet deep, eight or ten feet across, & boils at a wonderful rate. We taried here 3 hours then put forward about ten in the evening. Just as we were leaving some of the boys set fire to a large pile of kegs and casks. They were soon in a great blaze, the light of which appeard to astonish the neighboring wolves. They set up a fearful howl while we drove on passing during the night lots of dead & worn down stock. At day break we struck the deep sand, & the axels & hubs were down, so we had to stop & rest an hour."

Dr. John Dalton was called upon on August 19 to treat a mother and son who had been seriously scalded at the Boiling Springs. They had reached the springs about 2 A.M., when the six-year-old-boy, "hearing the noise ran to see what it was. His mother took after him to bring him back, and just as [she] came up with him, in they both went—scalding all of one side of each of them from head to foot, the skin peeling off. They were just alive, the last I heard from them, and not expected to survive."

The worst part of the desert was the last eight miles of deep sand. "It took hard whiping to get the oxen along," Clark of

Virginia continued. "Their backs and hips were cut with the lash so the blood was all the time trickeling down, while many were lowing as they woried along until 2 P.M. We reached the little stream, Trucky River, 80 feet wide and 30 miles beyond the spring, making the desert only 55 mile on this route, while it is 60 or 70 on the Carson trail. Here at the crossing we find a great many emigrants in camp. Lots of Indians and worn down stock. Dirty & hungary looking men, ragged & sunburnt, perhaps lowsey at that."

Eliza Ann McAuley passed the Boiling Springs about midnight, September 4, and early on the fifth stopped to rest before crossing the heavy sand to the Truckee. "Made our breakfast on bread and milk having no wood to cook with, and one of the cows stole all of the water we had, so we are obliged to put up with light diet. We are now seven miles from the Truckee River, but the road here becomes very sandy and heavy. After traveling three miles the teams begin to give out, so we had to unhitch them from the wagons and send them on to grass and water. The boys went on with the cattle, leaving Mr. Daugherty, Margaret and myself with the wagons. After resting awhile, Margaret and I started on, taking with us a cow that had given out and been kept behind. We took a bucket a short distance before her, and the poor thing, thinking there was water in it would get up and struggle on a few steps and then fall exhausted. After resting a few minutes we would get her on again a few steps. In this way we gained about a mile, when we met Thomas returning with a canteen of water. We took a drink and gave the rest to the poor cow, which revived her so that she was able to get to the River.

"Thomas said that when the cattle were within three miles from the River they smelled the water, and lifting their heads started on a run for the river and never stopped until they had plunged in and rushed half way across. It was about noon when Thomas returned with the water, and Margaret and I then lay down on the bare sand, with the hot sun pouring

[267]

down on us and slept until the boys returned with the teams. We then started for the river which we reached about five o'clock. This is a delightful stream of pure, cold water, about two rods wide and two feet deep. The current is swift and the banks are lined with a fine growth of cottonwood which is quite refreshing after such a long tedious desert. There are several trading posts here and a relief station. After crossing the river we went up it about two miles and found good grass."

Mariett Cummings reached the Truckee on August 8: "There are great numbers of Indians about here. They call themselves Piutes. Their country extends from Pyramid Lake to the Sink of the Truckee. They are very friendly and more intelligent than the Root Diggers. They procured for me great numbers of little fish resembling a sardine which they caught with ingenious little hooks made of a little stick one fourth of an inch in length to which was fastened nearly at a right angle a little thorn.

"These they baited with the outside of an insect. The line was simply a linen thread with six of these little hooks attached. They gathered also quantities of bear berries said to be very wholesome.

"We stayed at this trading post the 9th and 10th. During both days I was very unwell, as well as my husband, but we were still and would not complain. This incessant traveling kills sick people."

"There is at this side of the desert a relief train (so called) but it is only to relieve the emigrants of what loose cash they may have, and if they have not money they take stock in exchange for their provisions," Richard Owen Hickman wrote. "Governor John Bigler, the present executive, appointed an old snub-nosed Pennsylvania dutchman to take charge of the station and also gave instructions with regard to disposing of the provisions. Now this relief train was made up by subscription of the residents of California, to be appropriated for the relief of the suffering emigrants who may have fell short of pro-

[268]

visions on the plains, but instead of being appropriated in this way, it is a plan of the Governors to strip and huckster the emigrants out of their last shilling and then get the remainder of their stock for a trifle. Such is the state of democracy in California. The Governor is speculating on the funds contributed by the citizens to the relief of those who may be in a suffering condition."

Although it is never an easy task—and sometimes it is an impossible one—to defend John Bigler against charges of peculation, in this instance he was not the chief offender. The California state legislature had appropriated $25,000 for the relief of emigrants, and the governor had appointed Generals James S. Rains, James W. Denver and James M. Estill to conduct the train and establish the various relief stations. Four stations were set up: one at the Sink where the Carson and Truckee roads diverged; one at Sulphur Wells on the Carson route; and one each at the Carson and Truckee rivers. General Rains saw to the stations on the Carson, and General Estill established the Truckee station, putting a man named Bodley in charge. California in this period was noted for corrupt politicians, and James M. Estill towered above his sticky-fingered contemporaries. Wherever Estill was, dubious profits could not be far away. It was not surprising, then, that the emigrants' complaints were directed toward the Truckee station.

An anonymous emigrant wrote the Marysville *Herald*:

"About the 5th day of August last, myself and company crossed the Desert, between the Sink of Humboldt river and Truckee river. About eight miles distant from Truckee river, we found a water station, kept by Bodley's son, and was told that we could have water for ten cents per pint, or one dollar per bucket, for drinking purposes only.

"My cattle being in a famished condition, I offered him three dollars for three buckets full of water, which he refused; and in consequence of this refusal, I was forced to sell two of

[269]

my cows at $16, which would have brought me $200 could I
have driven them through. These cows I sold to one of
Bodley's men.

"At this station, kept by a son of Bodley's, provision was distributed at the following rates to the suffering emigration:

"Bacon, 40 cents per pound; flour, 25; fresh beef, 30; dried
apples and peaches, 35; tobacco, $1 per quarter pound; sugar,
50 cents per pound; coffee, 50 cents, whisky, $8 per gallon;
pies, $1 each; meals, $1 each.

"The above articles constituted the entire stock in trade, except the water, of which I have already spoken.

"Men, who were without money and in a starving condition, were refused; even a drink of water could not be had
without pay. People were told, that an ox or a horse would be
taken in exchange for provision; and many a sufferer was compelled to part with his team to raise means to procure the necessaries of life.

"I saw, myself, ten or a dozen wagons left on the Desert, in
consequence of the cattle, and horses failing for want of water;
and when applied to for assistance, Bodley and company
would answer, 'I will buy your oxen at $10 each, and haul you
through in the bargain.' . . .

"No notices were posted up at any point on the Desert, noti-
fying the emigration that a government relief train was in the
neighborhood; nor, until we arrived in the settlements, were
we informed that Bodley & Co.'s station was a government
station, or that any supplies had been sent to us.

"One thing is very certain—no relief was afforded us, except
what we paid for, and that too, at a tremendous rate."

On August 23 John Clark of Virginia started up the
Truckee River toward the meadows, thirty-five miles distant:
"Our start is late & the road goes up the river between two
dark & ragged looking mountains. We soon begin to cross &
recross the darndest rough & rocky fords ever attempted before. The water swift, deep & full of round boulders from the
size of a dinner pot to that of a four foot stump. Here was cur-

sing of the hardest kind. The cattle got astraddle of some & were completely on a balance for some time, then fell off our waggon on coupled [uncoupled] the hind part & bed went down the stream some of the donage floated off Bill Morton lost his carpet-sack, Kinsey his bundle & Perin his gun. After crossing four times we follow up to the Grizzly cliffs 10 miles. Here is a place of teror. Wild & fearfull looking mountains high on each side, then closed in to a narrow kanyon. For some distance we pass up what we shall term the Lime Kiln Hollow over White's Mountain down what they call Hell's Hackle to the river, 5 miles. Here we camp & are soon joined by a small band of Piute Indians. They were friends & proposed a dance. The music was brot out, the circle formd. . . . Oh, what a flaping of lether legins & wet mocasins. Now & then a keen yell & a whoop, with a heavy tread until the tune was done. Then all to our blankets save the guards on duty."

The next day the Truckee had to be crossed again, "on a pile of rocks. The first plunge, under went the cattle, next came the waggon, driving them upon a thundering boulder, then a surge & the couplin broke. Here was hell again & the Elephant afloat. In jumt the men & mored the wreck ashore away below the ford. This was not the real crosing but the cursing of the Truckey. We were some time righting up our injured waggon, then followed up the stream 2 miles & camp in the edge of the great meadow."

The Charles Schneider company made the crossing of the river without trouble, but on the mountain leading to the meadows: "Half a mile over stones. No track visible. Over a very high hill and zigzag downward, so steep that when one wagon left the train it fell down the hill, a total wreck. We see blue wonders here, and wrecked wagons hanging over the edge and lying in the canyon bottom. Through canyons. Many broken wagons. Arrived at Truckie meadow. Good grass, On guard."

Dr. Dalton's train was approaching the meadows at dusk on

[271]

August 21: "Bailey & myself had walked ahead & passed up the meadow about 2 miles, to where a Mo. train had camped. We tried to get supper & lodging with them but they refused; and we started after dark to go back & meet the train, our way being along the side of the river opposite that of the road & on the side of a tremendous mountain partly through the willows & very rough and rocky—After walking about a mile we discovered several Indians sculking about in the bushes, they came into the road after and followed us a piece but as we had no weapons we walked tolerable fast and soon left them in the rear—I had no fears of their hurting us; but have no doubt that if they could rob or steal any thing or everything from us, they would be certain to do so—although the many foolish, alarming & bugbear stories about their being so dangerous & bad, is all *Humbug*."

"We are now in camp at the Truckey Meadow, a small valley of some four or five mile square surrounded or enclosed by high & raged mountains with spots of snow," John Clark of Virginia wrote. "No timber whatever or vegitation upon them. . . . The Piute Indians are quite numerous here & prowl about in great bands, although we see but few. So many emigrants on this Beckworth trail they keep rather shy. We can only see them looking down from the face of the mountain, while the smoke raises from their campfires far up the Canyon. Well we have had our scanty breakfast, & the poor steers this morning looks larger than comon. The grass has sweld them out so I fear the skin will split if we dont drive on."

"The sierra Nevadas lie before us, majestic and reaching to the skies," Charles Schneider wrote on September 10. "They are heavily wooded with pine. One of the mountains is afire and presents a great sight at night."

From the Truckee Meadow, the Schneider train took the Henness Pass road to Downieville: "The way passes alternately through pinewoods and valleys rich with good grass and wild clover. The whole region is the most attractive we have yet seen." They crossed the Sierra summit on September 14, and the next day: "Today Biebrich went ahead to Downieville and we have only five men in our party. Tonight there was a hard freeze. The woods become denser, the trunks higher— twenty feet in circumference and 200 feet in height common. In the valleys are ranches. The way leads three miles over hills covered with broken stones. See many abandoned wagons, and one family of emigrants, the man sick and with no food. *Gray bears (grizzlies) occupy this district. Their weight runs from 600 to 1600 pounds. Saw their tracks in the road.* Cut hay and took it along." Two days later: "The cattle are exhausted, and do not want to proceed. The worst traveling spot on the entire trip. At 5:30 we arrived at Galloway's tavern, five miles this side of Downieville, where Biebrich came towards us. He had taken up claims, and brought a bit of sample rock with him. We do not wish to and cannot travel further."

From Truckee Meadow another road ascended the mountains through Beckwourth's (or Beckwith) Pass, past the headwaters of the Feather River to Beckwourth's ranch, then over a steep mountain into the American Valley.

Mariett Cummings reached the summit on August 14: "I am yet sick. Sometimes think I shall not live long. It is hard to die so young and William, my William, who will console him? Passed up the creek nine miles and crossed and two miles brought us to the summit of the Sierra Nevada mountains. I walked a few rods and feebly did my feet press California soil for the first time. The goal of my ambition, and I said to myself: 'Will my bones rest here in this strange land?' Six miles across a beautiful valley to one of the head branches of the Feather River, near a ranch, and camped for the rest of the day."

D. B. Andrews reached Beckwourth's Ranch on August 11: "Here is the first cabin on this route to the mines. Here the

Scenery of the Sierras, Near the Summit

roads fork, the left hand leads to Seventy-Six, 13 miles distant. This is a quartz mining town. The [right] hand or Beckwith leads to Marysville." Andrews was going to Marysville, but on August 19 Edward Kitchell took the left-hand road to Seventy-Six.

John Clark of Virginia came to the ranch on August 28, and in his diary reached an uneasy compromise on the spelling of the name of the fifty-four-year-old mulatto mountain man who lived there: "The stock was gathered in & on we went to the Beckwith ranch, 2 miles. Here we found Old Jim Beckworth, once a mountain trapper, then a miner, now a packer & speculator in provisians, drinks, &c. for the emigrants. He had at this time but two quarts of poor brandy about his shanty. This I gave him $6 for, & it hardly gave the boys a taste. We sat around the cabin for some time looking at the lanlord & the monster pines that overhung his shantie. These were all objects of curiosity, particularly the trees six & eight feet through & two hundred high. Old Jim remarkd that these were mere saplins compared with the big trees of Calaveras."

"Started at 8 o'clock and traveled down Beckwith's Valley 16 miles to *War Horse Ranch* [Beckwourth's] and camped," Dr. Dalton wrote on August 25. "Excellent grass wood and water —This is a very large & beautiful valley with an abundance of excellent grass, surrounded with high mountains covered with Evergreens, very large Pine & Cedar; the tops of which are covered with snow. We here strike the timber & pass through thick pine & cedar woods for several miles—The fuss and jangling between the Captain & his boys, and several of the Company, which has been kept up for a long time, about the Provisions, is still getting worse; & this evening came very near a fight When the Capt. sold the flour at Truckie River he promised to buy whatever provisions the Company needed according to Handbill, and as for security for his doing so, he promised to put into my hands the Cash received for the flour. Not yet having done so, the Company this morning were about to pass a vote allowing any team to drive out when they pleased if he did not put up the money; he immediately put the amount not expended $70.00 into my hands—We then purchased 10½ lbs. of shugar, at .75 cts.

"Aug 26th The jangling about the Provisions & the laziness of the Drivers caused us to get a very late start this morning; which was not until near 10 o'clock. . . . The Captain refusing to buy any provisions this morning the Committee bought 20 lbs. of Sugar at .50 cts. & 1 Gallon of Vinegar at $4.00, which was paid out of the money deposited with me— James Beckwith, (The *Old War Horse*) has a light frame house about 50 by 20, the roof covered with pine boards & the sides with muslin; and well divided into four rooms; a Bar room, store room, dining room & Kitchen. It is the first house, we have seen, covered with boards, since leaving Fort Laramie. He is a dark swarthy, keen looking, shrewd old fellow; 54 years old & is of four different Nations: French, English, Indian &

Nigro or Mexican—says he has traveled across the mountains 14 times, and expects to live to cross them 24 times more—He gave us a diffinite discription of the route where the Rail Road would have to be located from the Atlantic to the Pacific."

After leaving Beckwourth's Ranch, the road crossed the most difficult mountain on this route. "We drove on 5 miles to the foot of the Great Sierra Mountain that looks so very high & steep we dread the task," John Clark of Virginia wrote on August 29. "But seeing the many teams ahead winding up the heights as if they were making for the clouds, we just stop a while, throw away all the spare donage & prepare the lash; for it took awful cracking to get up the 2 miles in Six and a half hours. Many teams with eight & ten yoke were seven hours. I saw one long team that stuck on the brink. They had to run a line from the forward yoke, make fast to a tree so as to hold, while the cattle could rest. Other teams, many oxen, would be on their knees holding while the drivers would whip & pound until the poor beasts would bawl under the lash, before they could raise and go forward to the sumit 14,000 feet above the level of the sea. On this narrow spot we rested two hours. A good portion of this time with our telescope in hand taking a general survey of the high & broken range, baren in spots, then low scrubby trees, banks of snow, savage looking points, long ridges, deep canyons that appear to yawn at every turn as they run down, until you can see no botom. Now look up again to the monster range of the wild Sierras. Far to the right & left is the prominant points & high peaks of snow. Upon the whole, our minds were drawn out in deep meditation upon the wondrous works of nature. Truly the mountains are high, cold & dreary looking. To give a thorough discription would not only require a pen but a mind thats deep & far beyond that of your humble servant. We now take down one of the ragged spurs, so long & steep, it was necessary to save the waggons from distruction to take all the cattle off but one yoke. Then a good sized tree, with considerable top made fast to the rear of each wagon; then let her went, with a shower of little rocks that followed down the trail & the dust that rose so high & thick it frightened some emigrants in camp several miles below. They took it for granted that an eruption of the mountain had taken place, & was preparing to leave. When we reach the Willow Ranch, 12 miles below, we came & buy provisions at the usual high price. Our Company lookd hungary, poor, dusty, sunburnt, & ragged. Our oxen nearly gone in. No cud, & two to make a shadow. And there lies poor Bill Morton, one of our way passengers from Greenup, thats traveled 1400 miles without a shoe; his feet so swolen they resemble two great glutts. He cannot ride on account of the feet not going in the stirups. With all this he is awful ill-natured with scratches the wool shirt put on at Salt Lake has gathered moth that have cut through so as to interfere with the skin. His case is considered doubtful, without a change. We are now in camp on the headwaters of the Rio de Plumas, or River of Feathers."

Eliza Ann McAuley reached the summit of the Sierras on September 14 but on a different route. On September 13: "This afternoon we passed Starvation Camp, which took its name from a party of emigrants, who, in 1846 attempted to reach Oregon by a southern route, but getting belated in the mountains, the snow came on and buried up their cattle. Here they were forced to remain several weeks, and were, it is said, reduced to the terrible extremity of cannibilism, and but six were living when relief came to them. It is the most desolate, gloomy looking place I ever saw. There were the ruins of two or three cabins down in a deep dark canyon, surrounded by stumps ten to fifteen feet high, where they were cut off above the snow.

"Donner Lake, a beautiful sheet of water, not far from here, was named in remembrance of the party. . . ."

The following day: "While the teams were toiling slowly up to the summit, Father, Mr. Buck, Margaret and I climbed one of the highest peaks near the road, and were well repaid for

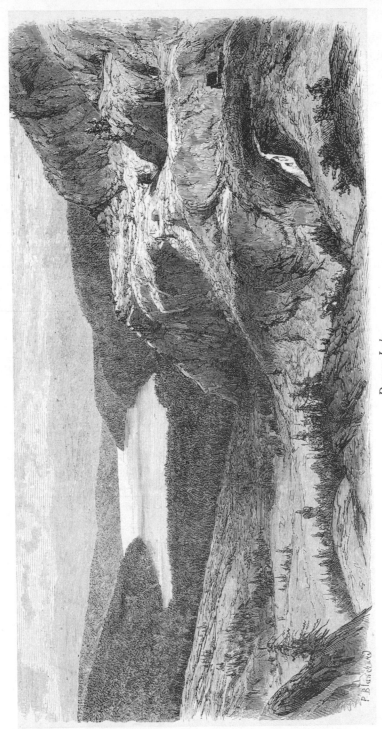

Donner Lake

P. Blanchard

our trouble by the splendid view. On one side the snow-capped peaks rise in majestic grandeur, on the other they covered to their summits with tall pine and fir, while before us in the top of the mountains apparantly an old crater, lies a beautiful lake in which the Truckee takes its rise. [Tahoe.] Turning our eyes from this, we saw the American flag floating from the summit of one of the tallest peaks. We vented our patriotism by singing 'The Star Spangled Banner' and afterward enjoyed a merry game of snow ball. Turning to descend, the mountain side looked very steep and slippery, and Margaret and I were afraid to venture it. Father, who is a very active man for his age (about sixty) volunteered to show us how to descend a mountain. 'Just plant your heels firmly in the snow, this way,' he said, but just then, his feet flew from under him and he went sailing down the mountain side with feet and hands in the air. After a minute of horrified silence we saw him land and begin to pick himself up, when we gave way to peals of laughter. We found an easier way down and rejoined the train, and tonight we camp in Summit Valley on the western slope of the Sierra Nevadas, and are really in California." On September 18 the McAuleys reached a fork in the road, one leading to Nevada City, the other in the direction of Little York, which they took. The next day they reached their father's cabin and the end of their journey.

On August 30 John Clark of Virginia came into the American Valley. "Late in the morning we turn down one of the rough & rocky branches of the North Feather 10 miles to the Illinois Ranch, at the head of the American Valley. Here some emigrants were building shanties & preparing to locate around. We continued down some 5 miles further to what is termd the Uncle Sam ranch, at a small grove of timber. We pitched our tents again. A feteaging journey, 116 days on the plain undergoing many privations & hardships. First the rain, wind, thunder & hail. Time & again no camp, tree or cabin to shelter under. Then days & weeks amidst Cholera, sickness and distress. The dying & burying of the dead were daily

[279]

Lake Tahoe

occurances for a long way out. My God, how thankful we should be that we are spared, even should we yet suffer in a strange land. Our provisions is entirely gone, but here comes Sam Thomas with a few pounds of fresh beef upon his back. We have no salt, but all hands cut & roast, except Bill Morton who is picking at his old quilt under the waggon. Richardson, Thomas, Paine & Perkins have sold their teams today and speculators in stock are in camp now to purchase the balance, if the price can be agreed upon in the morning."

The next day: "Two more teams are sold before the balance of our meat is roasted. Price, Robinson, Gilman & others are hired to take the stock to Sacramento, which is 150 miles yet. It is just now we begin to feel sorry to see our crowd break up & leave for different points. Although sour looks & hard words had often past between us on the way, now a heartfelt calmness appeared in every bosom that began to swell with forgiveness as they leave to make new acquaintances in the Eldorado of the West. We now proceed to settle our way-bill and Company affairs, sell a portion of our stock. The balance

[280]

View of the Town of Marysville, California

we keep for better prices. As we are now in the neighborhood of the mines we shall prepare on the morrow and leave."

In the American Valley on August 31 the Dalton party also began breaking up: "Started at 8 o'clock and in 1 mile came to another Ranch Greenwood's where Capt Stephens sold three Waggons for $10.00 each, (having sold one last night for the same) and thirty head of Stears for 920 dollars; leaving but three Waggons and thirty Steers; four Cows and twenty men—Rearranged our men into three Messes; loaded up accordingly and passed on 1 mile to the mountain; thence 2 miles up a very steep mountain & thence down 8 miles, quite steep but smooth road, to the Spanish Ranch & Camped. Tolerable grass, good water & wood. Gold Diggings all around us."

One of the remaining party, Philip Linthicum, was taken ill and on September 4: "Started at 8—passed over a small mountain, thence across a Brook with high banks where Squire Stephens upset the Waggon he was driving in which was Philip Linthicum, and he was hurt *very badly*—passed on to a small meadow on a branch at the foot of a very steep mountain, about two miles, when observing that P. Linthicum was getting worse, requested the train to stop which was done & the cattle turned out—Mr. Linthicum continued to sink very fast and at 12 o'clock breathed his last—We dug a grave, wrapt him in his blankets, spread over him a tent & a waggon sheet and burried him in the most decent manner we could in a small prairie meadow a few feet East of a Spruce Pine Tree, on which we cut his name &c. about six miles West of Rich Valley Ranch."

Charles Schneider encamped at Galloway's Tavern on September 18: "Early today we sold our wagon for $10.00 while still sleeping in it. . . . At 9 o'clock we sold the oxen, practically all of them being sick from poison herbage eaten the day before. We got $55 for them, per yoke. Now we are freed of our wagons and cattle. We proceed to divide. The articles are auctioned. . . . Certain articles that we could not divide, and which cost $15, and were sold for $31. The whole proceeding was very laughable. Each packed his things in a given spot, and he who had the least was really better off, because he had less to carry."

Alpheus Richardson, on September 15: "This morning as we was about to start several Chinamen passed along the road with their mining tools such as cradles, pick, pans, and shovels, all tied to the middle of a pole and a man at each end of the pole. This is the way—two and two with their implements and with broad brimmed hats, short breeches, wooden shoes, pipe in the mouth, and long hair plaited and laying down on their backs—quite a show for a green Californian. . . . In 3 miles from the canyon we came to Feather River at Bidwell Bar. Crossed our wagons here on a ferry boat for one dollar per wagon and swam the cattle across the river, which is narrow but rapid. Considerable mining done here, and on the south side of the river is a small mining town."

Dr. Dalton passed through Bidwell's Bar on September 6 and on the eighth, near sundown, arrived in Marysville: "Found Capt. Stephens & his family there. Drove into a large Hayyard & Camped—Went immediately to a Bath House on the Yuba River (being covered with dust) & washed off clean; then to a Barber's shop & got shaved . . . & then to the Bee Hive Tavern—a pretty good House. Found Mr. Hart Mr. Baily & several other of our boys there. This is a fine flourishing, business place."

To the north, Solomon Kingery wrote on August 22: "Traveld 12 miles & landed in Shasta City. Here we Soon was informed that the Citizens of Shasta had prepared A dinner at the St. Charles hotel for the Emegrants so we partook of a very Sumtous dinner, Much better than I Expected that they Could raise in California. We were treated with great Respect as we was the first train of Waggons that ever Come into Shasta on the Shasta or Knobles rout. You can See according to this that we have had a very lucky Successfull Jurny. We had provision Enough & very little left. Our teams done very

[283]

well. . . . Provision are very high here: flour is worth $18.00 pr cwt, Bacon 35 Cts pr lb, Beef 20 & 25, Beens 18, potatoes 12, dried apples 25 Cts lb. . . . The prospect for mining at pressent is not very good as the Creeks are nearly all dry. There has not been any rain in Cuntry Since the first of June. As soon as the rainy Season Commences mining will be better buizness."

Richard Owen Hickman, writing his stepmother in December, closed his journal and summed up his impression of the land he had crossed the plains to reach. He had visited Sacramento and then returned to Nevada City: "I must acknowledge I was badly deceived in the valley. It is so far behind the prairies of Illinois, that it would never have been thought of if the mining region had not been so close. It all overflows and there is but a small portion of it fit for cultivation. . . . I have no anxiety to settle in California at present, but I would like to explore some of the country before I take my leave for the far off land, Sweet Home."

XI

FROM THE SINK OF THE HUMBOLDT TO PLACERVILLE VIA THE CARSON RIVER

———◄◄●►►———

THE greater part of the emigration took the Carson River route to the Sierra Nevada and over Carson Pass by way of Hope Valley and Tragedy Springs. There was a new road this year, Johnson's Cutoff, which crossed Echo Summit, but it was only used by packers. John Hawkins Clark was at Humboldt Sink on August 18: "To-day we make the last grand effort of this wearisome trip; this is considered the hardest bit of travel on the route, and consequently more preparation is made for the journey. We have grass and water on board for our teams which is now universally carried, the distance about forty miles. Very few animals that have made the travel of the Humboldt could endure the journey without some nourishment. Started about four o'clock in the morning, weather unusually cool and the roads good. About ten miles out the dead teams of '49 and '50, were seen scattered here and there upon the road. Very soon, however, they became more frequent and in a little while filled the entire roadside; mostly oxen with here and there a horse and once in a while a mule. Wagons, wagon irons, ox chains, harness, rifles and indeed all the paraphernalia of an emigrant's 'outfit' lay scattered along this notorious route, reminding one of the defeat of some great army. In many places the teams lay as they had fallen; poor beasts—they had struggled on over mountains, plains and through the sands of the barren deserts for days and weeks with but little or no food, but still with strength sufficient to make this their last effort to gain a haven of rest. Good water and plenty of food lies just beyond; but alas, strength failed and here they lie, and sad memorials of a grand crusade to 'the land of gold.' Although dumb brutes and created for the use of man, I could not help but deplore their sad fate as there they laid in mute silence, marking our course through the great desert they had not the strength to cross.

"Camped at ten o'clock in the forenoon, made coffee and gave our teams a little water and hay; while eating our dinner one of our stragglers came up and declared he had made one of the greatest discoveries of the age. He being a candid kind of fellow, all hands were eager to hear of so great an event. 'What is it?' was asked. 'A dead mule.' 'Impossible' we all axclaimed; 'a mule was never known to die.' 'Did you see the dead animal yourself?' we asked. 'Yes I did, and I also saw a fellow tickle his heels with a long pole and he never budged and that is the surest sign on earth.' We gave it up; a mule that could stand to have his heels trifled with and not resent must surely be a dead one. After an hour's rest we were again on the road and traveled until near sundown. Camped and boiled our coffee with broken wagons that had been left on the road, gave our teams the remaining hay and water and pushed on again. So far our road has been good but from this out, ten miles, it is deep and heavy sand and consequently heavy traveling; as much as our fatigued teams can do to make any show of progress. But patience worketh many hard questions, and as we have a respectable supply as yet, I think it will last us through. Nine o'clock and as dark as hades; our teams just crawling and for fear they would stop of their own accord we called a halt, gave each animal a pound of hard bread and moved on. Ten o'clock, a bright, blazing fire that shot heavenward through the gloom in our rear, arrests our attention; it is a company of ten wagons which their owners dispair of getting through, have concluded to desert; so hauling them up, side by side set fire to the concern. A huge blaze of ten or fifteen minutes' duration, startled the astonished wilderness, revealing a long line of pilgrims, progressing slowly, but surely, toward the end of a hard day's work. The great fire has gone down and darkness again reigns triumphant. Could we but catch a view of the river with its volume of pure, cold water, 'twould be of some comfort. We are now within two miles of our destination and our teams have caught the fresh scent of pure, cold water, and it is as much as the tired pilgrim, who is on foot, can do to keep up. Eleven o'clock and we are on the banks of the long-sought-for river and more than all, at the end of a long and toilsome march. I never saw a dumb brute so eager for water as ours are to-night; they thrust their heads in water nearly to their eyes, so eager are they to slake their thirst.

"The passage of this desert would be no hard matter to old

and experienced travelers well fixed, but to the untutored pilgrim, with worn-out teams, poor feed and bad water, it is a matter of some importance, the men who burnt their wagons for fear of not getting through were very foolish. In the morning they could have returned and brought them through with leisure. . . . Most of the dead animals now lying on the desert have laid there since '49 and '50; the pure air of the desert has almost preserved them in their natural forms."

Richard Keen's company crossed the desert over a month before Clark, on July 12: "this is a very favorable day for Crossing it being Cloudy we Rolled Out at 3 Oclock the Road excellent . . . the further we proceed the more dead stock we seen although it was a dark night and it proved quite difficult to wind our way through the Carcasses . . . I can see Where some of our fellow travelers who have gone this road before us were in possession of the Emigrants requisite Mirth of Cheerfulness I notice where they have been playing their pranks by tying dead horses tails together log chains about their necks &c. . . . we stop and feed at 2 Oclock again cut up a wagon to make a fire and seated Our selves around. I was meditating my thoughts had wandered back over the many wearisome steps I had traveled and I was at home again then came the truth of my situation I was in the great desert (and just waiting a few minutes to allow our Jaded animals to rest) when we were to resume our Journey on to ward the land of Gold I was interrupted in my abstracted thoughts by hearing Solon Lacy exclaim Here boys is a cake that my Sister made and gave me when I started and requested that I should keep it until we came to the desert. so Accordingly the Cake was served up it was a delicious One and that dear Sister the doner of that delicacy was Remembered with thankful hearts and tearful eyes the Repast being over in silence we started on . . . we arrived at Carson River about Sunrise and Judge of My suprise to see quite a Village here of tents traders that had come from California to buy stock."

An anonymous correspondent to the St. Louis *Republican* wrote: "Little trading posts were established at the ends and all along the road over the desert, where they sold water at one dollar per bucket, and very bad whiskey at twenty-five cents per drink. The whiskey greatly enlivened the spirits and energy of the drivers, while the poor animals drinking only water, and but little of that, were unable, in most instances, to go ahead as fast as the drivers desired. So they went cutting and whipping, frolicking, and rushing on at a furious rate, leaving a wagon here, a horse there; and an ox yonder, as monuments of their haste; folly and bad management. Thus it has been, no doubt, night after night, previously, for the road was lined with dead carcasses and abandoned wagons. . . . Just at the break of day, and when we had ten miles of the very worst of the road to travel, my best carriage mule showed signs of giving out. He trembled at every joint, his ears fell, and his feet seemed as sore as if burned with hot sand.—At the same time, oxen, horses, mules, and cows were down all around us, and the impression seemed to be, that unless we got over before eight in the morning, that we would not get over at all. So every one almost, rushed ahead, as if for dear life. But among the throng thus pushing along was a character. Just ahead of us lying in the middle of the road was a fine large ox, unable to go a step further. His owner had resolved not to leave him in that situation, sent the team on, got out his violin, dismounted his horse which stood quietly by his side, got down on one knee in front of the ox, and talked to him, and told him that it would 'never do to give up so,' and then played away on his fiddle, until the ox got up and went on! . . . I hauled off the road, and let our train go on to Carson river, and was relieved in due time by a fresh team sent back, and got over the same day all safe with all our stock."

Thomas Turnbull, starting across the desert on July 27, passed the relief train station: "here are State officers sent on from California with Flour & every thing a family or single man wants to give them for nothing to carry them to carson Valley & then from the Valley to be supplied & sent through they seem to be fine men & think nothing of money."

"We made a start across the great desert this morning a little after sunup and took, as Mr. Sawyer thought, the old Truckee route," Mrs. Sawyer wrote on August 2, "but in about six miles we came to an alkali pond, which it was impossible to cross. We then went over to the Carson route. This mistake tired our mules that much more than they ought to have been, but we traveled slowly, to save them all we could. . . . We stopped at a trading post in the afternoon and bought some water for the mules, paying seventy-five cents a gallon for it. The gentleman who keeps the post, sent me a glass of port wine, and I drank it with good grace, for I was tired too."

James Carpenter and a companion took some provisions and set out on foot across the desert. "Before we got to the River we were so nearly famished for water that our tongues were Black and neither one could talk. We got to the river and such water we could not drink our tongues were so swolen but we burried our faces in the clear bright water guzeled it us as best we could then wait a few minutes and guzel again. Before we got through there was a drove of cows came down on us but we wanted to drink as bad as they did and laid there and drank with a cow on each side of us."

Richard Keen met the relief train on the Carson River on July 16: "they enquired if we had provisions enough to last us through on being told we had they started on when some of the boys that had no great variety wished to buy they would not sell a pound as it was sent by Governor Bigler to supply those emigrants that were out of provisions and money they would neither give or sell to those that had plenty."

But when John Verdenal went to the relief station on September 23, "we inquired for provisions. but they had none. We now live on crackers & beans."

The settlement on the Carson which the emigrants reached

[290]

after crossing the desert was called Ragtown, and an emigrant signing himself "Justitia" described it for the Sacramento *Union*: "Perhaps a letter from this place, the dividing line between civilization and barbarism, might not prove uninteresting to your readers. First as to the town itself—it comprises some thirty or more houses made of boughs and *rags*—hence its euphonious appelation. The population are enterprising and industrious in their vocation, which appears to be supplying emigrants with provisions . . . purchasing their broken down stock at prices 20 per cent. above the Sacramento market, and selling very poor whiskey at a remunerating advance. In this last branch of their business, they exercise a christian benevolence and brotherly philoanthropy, that is truely commendable.—Knowing, as they do, that emigrants do not practice temperance except under compulsion, and that they invariably get *alkalied* by the poor liquor sold by traders upon the Humboldt; and being, moreover, firm believers in the *Hydrio*pathic principle of medicine, they mix their whiskey with the pure waters of the Carson River, and thereby enable the thirsty traveler to drink to excess, after crossing the desert, without any particular injury to his health. . . ."

From Ragtown the road followed twenty miles up the river and then cut across a desert of twenty-six miles. Meeting the river again, the emigrants, five miles farther on, passed Gold Canyon, where they saw the first miners. Richard Keen, on July 16, thought there were about fifty miners there: "they are a hard set of Custimers And if I must express myself I would suppose they were not making Much although they advised us to stop for we Could do better than we Could in California they stated that they were averaging 8 dollars pr day they have a railway to carry the dirt to the River to wash it they have a Grog shop here boarding house &c."

Addison Crane was there on August 20: "Found good grass at our encampment to night which is near the 'Rail Road

Winnowing Gold, Near Chinese Camp

House'—a large log cabin where supplies for miners are kept, including of course the ardent. . . . (In entering the door of said log cabin, struck my forehead square against the top— like to have broken my neck—*con*found all low doors.)"

Three days later, John Hawkins Clark camped nearby: "Chinamen were mining for gold at this place; they told us they were making from four to six dollars per day to the man. We did not believe the story. Here is also a trading post where vegetables, canned fruits, bacon, flour, mining implements and bad whiskey are kept for sale. It is but a small affair and established for the accommodation of the few miners who are at work in the neighborhood and any transient custom that may happen by. . . .

"The boys have killed a large rabbit and some wild fowl, determined to have a pot pie; it was something of a job to make it, but made it was, after a fashion. But if anybody could tell what it was, or how it was made, he would be much wiser than those who ate it; for never before did anyone see such a conglomeration of fresh meat, fish, bacon and hard bread; but it was a change in the dull routine of our every day fare, and that was something."

The Sawyers were at Gold Canyon on August 7: "Mr. Sawyer sold our four-horse wagon and harness this morning for $25.00. He thought it was not worth taking over the Sierra Nevada mountains, besides it would be very hard on the mules. The men have been getting ready all day for 'packing.' They will put some light things into my carriage, and drive it as far as it will hold out. Mr. Sawyer will walk and drive over the bad places. I will ride a mule, and the boys will ride another. The remainder of our things will be packed on the backs of the other animals, and we will thus be converted into a pack train."

Addison Crane was nearing the Carson Valley on August 21. "I found young Vigus, formerly clerk for E. H. Halliday. He came overland this season & arrived at his present location June 27, where he has since been selling provisions & liquors and buying cattle of emigrants. He told me he thought of returning this fall, and should make some money. He gets his supplies from Sacramento." And the next day: "We are to day in Carsons Valley, and find trading posts very plenty. Several families are also settled here who are raising vegetables. Could have bought a bushel of potatoes to day for $45.00 only (i.e. 75¢ per lb.) but not having the odd 5 (to say nothing of the 40) to spare, concluded not to invest. The most important place is the 'Mormon Station' which is a fortified post—where goods are kept for sale at enormous prices—Flour $.50 per barrell, & other things in proportion The upper portion of this valley is very beautiful, and plenty of fine timber on the mountains for ages to come—but it is in Utah and of course no sensible white man would settle here We stopped 3 hours at noon under the shade of a large pine near the mountains base and besides one of those clear, pure & pearly mountain rills that it does one good to look upon. Cooked and eat some fresh beef, 4 lbs of which I bought to day at 25¢ per lb. Roads generally good but sandy—& grass old & ripe, but cattle will eat it. . . . As I went into a log house trading post this morning a young man came up to me and seizing me by the hand called me by name and appeared quite glad to see me. I did not at first recognize him, he had changed so much in two years, but he was no other than Marshall Taylor. I was quite gratified to meet him, & even he and Albert were like old friends—had a long chat with him—the most material points in which were that he had cleared about 1700 dollars & was going home this fall. Well done Marshall! Better done than many a man of more maturity. A true chip of the old block. He is down in this valley exchanging a few horses of emigrants with which he will return soon."

Among emigrants disposing of stock to traders like young Taylor were the Richardsons at Mormon Station on September 9: "stayed here to day to cut hay and get our wagons fixed sold two of our horses and wagon for three hundred dollars but we are to take them into hangtown."

George Wilkes, founder and editor of the New York *Police Gazette*, had accompanied the relief train from California and was at Mormon Station on August 4: "A great number of emigrants entered Carson Valley during the course of this day, and as they all filed past the Mormon Station, and most of them stopping there for supplies, we had a good opportunity of inspecting their condition and getting the experience of their trip. Most of them were in fine case and spirits; though few had lugged misfortune on their backs, and some had frequently been obliged to endure hardships in the stomachs. In one case I saw two Germans who had truged the entire journey to this point, with bedding suitable for themselves and wives, strapped upon their shoulders. Their partners walked by their sides, with staff in their hands, and carried packs on their backs, out of which came the cupboard furniture that graced their meals.—They looked sullen, but as an air of depression or indifference is common to most emigrants at this stage of journey, that expression did not distinguish them from the rest so much as their burdens."

"A late start this morning," Richard Keen began on July 17. "Solon Lacy. Doc Humley Doc. Weatherly, Theron Ink, and Anthony Rogers left us this Morning they pack through. and we had a two legged Stampede last night Doc Humly played the Violin and the Boys danced Vigorously they kept it up until Midnight. We also leave the Illinois train there was quite a debate in Camp whether we should stop in this Valley and recruit our stock or proced directly on to the gold diggings those that Owned stock were generally in favor of recruiting However after some hard words it was decided that we proceed so about 10 Oclock. we bid Good bye to our Illinois Comrades. they thought their teams too weak to Cross the Mountains and their stock Owners told us they would Overtake us after stopping a week. We parted in good fellowship. Our little Company now Consists of 16 men and One Woman all told. We are now in Carson Valley . . . the soil is excellent and the Mountains are covered with timber on either side . . . the Grass three or 4 feet in height and the Water is the best I have ever seen. about every three or four hundred yards we find most excellent streams of Water perfectly Clear dashing down the hill side over pebles of a snowy whiteness. there is a mormon settlement here they are raising a few pottatoes &c. . . . there is a couple of Men here that have been shot by the Indians One is mortally Wounded having been shot with five Arrows the Other will Recover he was shot with three Arrows the circumstances were these as near as I could learn they were from California Coming out to buy horses they staked their Mules and layed down to sleep they were armed with Colts Revolvers and also carried a hatchet which they placed under their heads Just before day they were aroused by a shower of Arrows they immediately had recourse to their pistols and the Indians fled when it became light they found that the Indians had stolen their provisions and also their hatchet they with

[295]

difficulty gained their Mules and proceeded on the Road until they came to this trader they Report a great many Indians in the Mountains Our guard is now diminished and but One Man stands on duty at a time."

Mary Medley's company was camped near the mouth of Carson Canyon, preparing to move into the mountains: "It was necessary to get an early start next morning so as to be ahead of all the other trains. It was the captain's orders that we must be ready to start our day's journey at daybreak. Long before daylight the camp was astir. The captain and father were sitting by the campfire when the cook was preparing breakfast. They heard something flying over their heads and remarked:

" 'How strange for birds to be flying in the darkness; what could have disturbed them?' And they heard it again and again.

"Day was breaking and we were ready to start, when to our surprise and horror we found arrows all over the camp. Some had gone through the covers of two wagons, but no one was injured. Several cattle had been killed and father had an ox wounded. The men at the trading post bought the killed and wounded cattle. The supposed birds captain and father heard were arrows shot by Indians on the hillside."

"This morning considerable excitement prevailed in the camp," John Riker wrote on July 25, "in consequence of Captain Mott informing us of his intention of remaining in the valley for ten days, for the purpose of recruiting his stock preparatory to crossing the Nevadas. When the Captain's intentions had become known to the company, several of them determined to make their way over as they best could; the Captain reluctantly gave his consent to the separation, and seven of the company began to make preparations for the journey; three of them preferred the old Carson routes; the remaining four chose Johnson's Cut-off, as it is called. A. D. Riker, D. E. Lichliter and myself were of the latter number. Before we left company the sick men were lodged in a good house, where it is to be hoped they will be properly cared for.

. . . After all were ready we bid our long endeared friends a kind adieu, and started over the most difficult and dangerous road between the Missouri River and California; soon we were ascending the first ridge of the Nevada Mountains, not like those heretofore crossed, but covered by a thick growth of tall and stately pine. . . ." R. H. P. Snodgrass stayed with Captain Mott and the wagons.

Dr. Wayman's party also laid over near Mormon Station, to the doctor's disgust and mounting impatience. After a week of idleness, he wrote: "Shit, Hell and Granny with a cock & ballocks Damnation and Hellfier Camphire Forx Fier and all else that is mean, low and shitting. May the Good Lord ever deliver me from such Asses for all Coming time, and I will thank him Kindly, and return the Compliment the first practical apportunity."

Thomas Turnbull described Johnson's Cutoff as "a pack road a little track like a foot path," and according to James Carpenter, there was another cutoff designed to be impassable: "we found some fellows that had (as they said) found a new Cutoff that would shorten the distance over the mountains 2 days so we joined them and started." Two days later: ". . . we went around a turn of the mountain and there we met a sight that set us to thinking. the road crossed the creek and the mountains came down on each side forming a gorge just wide enough for the Creek and no way to get a wagon any farther of course we had no wagon with us but there was a lot that had and they had to leave them there. a lot of sharpers had made this rout so as to Cause the Emigrants to throw away their wagons & Harness and they would gather them up afterward."

From Mormon Station the road led to the mouth of Carson Canyon up which the emigrants would have to travel to Hope Valley. "Passed on 10 m up the valley to the mouth of the Canion," Addison Crane wrote on August 23, "where we followed up the most wild looking chasm eye ever rested upon, and over the worst road the human imagination can conceive for 8 m. crossing the W. fork of Carsons R. 4 times—3 times on bridges. This valley is about ½ to ¾ m wide—perpendicular mountain rocks on each side said to be 2000 ft high. . . . Rocks as large as a farming mill pilled together in admirable confusion sometimes for rods & over these our wagon had to pass—or be lifted, again such rocks lay so near together that the cattle could pass between but the wagon must be lifted over. Once we took our cattle off and rolled over by hand we ascended a very steep hill, and then went on to the valley beyond called hope valley & encamped. . . ."

Alpheus Graham made the ascent on August 17. "Drove into the Canyon about 9 o'clock, found a large creek running down through it. This creek is 3 rods wide and 4 feet deep and falls 300 feet per mile, the creek is so filled with large rocks that I walked over it in a hundred places the water dashing and foaming between the rocks. One mile up the canyon the pass is very narrow and entirely filled with rocks that have rolled down from the mountains. The road is now very bad as there is no chance but to drive over them. . . . In many places we drove over rocks 3 feet high, some times one ox was down, sometimes all but we kept moving, about 4 miles out of 6 of this canyon is nothing but rocks . . . we got to Hope valley before sun down."

Mrs. Sawyer entered the canyon on August 11. "Our road is very rough, rocky, and difficult to travel over. Some stones, right round and as large as hogsheads, lie right in the middle of the road. Our carriage broke down, and we have abandoned it. One wheel got fastened between two rocks and broke all to pieces. We packed everything on the mules and went four miles further, where we are in camp on the bank of a beautiful mountain stream of pure, good water. Our men are making more pack saddle."

R. H. P. Snodgrass camped at the mouth of the canyon the night of July 29. "Last night either two Indians, or two white men disguised as Indians attempted to get a few of our horses, but a well directed shot from a revolver altered their minds,

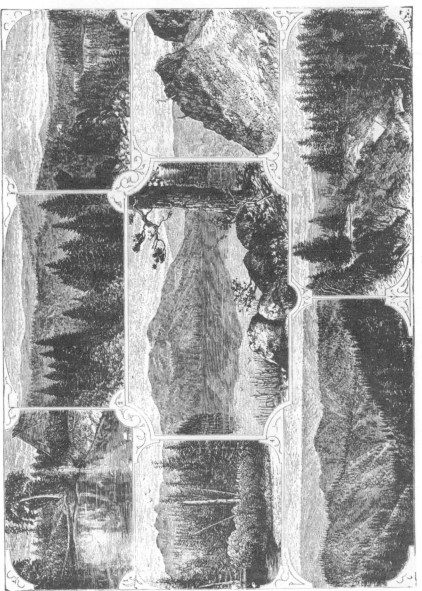

Scenery Across the Sierras

Summit of the Sierras

and one of them went off howling as though he had been nipped by a shot. It was laughable when the pistol cracked to see the boys pile out of the waggon, with their pistols, guns and knives eager for the chase, and it was hard to restrain them from pursuing the Indians."

"This afternoon's work was a hard one, but by industry and perseverance managed to make five or six miles," John Hawkins Clark wrote on August 25. "It was now nearly dark and a little wider space in the valley offering us room enough to spread our blankets and put up for the night. Huge rocks that had fallen from above lie around and about us. The little river is bounding from rock to rock, making a terrible noise as it vibrates high up on the rocky walls above us. . . . wierd, wild, dark and noisy is our camping place to-night. The little valley about fifty yards in width is almost choked with big pine trees and boulder stone, some of the latter as large as a good sized house and gloomy enough to frighten a mule. The moon is shining on the outside world, but it never has, or ever can, penetrate this dark recess. . . .

"Nine o'clock; a break in the mountain wall on our left; we cross over a bridge and bid goodbye to the dark canon and the mountain stream. We are now in the sunshine and the outlook is more pleasant; but the road—if it can be called a road—is the worst on the continent I guess. Rocks four feet high and so close together [they] fill the entire roadway. We unhitch our teams, lead them through and over them to a place of smooth earth, then go back, pull [off] our coats and lift our wagons from rock to rock, a distance of several hundred yards. Again we are on a smooth surface, hitch up and drive on to 'mountain camp.' Here is a meadow; a meadow in the mountain. We drive our stock into this meadow and build our camp fire for the balance of the day and night."

The Richard Keen company stopped at the mouth of the canyon for dinner on July 18. "We have slap Jacks and bacon for breakfast Bacon and Slap Jacks for dinner and for supper we have the same that we had for Breakfast Slap Jacks and

Bacon some of the boys begin to talk of Scurvy in fact I hear of considerable in Other trains O how we Yearn for something fresh Vegetables &c. . . . . there is a trader here that said he was authorized to collect toll for the crossing of the three bridges on this stream which is the west fork of Carson River the majority of our Company disputed his authority. he stated his authority was vested by a Company that had rebuilt the bridges that they had been burned by the Indians last season and rebuilt by this Company the present summer he and some of Our Company disputed some time the trader became very wrathy and swore he would take his gun and Knife and defend the Bridge until the toll was paid the Stock Owners held a council and concluded to pay the toll if he would go up to the first Bridge with us this he objected to on account of the Indians he said he was afraid to venture so far from his camp but there was no alternative he either had to go to the bridge which was about a mile or loose the toll which was One dollar pr wagon. in fact we began to doubt the existence of a Bridge. however he shouldered his gun and conducted us to the first bridge here he received his Money and he returned."

According to Caroline Richardson, who went up the canyon on September 12, at least one of the bridges had been burned. The three had been built, she erroneously thought, by the government, "but the co took the privelege to convert them into toll bridges and because the travelers refused to pay toll they burnt them the first is not so bad to ford we were alone in the worst place I ever saw and to render it more fearful a storm had gathered over the mountains with heavy thunder and gusts of wind came to last bridge where we found the company who had proceeded us they were obliged to wait at least half an hour for each ox wagon the de[s]cent was very steep and rough the river filled with large rocks and the banks steep besides."

John Verdenal was camped at the mouth of the canyon when a heavy snow commenced to fall, and on October 3: "Still snowing started at 9 had to travel a road that if not seen cannot be described over rocks three feet high. one wagon had to be taken about a hundred feet & then stop to bring on the other and so on every moment the wagons were expected to upset & go to pieces. we were now in the Canon, it stopped Snowing at 2 o'clock road continued to get worse. Stopped for the night under the tall fir trees came during the whole day 4 miles."

Addison Crane was in Hope Valley on August 24: ". . . we found most excellent grass about a mile from the road & concluded to lay by and let the cattle rest and feed. Moved from our encampment to the base of the mountains among a grove of young poplars, near a beautiful cold stream, and remained until 3 P.M. Here Mr Russell shot with Alberts 4 in revolver a very fat partridge as large as a common hen, the ball passing through the head. Of course we had a prime dinner. Had also plenty of wild gooseberries stewed in sugar. They grow in great abundance all about our camp. This valley is about 3 miles in circumference, almost circular and surrounded on all sides by the mountain wall of the Sierra Moved on at 3 P.M. and went 7 m. to red lake and encamped at sun set, near the lake, among heavy pine timber at the foot of the great mountain which we must attempt to ascend to morrow. We are encamped alone in the wildest looking place we have seen."

John Hawkins Clark passed Red Lake on August 27: "Teams well fed and to make a good day's work started early; the way tolerable for two or three miles. Passed near a beautiful lake fringed with green grass; wild ducks and other fowls were flying about or disporting themselves on the little islands that set like gems upon its bosom. Soft, pleasant and tranquil, lay this beautiful sheet of clear, cold water. Immediately after passing the lake above described we came to the foot of an immense elevation. We first looked at the high, steep and rough mountain road, then at our teams, and lastly we looked at one another. However, it was no use looking; the work had to be done. To throw off our coats was the first move, to unhitch part of our teams and attach them to others was the next

Winter Forest Scene in the Sierra Nevadas

move, and when all was ready we began the steepest journey we had ever before attempted. The starting point was quite smooth and gradual, but the way soon became very steep and rocky; indeed, the rocks monopolized the entire surface of the great mountain, first one way, and then another, zigzag fashion. We slowly made our way towards the summit; every rock we lifted our wagons over made one the less before us. After two hour's hard work lifting at the wheels, whipping our tired teams, and using language not becoming church members, we gained a resting place and well did we need one. If ever we had worked it was in the past two hours.

"After a short rest we are again on the move; the way is now more smooth but very steep and crooked; a man to every wheel, and one to every horse and mule; a few steps and then a rest. As may be imagined, our progress was very slow, but as it was a sure one our teams and ourselves kept up a steady courage. Eleven o'clock came to a dead halt at the foot of a large, flat rock, smooth and so very steep that it is impossible for our teams to even stand upon it, much less to climb and haul a wagon over. Unhitched, led our animals around and above the steep incline, then attached a long rope to the end of our wagon tongue and hauled them up. The big end of our day's work was now done; the worst for the day was over; made a few more hundred yards and stopped for dinner. At one o'clock rolled out again; the road is now passable, but here and there a steep grade to worry our worn-out teams. Camped for the night near the shores of Mountain Lake where the mules and horses fared well upon good mountain grass. This is a beautiful location; high towering peaks surrounding a beautiful lake upon whose shores the green grass grows so beautifully and where the tall pine trees give such a welcome shade. There are many pilgrims lying around and about us feeding their teams and making preparations for climbing the second and last steep grade over these great mountains."

Addison Crane began his ascent on August 25: "When about half way up our wagon uncoupled & the hind wheels

[305]

the box attached took the back track in double quick time, down a steep declivity and there ensued a scene which certainly ought to illustrate next years comic almanac. First it struck Kate, and half knocked her down & entirely frightened her—second it then made an entire sumerset, & lastly brought up standing against a big pine, the load having been entirely cast out by the sumerset. Sitting on a fallen tree by the road side I had a full and fair view of the catastrophe. Of course I supposed every thing had gone to smash, but to our great surprise the only injury done was the breaking of 2 of our hoops which supported the wagon cover, & breaking one glass bottle, the wagon not being injured in the slightest degree. An hours hard work in packing the load on our backs & rolling up the wheels & carrying up the box—put things to rights again, and we continued the steep toilsome rocky ascent, stopping our oxen every few rods to take breath, and we finally rolled to the summit. . . ."

Mary Stuart Bailey crossed the summit on September 29: "Have got over the first mountain—& are not killed any of us. Are now encamped on the margin of the mountain lake—The scenery today has been truly sublime—Mount rising to the skies—covered with snow the fine old pines—in every direction a great variety of evergreens—It seems quite like snow, cold & chilly how I wish we had a home to live in now—if it were not for hope the heart would break—"

Of crossing the Sierras, the St. Louis *Republican*'s correspondent thought: "But, all in all, this part of the journey was delightful, when compared to Humboldt and the Desert. We had delightful cool water, fresh green grass, plenty of fuel, fresh fish, and even grouse, in abundance. With such appliances, we felt able to haul up with ropes, to pack our plunder on the backs of mules, and fairly lift our wagons over the rocks. No day laborers on canal or railroad ever worked harder than we did. A knowledge of the sciences and polite literature was of no particular value here; law and land titles of no use; and it was interesting to see young men who had been all their lives in college or behind the counter, lifting at a wheel, holding on to a rope or a mule's tail, according to the circumstances—for the circumstances were various, and sometimes very trying. There was not much starch left in a person after travelling over so great a part of the journey, and the most elegant and accomplished of our young men became good teamsters, handy workmen and fine cooks."

After resting at Mountain Lake, the emigrant crossed the second, and last, summit of the Sierra Nevada. This second mountain was not as bad as the first, but it was quite bad enough, especially early in the season. "Started at sunup," Richard Keen began on July 21. "we are in Company with a train from Peoria Ill. they have splendid teams all large fine Mules. We are in the lead and o Shocking such Roads. We are now ascending the second summit and have to pass over a great quantity of snow almost perpendicular the horses sinking almost up to their bodies in the snow I had the good fortune to upset the Wagon that I was driving turned bottom side up and broke all the bows however we turned it back and threw in our goods and started minus Wagon Cover, whilst I was reloading all the teams passed me but I passed several of them in Return they were stalled in the snow by noon we were all up an[d] started on the de[s]cent very hard on our teams drawing our wagons through *he snow about 3 O'clock we came to a small clear spring of water apparently on the top of the Ridge this spring bears a startling name some two years ago three weary travelers halted at this beautiful little spring to quench their thirst when they were suddenly summoned to another world. a party of Indians lay in ambush here who made sure work with their Victims they murdered them and left their corps lying beside the spring to tell their comrades who were behind of the hard fate they were doomed to meet. and the thousands that have passed this way since I will venture to say can each and every one tell the sad tale of Tragedy spring we are camped on a high Ridge in a heavy grove of pine timber the weather is quite cool will freeze hard to night."

[307]

Perry Gee was packing over the Sierras on September 21: ". . . passed over second mountain the summit of the Nevada mountains passed over snow some three feet Deep saw flowers by the snow traveled on, over roads which if they were in the states people would think that they ware impassable the mountains and valleys ware covered with lofty pines so thick in some places that it is Difficult to pass through them . . . this morning the ground was covered with frost as white as snow and the ponds of water was frozen over. . . ."

When John Verdenal made the ascent on October 6, the newly fallen snow on the summit was a foot deep: "we found a negro man frosen to death by the cold and snow he had belonged as we heard to Pepbles train."

As for the descent from the summit, Holmes Van Schaick called it "one of the most God forsaken waggon breaking mule provoking drive perplexing: heart sickning roads ever saw. Over rocks & down short & steep pitches over logs & through mud nearly deep enough to take a mule in out of sight, we pushed along fully determined that the Sierra Nevada should not conquer the N Y boys."

John Riker, packing over Johnson's Cutoff, had hard going on July 27: "Soon after leaving camp we came to a very high mountain, which seemed inaccessible on account of its perpendicularity, together with the immense quantity of detached rocks which literally covers its sides. Presently a trail was discovered, leading towards the summit, which was sufficient evidence that others had passed before us, and why should not we? The ascent was commenced,—from rock to rock we were forced to climb until, weary and worn down by the constant exertions essential to the advancement of our desires to reach the summit, where we arrived in safety.

"I am now quite unwell, which renders traveling a double task to me. After leaving the summit, the road was good for some distance; then we descended another steep and stony mountain to the first waters of the American River, down which we followed a short distance, and then began the ascent

[308]

of another very high mountain, up which we traveled until night put a stop to our toils for the day. At nine o'clock we built a small fire by which we lay down to rest and await the dawn of day, that we might proceed with more safety. Our stock of provisions is now reduced to a very small allowance to each man, and for this, scant as it is, we are indebted to some packers who kindly shared their own small allowances with us. If we do not soon reach the settlements, all must soon feel the torturing pangs of hunger, as our provisions will not last another day. Distance twenty miles. . . .

"This morning, at daylight, continued the ascent of the mountain, and reached the summit at a late hour; then gradually descended to a small stream, where we prepared our morning's meal, consisting of pork and crackers, which was all we had. Our pork we sometimes eat raw and sometimes broiled. Our scanty stock of provisions were now exhausted, and still we were in a large wilderness and surrounded by hordes of savages and beasts of prey. Continued our course over rocks and hills until a late hour, weary in body and low in spirits, when, to our inexpressible joy, a house was descried a short distance in front. One long and joyful shout arose from the company as we neared the long-wished-for tenement. Upon entering we found it to be a boarding-house, and we were soon provided with food, which stayed the cravings of hunger. At this house we stayed all night. There happened to be a vacancy in the house for a cook, A. D. Riker accepted the offer at a compensation of one hundred dollars a month."

Addison Crane left the main Placerville road on August 26 and took a newly opened road to Volcano: "Friday Aug. 27. (115th day) Started at 7 & drove on through heavy hemlock woods over a passably good but very dusty road 5 m. & came to a spot of most excellent grass, and stopped to feed—where we now are. I am sitting near the base of a monstrous hemlock · penning this. Rested & fed 2 hours & passed on—small bushes covered with red cherries very plenty—could have picked hundreds of bushels—but they are worthless being bitter. Wild plum bushes are also abundant, and the fruit is much better. The mountain cedar, a large straight tree, growing up like the pine 100 feet high—appear quite common, also some small scrubby black oaks The soil through these forests is very loose and porous, so that a horse will sink in in 6 inches. . . . Encamped at sun down amid the dense hemlocks our wagon being entirely alone. The light of the bright full moon gave interest and romance to the scene. Still we spent an uneasy & watchful night—A party of these mountain indians could easily have cut us off—and we frequently heard a rustling and cracking in the underbrush close by—perhaps the work of some wild beast. No grass here. Fed out a little which we cut and brought along from where we fed last, after eating which our tired cattle soon laid down around the wagon—Albert & I in it, and Russell & son outside in the open air, the weary they have to sleep. . . .

". . . after 4 m travel found a place to feed & stopped & got break fast—of ham—slap jacks, coffe, sugar & stewed fruit. From here went on 10 m. to Volcano, a mining town in a deep hollow among the mountains & put up for the night. Cost to feed cattle $4. Slept in the barn—saw divers sights . . . near 200 m. yet to go but as I am *in* Cal. must stop my journal here."

William Lobenstine arrived in Volcano August 23: ". . . sold our stock the next day for the sum of three hundred dollars, making my share with our previous receipt for horse and one yoke of cattle, eighty-seven dollars and subtracting this from the whole of my expense leaves me ninety dollars debit to the journey.

"At Volcano is the first mining district met this side of Nevada and provisions being tolerable cheap and some of the digging middling favourable some five of us concluded to stay here a while and try our luck."

Mary Stuart Bailey said of Volcano on October 6: "We arrived in the first mining town in Cal took dinner there had a variety of vegetables. The buildings are very rude some of logs

Hangtown or Placerville

others covered with cloth—the vilage is without form. . . . Saw a good many mining it seemed like very hard work & rather poor pay but some do very well."

John Hawkins Clark kept to the main road to Hangtown, or, more formally, Placerville, and before arriving, paid his last tribute to the hardy mule: "Good horses, good mules and good oxen are everything on a journey like this. Job in his day, immortalized the horse and clothed his neck with thunder; but he was silent on the mule, and for what reason I am unable to say. If he had made this journey and had used the mule as motive power, he would no doubt have done him justice and left to succeeding generations his testimony of the mule's virtues. For our part we love the patient and hardy animal; their ears do not seem half so long as they did at the commencement of this journey. In every way they appear more endurable; if one gets stubborn and kicks our hats off once in a while we let him kick, but are very careful to stop in his way no longer than we can get out of it. Oxen are very reliable, patient and enduring. Thousands of them have made the entire trip and stood it nobly; but they are more liable to get lame than either the horse or mule. They will drink the poisonous water at every opportunity, and many of them are lost in that way; but with good watching they will make the trip. One would think a dog would make the journey very easily, but of the thousands who made the attempt very few succeeded in getting through. Those who had valuable ones let them ride. I know of no dog that has made the entire trip on foot."

Mrs. Sawyer wrote on August 15: "We came to Placerville to-day about noon. On our arrival it was discovered that our dog had been left behind somewhere, and Mr. Sawyer had to go back twelve miles before he found him."

It was a tattered and hungry James Carpenter who walked into Placerville: "Well the last two days we did not have anything to eat and I want to Record here that I made a solem vow that if I ever got home and could get a piece of Cornbread and it cooked by a woman I would not complain. We got into Hangtown California on the 7 day of Aug 1852 about 4 oclock in the afternoon. I will try to give a short description of how I looked when I got there. . . . my left britches leg was off above my knee. I only had one shirt and that I have worn from Salt Lake City. my hat had lost its rim I had no vest, my coat was ripped up the back to the collar, I had had nothing to eat but the grease for two days and the worst of it all I did not have a cent to my name. I didn't know what to do 3 thousand miles from Home a stranger to everybody what should I do? I didn't sit down and cry but I went into a Hotel and told the landlord I was strapped and wanted something to eat. I was willing to work for it, that I had not had anything to eat for 2 days. He said I have no work for you but as you look like an honest boy I will give you something to eat and at that time someone touched me on the shoulder and I looked up and *Phil* March stood there. he said Jim I have got a little money and as long as it lasts you shall eat. stay with me, and I stayed with him you bet. . . ."

Richard Keen took a new road to Placerville through

[312]

Grizzly Flats and Weaver—a settlement of which G. A. Smith said there was "not much a going on but card playing and drinking"—on July 23. "I discovered there are a good number of Miners here, I cannot refrain from saying that they are the roughest lot of fellows I ever saw they universally wear woolen shirts with pockets in front slouched hats and long flowing beards that have never been disturbed with combs or Razors. I have taken a walk through the mining Region and have gained an idea of Mining the miners appear very clever and gave me the name of their different tools &c. the most interesting portion of their camp was their store. a tolerably large one which was composed of provisions and miners tools they endeavored to pursuade us to stop here as wages were better than they [are] in any of the old mining Camps however we concluded we must go on to Hangtown and maybe the Prospect will be better there. . . ."

On July 24: "All up by times and anxious to reach Hangtown a change of diet &c. We have lived so long on slap Jacks and bacon that the sight of them almost sickens me but very little breakfast eat this morning Rolled out by sunup. Roads excellent and about 10 Oclock we hove in sight of Ringold which is a small town situated in a Ravine some 400 inhabitants I hear. I see a great many mining along the Ravine I see a great many Chinese or Chinamen mining . . . we passed through this town and in about One Mile we came to weaver town this is a small place not as large as Ringold . . . we passed through this place and in about one and a half Miles we Came in sight of the long talked of or wished for Hangtown this as the others is situated in a Ravine it is quite a town of some 6000 inhabitants Placerville is the proper name but it is universally called Hangtown I must acknowledge that I felt as if we were drawing the attention and remarks of all the people in the streets which were crowded with well dressed men they all appeared to notice us we were Ragged and dirty and as a Californian would say about strapped and no friends however we marched boldly along until we came to the

[313]

Sutter's Fort

Eldorado a large neat looking frame house we Called for dinner and in the course of an hour we were served with an excellent dinner to which we did ample Justice here was Vegetables of almost all kinds it appeared to be the best Meal I ever eat after dinner I took a stroll about the town it appears that every house in the place is a grog shop. I visited the Post Office and Received a letter from Home.

"Visited several Smithshops thought I would work awhile at smithing if I could get a birth but they were all full and times were dull. the greater portion of our boys are Alkalied already. Overhauled my purse and found but 42 dollars board was worth 16 dollars pr week went out in the hills a Mile or so and prospected some little water is scarce none to be had I see hundreds of claims staken off which is done this wise along Ravines a Claim is 100 feet and back to the hill they drive stakes with written Notices stating that the undersigned claimed this 100 feet for mining purposes &c. came in about dark. peter Calibaugh and I slept in the Wagons."

Dr. Wayman slept the night of August 28 in Hangtown, and in the morning: "I woke up this morning and found somebody in the city of Hangtown went down stairs and look about took

[314]

a snorte of Brandy and found out that it was 'me' a matter that has been in dispute for some Months I could not deside it satisfactorily:—for I never drove cattle nor wa[l]ked bare footed through hot sand and dust; so the thing went on until this morning after washing myself & drinking about 3 inches —the matter was satisfactorily settled and I found that it was 'me' *my self* forked and down right in the City of Hangtown California. Well I took an aspect of this place, and found it to be situated in a ravine long & crooked with but one street & that very narrow—some 2 or 3 M.s. containing some 3 or 4000 inhabitants made up of all kinds of people. They were mining all along the main ravine and several small ones pointing into the main one. Making tolerably good wages. Gambling going on by the whole sale."

John Hawkins Clark reached journey's end on September 4: "Only twelve miles to the end of our destination. Our road now is side by side with the American river, a somewhat different stream than when we crossed it in the mountains. To our left stands Sutter's Fort, and ancient and dilapidated-looking concern, all gone, or going to decay. To our left is a grave yard where monuments and tombstones stand like out-door sentinels to the entrance of a great city. Soon the spires of churches and the masts of shipping become visible. The breeze now brings the busy hum of the city together with the voice of the steamboat bell, all old but familiar sounds. How earnestly did we gaze at the sight and signs of civilization; from the first of May to the first of September we had been wanderers in the wilderness; everything we heard or saw appeared new. It was indeed a new world and we were, in reality, in the midst of it. We had, as our looks indicated, crossed a continent, but in crossing had nearly lost our nationality, for to the unpracticed eye we looked more like Hungarians than American citizens. It was only by the voice that the universal Yankee nation would have recognized us as brethern of the same race. At 12 o'clock, we entered the city of Sacramento, dirty, dusty and hungry, our teams and ourselves

[315]

The City of Sacramento

worn down with fatigue and looking for all the world like the remnant of a disorganized army that had just escaped destruction.

"In closing up I am happy to say that we brought every man and every horse and mule safely through the long and tiresome journey. We are now in California. No more traveling day after day; no more standing watch by night. It is here that we separate from our companions. The bond that held us together on the long and toilsome road is canceled. Each individual has his own way to choose and travel, whether for good or evil, time only will disclose. A shake of the hand and a good-by and the company of C.[lark] and B.[rown] are separated."

APPENDICES

—————◄◆►—————

I

It is impossible to know with any precision how many persons crossed the plains in 1852, but there are some indications. The Lexington (Missouri) *Express* reported the number of persons, wagons, and stock that left from Lexington and St. Joseph between May 1 and June 6 to be: men, 16,302; women, 3,242; children, 4,260—for a total of 23,804—and wagons, 5,325; horses, 6,538; mules, 4,686; cattle, 59,393; sheep, 1,523; turkeys, 152; hogs, 11; ducks, 4; guinea fowls, 6.

The army at Fort Kearney kept a count of emigrants (if they signed in) on the south side of the Platte, which, if the figures can be trusted, would give some idea of the size of approximately half the migration. No count of any sort was kept on the Mormon Trail. But the count at Fort Kearney as reported by emigrants and in the press is wildly discrepant. For instance, Caroline Richardson reported the figures as of May 25 to be: 2,750 wagons, 27,025 head of stock, and 9,075 persons. But on May 26 Lodisia Frizzell said that 2,657 wagons had passed, and John Clark of Virginia on the same day claimed that no less than 33,176 wagons and 16,880 persons had passed.

Perhaps somewhat more reliable are the figures published in the New York *Tribune* taken from a letter of August 6, 1852, by Corporal F. Longfield, Sixth Infantry, who was stationed at Fort Kearney. He stated that at the time of writing the emigration had passed and the trail was deserted. He gave as the total number of the migration: 19,000 men, 4,400 women, 5,555 children—total 28,955. 7,800 horses, 5,000 mules, 74,538 cattle, 23,980 sheep, 1 hog—total stock 111,319; wagons, 6,479. And, according to Longfield, the emigration

[317]

on the north bank of the Platte "is computed to be equal to the above."

Delazon Smith, an emigrant to Oregon, estimated the total emigration at 50,000 people with 100,000 head of stock. Other emigrants estimated between 50,000 and 60,000 people, which, lacking better evidence, may be taken as a fairly reliable approximation.

II

THE EMIGRANTS

ADAMS, MRS. CECELIA EMILY McMILLEN

Born February 16, 1829. From Du Page County, Illinois. Company of sixteen men, ten women, plus children, with eight wagons and ox teams. The party included her husband, twin sister, parents, brothers, brother-in-law and wife. Kanesville to Oregon.

AKIN, JAMES, JR.

From Salem, Iowa. Family in party: Father, James Akin, Sr.; mother, Eliza Richey Akin, age thirty-seven; uncles Stuart Richey, forty; Caleb Richey, thirty-five; their wives, Louisa and Alice; and his sisters, Frances and Mary Ann. From Kanesville to Oregon with ox teams.

ANDREWS, D. B.

From Indiana, he traveled in a party of four men from St. Joseph to California, with ox teams.

BAILEY, MRS. MARY STUART

From Sylvania, Ohio, she accompanied her physician husband from St. Joseph to California via Salt Lake City. Horse teams.

BOWERING, GEORGE

Clerk of the Mormon Council Point Emigrating Company, a Mormon train of 319 persons, 61 wagons, 213 oxen, 164 cows, 25 sheep, 14 horses. Kanesville to Salt Lake City.

BRADLEY, HENRY AND JANE

From Elkhorn, Wisconsin. Kanesville to California via Salt Lake City, with horse teams.

BROWN, JOHN

From Ray County, Missouri. He left St. Joseph with his family for Oregon.

CARPENTER, JAMES C.

Born December 11, 1832. A blacksmith. From Battle Creek,

Michigan. Kanesville to California via Salt Lake City, with one wagon, two ponies.

CHADWICK, SAMUEL

Probably from Wisconsin. Kanesville to California, with ox teams.

CLARK, JOHN HAWKINS

Thirty-nine years old, from Cincinnati, Ohio. St. Joseph to California via Salt Lake City. Co-captain of his company of twenty young men, with one ox team, two horse teams, one mule team.

CLARK OF VIRGINIA, JOHN

Although so styled by himself, he was living in Ohio before traveling from St. Joseph to California by mule teams.

COLE, GILBERT L.

From Monroe, Michigan. St. Joseph to California in a train of twenty-four men, one woman, eight wagons, forty-four head of mules and horses.

CONYERS, ENOCH W.

From Quincy, Illinois. Kanesville to Oregon in a train of twenty-four ox teams, sixty-five men, two women.

COOKE, MRS. LUCY RUTLEDGE

Born 1827, in London, England. From Dubuque, Iowa. With her husband, William, infant daughter, father and mother-in-law, she was a member of the Dubuque Emigrating Company, of seventy-two men plus families, with thirty wagons and ox teams. Kanesville to Salt Lake City.

CRANE, ADDISON MOSES

Born Litchfield, New York, July 2, 1814. Married in 1839 and moved to Indiana. In 1850 was judge of the Court of County Pleas, Lafayette, Indiana. Traveled with his brother Albert (born 1824), leaving his wife and six children in Indiana. St. Joseph to California via Salt Lake City, with ox teams.

CUMMINGS, MRS. MARIETT FOSTER

From Plainfield, Illinois. Company included her father, Isaac; mother, Grace; husband, William; son, Billie; and brothers, Vincent and Arthur. Isaac Foster was making his second overland crossing. St. Joseph to California via Salt Lake City, with mule teams.

DALTON, DR. JOHN

From New Vienna, Clinton County, Ohio. In a company of about fifty men with twenty yoke oxen, traveled from Westport to California.

DAVID, JAMES C.

From near Belmont, Wisconsin, he was one of a party of three men traveling from Kanesville to California, with four yoke oxen.

DAVIS, MR.

Born January 14, 1825. From Lockport, Illinois, where he had been a clerk in a mercantile warehouse. Party of nine men with forty oxen and cows, traveled from Kanesville to Oregon.

DODSON, JOHN F.

Seventeen years old, from Buffalo Grove, Illinois. From Kanesville to Fort Owen, Montana, in an ox train.

DOWDLE, JOHN G.

From Iowa, a member of the Eighteenth Mormon Company, Captain James C. Snow. Kanesville to Salt Lake City, with ox teams.

FOX, JARED

From Delton, Wisconsin. From Kanesville to Oregon with horse teams.

FRIZZELL, MRS. LODISIA

From Ewington, Illinois, traveled with husband, Lloyd, and four sons. St. Joseph to California, with five yoke oxen.

GAGE, STEPHEN T.

From Ohio, he traveled with a small all-male party with oxen and two riding horses from St. Joseph to California.

GEE, PERRY

From Madison, Ohio. Independence to California with ox teams, five mules, three horses.

GILLESPIE, AGNES LEONORA

From Lafayette County, Missouri. Her father, the Reverend Jacob Gillespie (born 1809) was captain of the train. His family who crossed to Oregon were his wife, Amelia, and their seven children: Polly, twenty, and her husband of one month, Walker Young; Agnes, eighteen, Margaret, sixteen; Parmelia, fourteen, Nellie, twelve; Matilda, nine; and Marcellus, seven. Also in the train of eight wagons with ox teams was John Day, whom Agnes Gillespie married ten days after reaching Oregon.

[320]

GRAHAM, ALPHEUS N.

From Ashmore, Illinois, he was of a party of seventeen men. Independence to California, with ox teams.

GREEN, JAY

In partnership with a Mr. Gray, he traveled with mule teams from St. Joseph to California. He may have been the captain of the company, which was of indeterminate size.

HAMPTON, WILLIAM P.

From Dover, Ohio. St. Joseph to California via Salt Lake City, with ox teams.

HANNA, MRS. ESTHER BELLE MCMILLAN

Eighteen years old, from Pittsburgh, Pennsylvania. The bride of the Reverend Joseph A. Hanna. St. Joseph to Oregon, with one ox team, one mule team.

HENRY, DR. ANSON G.

From Springfield, Illinois. He, his wife and family traveled from Independence to Oregon in a train of ten wagons with oxen.

HICKMAN, PETER L.

From Allegheny City, Pennsylvania. Member of the Wellsville & Pittsburg California Company, twenty-one men with ox teams. St. Joseph to California via Salt Lake City.

HICKMAN, RICHARD OWEN

Age twenty, from Illinois. Independence to California, with oxen.

HOSLEY, DEXTER P.

From Greenfield, Massachusetts. St. Joseph to California, with oxen.

KAHLER, WILLIAM

From McConnelsville, Ohio. Two wagons with ox teams. With his wife, Rachel, son, Robert, and other children went from St. Joseph to Oregon.

KEEN, RICHARD

From Logan, Indiana. A blacksmith. Paid $100 to join a train organized by B. T. C. Brandon; twenty-four men, one woman, with five wagons, one carriage, horse teams. St. Joseph to California.

KERNS, JOHN T.

From Rensselaer, Indiana. In company of thirty-five persons, with nine wagons, ox teams. Kanesville to Oregon.

KINGERY, SOLOMON

Born March, 1831. From Pine Creek, Illinois. Native of Dauphin County, Pennsylvania. Kanesville to California, via Nobles' Road with ox teams.

KITCHELL, EDWARD

From Fort Madison, Iowa. Kanesville to California, via Salt Lake City, in a train of twenty-six ox teams, four horse teams.

LAIRD, MOSES F.

Born February 26, 1835. A saddler and harness maker from Zanesville, Ohio. Savannah to Oregon in an ox train of sixteen wagons.

LAWS, ROBERT C.

Born June 14, 1830. From Jamestown, Green County, Ohio. St. Joseph to California, via Salt Lake City, in the train of Major Ormsby, eighteen men, five women, ten children, with horse-drawn carriages, buggies, and three light wagons.

LEWIS, JOHN N.

From Sandcreek, Indiana. To Oregon, with oxen.

LEWIS, Thomas C.

From Portsmouth, Scioto County, Ohio. St. Joseph to California, with two mules and one mare.

LOBENSTINE, WILLIAM C.

Born November 8, 1831, a native of the duchy of Meiningen, he was a tanner and leather merchant from Pittsburgh, Pennsylvania. In a company of forty men with ten wagons and forty oxen, traveled from St. Joseph to California.

McALLISTER, REVEREND JOHN

From Louisiana, Missouri, he traveled by ox team from Kanesville to Oregon.

McAULEY, ELIZA ANN

Age seventeen, from Iowa. With her were her sister Margaret, thirty; brother Thomas, twenty-two; Winthrop Cheney, twenty; and his brother Merrick Cheney, sixteen. From Kanesville to California to meet her father, who had gone out in 1850. Two wagons, with ox and cow teams, two saddle horses, and a herd of twenty dairy cows.

MEDLEY, MARY E.

Born at Winchester, Missouri, January 9, 1842. Traveled with her parents; her older sisters, Annie and Margaret; and her brothers,

John, seven, and James, four. In two wagons with ox teams, they went from Kanesville to California, via Salt Lake City.

RICHARDSON, ALPHEUS

From Caledonia, Ohio. Traveled with David Zuck and family with three wagons, ten yoke oxen. St. Joseph to California.

RICHARDSON, MRS. CAROLINE

From Detroit, Michigan, she traveled with her husband and sons with horse teams from Weston to California via Salt Lake City.

RIKER, JOHN

From Piqua, Ohio. A company of sixteen men, including R. H. P. Snodgrass and two women, with horse teams.

SAWYER, MRS. FRANCIS

Born June 13, 1831. From Louisville, Kentucky. She accompanied her husband, who was making his second overland trip, from St. Joseph to California, with mule teams.

SCHNEIDER, CHARLES G.

Native of Germany; from Milwaukee, Wisconsin. Four wagons, twelve yoke oxen. Kanesville to California via Salt Lake City.

SCOTT, HARRIET

Age eleven, from Illinois. Her father, John Tucker Scott, and mother had besides herself, eight children ranging in age from nineteen to four. St. Joseph to Oregon.

SHARP, MRS. CORNELIA A.

From Jackson County, Missouri. With her husband, John, their seven children, her husband's sister, brother-in-law and their three children, traveled to Oregon with one wagon, five yoke oxen, riding horses, and loose cattle.

SHORT, GEORGE W.

From Waukesha County, Wisconsin, he traveled in a horse train from St. Joseph to California.

SMITH, G. A.

He left St. Joseph with a horse train for California.

SNODGRASS, R. H. P.

From Miami County, Ohio, he was in the same company as John Riker.

STABAEK, TOSTEN KITTLESEN

A native of Norway, he was from Rock Run, Winnebago County, Illinois. His party of eight men, three wagons, eleven yoke oxen, and

[323]

six cows traveled from Kanesville to California via Salt Lake City and Nobles' Road.

STOUT, LEWIS

From Van Buren County, Iowa. He went from Kanesville to Oregon with his parents, three sisters, two brothers-in-law, and six children. Seven wagons with ox teams.

TAYLOR, WILLIAM

Born 1804, in Tennessee. With two sons traveled from Independence to California, in one wagon with oxen.

TURNBULL, THOMAS

Born c. 1812 in Northumberland, England. Farming near Glencoe, Illinois, when he left for California from Kanesville, with horse teams.

UDELL, JOHN

Age fifty-six. From Gentry County, Missouri. Crossed with oxen and cows from Old Fort Kearney to California.

VAN SCHAICK, HOLMES D.

From Manlius, Onondaga County, New York. In a mule train of twenty-seven men, traveled from Independence to California.

VERDENAL, JOHN

From St. Louis, Missouri. He paid $100 for passage with P. H. Elsworth's "El Dorado Train," consisting of 13 wagons, 200 head of cattle, 15 horses, 75 persons, including — families, 10 women, 5 children. Kansas (City) to California via Salt Lake City.

WAYMAN, DR. JOHN HUDSON

Born 1820. From Cambridge City, Indiana. In a party of seven (or eight) men, with horses and one ox cart. St. Joseph to California.

WHITE, FRANCIS B.

Probably from Missouri, he left St. Joseph for Oregon in a company of thirty-three men, nine women and from twelve to fifteen children. He later joined the Hanna party for Oregon.

WIGLE, A. J.

Born March 4, 1830. From Adams County, Illinois. He, his wife, Mary, his parents, and two uncles were in a company of thirty-four, in an ox train. St. Joseph to Oregon.

James Carpenter joined his older brother in the mines, made a profit of $815 in a year and sailed for the East. He married in 1858, enlisted in the Union Army in 1862, and served under Sherman in his march to the sea. In 1870 he settled in Council Grove, Kansas, where he died in 1912, aged seventy-nine.

John Hawkins Clark worked in California as a contractor, returned east via Panama in 1857, moved his family to Kansas, where he died in 1900, aged eighty-seven.

John Clark of Virginia settled in Sierra County and served two terms as County Recorder, 1854–55, before returning to Portsmouth, Ohio, in November, 1856.

Lucy Rutledge Cooke and her husband reached California from Salt Lake City in the spring of 1853. The infant daughter she brought across the plains was joined in time by three sisters and four brothers. Mrs. Cooke died in San Francisco, in 1915, aged eighty-eight.

Addison Moses Crane was joined in Oakland by his family in 1853. He served as an Alameda County judge, was a state senator, 1861–63, and was elected a judge of the Superior Court of Alameda County in 1879. He resigned from the bench when he lost his sight, and died in Oakland in 1887, aged seventy-three.

Mariett Foster Cummings lived first in San Jose, then Columbia. Moving to San Francisco in 1864, her husband opened a furniture store. Mrs. Cummings died in the 1920's.

Alpheus Graham returned to his home in Ashmore, Illinois, in the summer of 1855. As a lawyer in Coles County, Illinois, he became well acquainted with Abraham Lincoln, and served as a captain of cavalry during the Civil War. He died in 1886, aged sixty-nine.

William P. Hampton did well mining and with his wife bought a Temperance House in Cold Springs, El Dorado County, where his daughter was born in 1853. The Hamptons returned east by steamer in 1855.

Richard Owen Hickman lived in Nevada City until his return to Illinois by steamer in 1863. In 1865 he settled in Montana, was elected to the territorial legislature in 1869, and was appointed territorial treasurer in 1871. A delegate to the Republican National Convention of 1876, he served three more terms in the territorial legislature, was a member of the State Constitutional Convention, and was serving as state land agent when he died in 1895, aged sixty-three.

Richard Keen worked at odd jobs and as a blacksmith at a sawmill near Murphy's Camp. He sailed for the east on the *Winfield Scott*, in December, 1853. The steamer was wrecked off Santa Barbara, but Keen was rescued and returned to Indiana.

Solomon Kingery stayed in Shasta, where he died, July 9, 1855, aged twenty-four.

John Lewis lived in Oregon and California and sailed for the East in February, 1859.

William Lobenstine worked in the mines until 1858, when he had accumulated $6,500. Returning east, he settled in Leavenworth, Kansas, where he was successful in the leather business.

Eliza Ann McAuley, Mrs. Egbert, lived the rest of her life in California, as did Mary Medley, who, in 1857 at age fifteen, married Warren Ackley. She published her reminiscences of her overland journey in 1928.

R. H. P. Snodgrass was living in Wyandotte, Butte County, in March, 1854, when he recorded that the Riker brothers were mining on the American River. He later returned east and as a captain of volunteers was killed in the Civil War.

Thomas Turnbull returned to Illinois, where he died in 1869, aged fifty-seven.

John Udell returned east and published the diary of his trip in 1856. In 1859 he made a second trip to California, via the southern route, and the account was published in 1868.

BIBLIOGRAPHY

———◆◀◆▶◆———

Manuscript diaries:

Andrews, D. B.—Coe Collection, Yale University.
Ashley, Mrs. Angeline Jackson—typescript fragment, Huntington Library.
Bailey, Mary Stuart—Huntington Library, HM 2018.
Baker, William B.—California State Library.
Bowering, George—Utah State Historical Society.
Bradley, N. J. and H.—Coe Collection, Yale.
Brown, John—fragment, Oregon Historical Society.
Bruce, Rachel C. (Mrs. Rose)—California State Library.
Chadwick, Samuel—typescript, State Historical Society of Wisconsin.
Clark of Virginia, John—Coe Collection, Yale.
Crane, Addison Moses—Huntington Library, HM 19333.
Dalton, Dr. John—typescript, State Historical Society of Wisconsin.
Daughters, J. M.—California State Library.
Fox, Jared—Bancroft Library.
Gage, Stephen T.—California State Library.
Gee, Perry—Coe Collection, Yale.
Hampton, William P.—typescript, California State Library.
Henry, Dr. A. G.—Illinois State Historical Library.
Hickman, Peter L.—typescript, California State Library.
Hosley, Dexter P.—Princeton University.
Humphrey, Luzerne—Princeton University.
Jones, Evan O.—Bancroft Library.
Kahler, William—Coe Collection, Yale.
Keen, Richard—typescript, California State Library.
Kingery, Solomon—Coe Collection, Yale.
Kitchell, Edward—Illinois State Historical Library.
Laird, Moses F.—Coe Collection, Yale.
Laub, George—Utah State Historical Society.
Laws, Robert C.—California Pioneer Society.
Lewis, John N.—Bancroft Library.

[327]

Lewis, Thomas C.—Coe Collection, Yale.
Richardson, Alpheus—Bancroft Library.
Richardson, Caroline—Bancroft Library.
Riker, John F.—typescript, Indiana State Library.
Sawyer, Mrs. Francis—typescript, Bancroft Library.
Schneider, Charles G.—typescript of translation from the German, Historical Society of Wisconsin.
Short, George W.—typescript, State Historical Society of Wisconsin.
Smith, G. A.—Missouri Historical Society.
Snodgrass, R. H. P.—Coe Collection, Yale.
Stout, Lewis—typescript, Oregon Historical Society.
Van Schaick, Holmes D.—Newberry Library.
Verdenal, John—typescript, Bancroft Library.
Zinn, Henry—typescript, California State Library.

Published diaries:

Adams, Cecelia Emily McMillen—*Oregon Pioneer Association Transactions*, 1904.
Akin, James, Jr.—*Oregon Pioneer Association Transactions*, 1909.
Clark, John Hawkins—*Kansas Historical Quarterly*, August, 1942.
Conyers, Enoch W.—*Oregon Pioneer Association Transactions*, 1906.
Cooke, Lucy Rutledge—Privately printed, Modesto, 1923.
Cummings, Mariett Foster—*The Foster Family, California Pioneers*, by Roxana Foster. Santa Barbara, 1925.
David, James C.—*Annals of Wyoming*, April, 1962.
Davis, Mr. (Alvah Isiah)—*Oregon Pioneer Association Transactions*, 1909.
Dodson, John F.—*Montana Magzine of History*, Spring, 1953.
Frizzell, Lodisia—New York Public Library, 1915.
Gillespie, Agnes Leonora—*Lane County Historian*.
Graham, Alpheus N.—extracts, *Kansas Magazine*, 1966.
Green, Jay—San Joaquin Pioneer and Historical Society, Stockton, California, 1955.
Hanna, Esther Belle McMillan—*Canvas Caravans*, by Eleanor Allen, Portland, 1946.
Hickman, Richard Owen—*The Frontier*, March, 1929.
Kerns, John T.—*Oregon Pioneer Association Transactions*, 1914.
Lobenstine, William C.—*Extracts from the Diary of . . .* privately printed, 1920.
McAllister, Rev. John—*Oregon Pioneer Society Transactions*, 1922.
McAuley, Eliza Ann (Mrs. Egbert)—*Pomona Valley Historian*, II, January, April, July, 1966.
Sharp, Cornelia A.—*Oregon Pioneer Association Transactions*, 1903.

Spencer, Lafayette—*Annals of Iowa*, October, 1908.

Turnbull, Thomas—*Proceedings*, 61st Annual Meeting, Wisconsin Historical Society, Madison, 1914.

Udell, John—*Incidents of Travel to California Across the Great Plains*, etc. Jefferson, Ohio, 1856.

Wayman, John Hudson—*A Doctor on the California Trail*. Denver, 1971.

White, Francis B.—excerpts, St. Joseph *Gazette*, April 10, 1932.

Reminiscences:

Carpenter, James C.—Manuscript, Kansas State Historical Society.

Cole, Gilbert L.—*In the Early Days Along the Overland Trail in Nebraska Territory, in 1852*. Kansas City, Mo., 1905.

Collins, Mary (Parsons)—Manuscript copy, Oregon Historical Society.

Dowdle, John G.—Typescript, Utah State Historical Society.

Ingrim, Godfry C.—Typescript, Kansas State Historical Society.

Medley, Mary E. (Ackley)—*Crossing the Plains and Early Days in California*, by Mary E. Ackley. Privately printed, San Francisco, 1928.

Meeker, Ezra—*Ventures and Adventures*. Seattle, 1909.

Palmer, Harriet Scott—*Crossing over the Great Plains by Ox-Wagons*. Privately printed, c. 1931.

Platt, P. L., and Slater, N. M. *Travelers' Guide Across the Plains upon the Overland Trail*. San Francisco, John Howell—Books, 1963.

Staebaek, Tosten Kittelsen—The Norwegian-American Historical Association, *Studies and Records*, Vol. IV, 1929.

Taylor, William—Photocopy, Bancroft Library.

Wigle, A. J.—Manuscript, Oregon Historical Society.

Newspapers:

Auburn (California) *Placer Herald.*

Chillicothe (Ohio) *Scioto Gazette.*

Cincinnati *Enquirer.*

Cleveland *Plain Dealer.*

Columbia *Weekly Missouri Sentinel.*

Kanesville *Frontier Guardian and Iowa Sentinel.*

Liberty (Missouri) *Weekly Tribune.*

Nevada City (California) *Nevada Journal.*

New York *Tribune.*

Galena *Northwestern Gazette.*

Placerville *El Dorado News.*

Portland *Oregonian.*

Sacramento *Union.*

Shasta *Courier.*
St. Joseph *Gazette.*
St. Louis *Republican.*
St. Louis *Union.*
Salt Lake City *Deseret News.*
San Francisco *Alta California.*
San Francisco *Herald.*
San Franciso *Whig.*
Springfield *Illinois State Journal.*
Stockton *San Joaquin Republican.*